Cleese Encounters

Cleese Encounters

JONATHAN MARGOLIS

ST. MARTIN'S PRESS
NEW YORK

Library of Congress Cataloging-in-Publication Data

Margolis, Jonathan.
    Cleese encounters / Jonathan Margolis.
        p.   cm.
    ISBN 0-312-08162-6
    1. Cleese, John. 2. Comedians—Great Britain—Biography.
    3. Motion picture actors and actresses—Great Britain—
Biography.
    I. Title.
    PN2598.C47M37   1992
    792'.028'092—dc20
    [B]   92-25779
                                                      CIP

First published in Great Britain by Chapman Publishers Ltd.

First U.S. Edition: October 1992
10 9 8 7 6 5 4 3 2 1

To Matthew Norman, whose idea it was,
Sue who made it possible,
and to Eleanor Mae Margolis who did
everything within her considerable and
growing powers to make it impossible

Acknowledgements

My thanks above all to Bryony Coleman, who researched this book so thoroughly, as well as worrying and kvetching about it even more than I did. Also to Victor Davis, Richard Heller, Oliver James, Stewart Steven, Michael and Vivien Robotham, Madeleine and Dave Harper, Richard Holliday and Sue Mills, Fiona Lafferty, Val Bethell, Barnabus Butter, June Webb of Weston-super-Mare public library, Brian Austin, Richard Caddell, Graeme Gourlay, Pat Gallagher, Ben Wordsworth, Graham McOwan of The Lighter Side book shop, Upper Richmond Road West, London SW14, Peter Hadfield, Carrie Nye, Dick Cavett, Judy Englander, Phil Easton of Orchard FM, Taunton, Alice Miles, Clare Collier, Philippa Leach, Jeffrey Taylor, Michael Paget, Angus Deming, Wendy Aldham, Peter Bell of Viacom, Peter Bellwood, Michael Filer, Vivienne Schuster of Curtis Brown, Mark Crean, Harvey Kurtzman, Everett Martin, Robert Christopher, Harry and Irene Chester, Barbara Metcalfe, Gene Saks, John Herdman, Stephen Albert, David Reid, Bruce Cohen, Doug Raffill, Duytch Pojowa, Olga Barbie, Jillian Edelstein, Julian Doyle, Stanley Speel, Claudia Cooke, Roger Nuttall, Tony Simpson, Paula Johnson, Peter and Andrew Nisbet, Alan and Chris Kettle, Stuart Hughes, Sinclair McKay, Jim Tavaré, Francesca Simon, Bob Tilley, Michael and Zoe Deakin, John Rowland-Hosbons, David O'Neill, Paul Nathanson, Peter Tory, Sandra Parsons, Miriam Margolyes, Jeffrey Archer, Dave Gelly, David Bromwich of Taunton public library, Deborah Lawrenson, Helen Minsky, Frances Hicks, Ruth Tipping, John Phillpott, Gabrielle Morris and the Associated Newspapers library staff.

In addition, the following publications contain a rich hoard of Cleesiana and I am extremely grateful to them: *Aquarian, Audio*

Visual Communications, Bristol Evening Post, Cambridge Evening News, Chicago Tribune, Christian Science Monitor, Current Biography, *Daily Express, Daily Mail, Daily Mirror, Daily Star, Daily Telegraph, Daily Telegraph* Magazine, *EGG* Magazine, *Emmy* Magazine, *Esquire, Evening News, Evening Standard, Film Comment* Magazine, *Films and Filming, Financial Times, GQ, Guardian, Hollywood Reporter, Independent, Independent* Magazine, *Interview, Life* Magazine, *Los Angeles Daily News, Los Angeles Herald Examiner, Los Angeles Times, Mail on Sunday, New York Daily News, New York* Magazine, *New York Newsday, New York Times, New York Times* Magazine, *New Yorker, News of the World, Newsweek, Observer, Observer* Magazine, *Oxford Mail, People* Magazine, *Philadelphia Inquirer, Playboy, Publisher's Weekly, Radio Times, Screen International, Stage and Television Today, Starlog, Sun, Sunday Express, Sunday Mirror, Sunday Telegraph, Sunday Times, Sunday Times* Magazine, *The Dial, The Face, The Times, Time Out, Today, TV Times, UCLA Daily Bruin, US* Magazine, *Variety, Vogue, Washington Post, Western Daily Press, Weston Mercury, Women's Wear Daily* and *YOU* Magazine.

Contents

Illustrations

Preface

If John Cleese is sure of one thing, it is that he does not want this book to exist.

Always with the utmost politeness, he declined to co-operate with it, and, when asked by friends whom I had approached if he minded them speaking to me, he would ask them to be 'restrained'. Some were, some weren't. Most saw no cause to ask his permission to talk.

At one stage during the research, Cleese's second wife Barbara Trentham asked me why I had taken on the task of producing the biography of a man who did not want one written: A question I had never been asked before. I blurted out something unimpressive about Cleese being a national treasure whose life story belonged in the public domain as much as that of any prime minister or royal personage.

The real reasons are that no one has yet written John Cleese's biography, I am an unreconstructed admirer, and, had I not undertaken it, somebody even less well-qualified than I would have tackled it. In the end, Cleese's unwillingness served me well, because I had to work harder than an 'authorized' biographer might have done.

I have come to appreciate that it must be very peculiar indeed to be John Cleese. When you are 6 ft 4¾ in. it is impossible to be inconspicuous. Cleese cannot put his head out of the door without being instantly recognized. Anything he does may find its way into a gossip column and, because his popularity crosses class barriers, he is at the peril of the entire press.

Thus did the janitorial comments of a plumber called Steve Jarrett come to appear in the *Daily Telegraph* recently. Mr Jarrett had been doing some work in a vacant house Cleese bought in 1990. 'Mr Cleese is very fastidious with his plumbing,' he commented, and somehow – I am serious – we increased our understanding of Basil Fawlty's creator.

Cleese has a complicated relationship with journalists. He responds to intelligent interviewers, typically recommending further reading to them and excitedly approving sensible questions. He tends to give better interviews to American writers, who seem to be prepared to think more deeply about his ideas. In late 1991, he rattled off a letter to the *Evening Standard*'s reference library ('Dear Cuttings Library,' it began) to correct a few factual points that reporters kept getting wrong. Most of the time, Cleese shows no particular desire to hide his private life, chatting away merrily about the most intimate matters. But he is as likely to round on the author of the most innocent paragraph. Peter Tory, one of the most gentlemanly and respected of journalists, was in charge of an elegant gossip column in the *Daily Mirror*:

If you ever wrote anything about John Cleese in the paper he would become very agitated and take himself terribly seriously. I wrote in the *Daily Mirror* diary about his going on the radio and having to have a massage. To me the humour of the situation was the fact that he simply needed a massage in order to speak on the radio, but he took that to imply that I was suggesting that he had needed sexual stimulation. He wrote to me and then to the editor, Mike Molloy, and there was a great coming and going. I was outraged by it because it was nonsense – there wasn't a sexual suggestion at all. It ended up with an apology going in the paper.

The sequel to this was that Cleese came to a boardroom lunch with about six of us, and we were all struck by how serious he was, and how unfunny, rather peculiar, and rather unnerving and unsettling – not someone whose company you enjoyed very much. He's one of these people who tend to put about a kind of unnerving social vibration. He makes you feel uncomfortable by saying things which are slightly oblique. Everyone expected him to be like Basil Fawlty, but he's not like him at all. He's rather strange. After this lunch, what concerned me was that my colleagues took him round the building and showed him my office where I was working. After Cleese had gone, Mike came to me and said, 'John Cleese says that behind the smiles you're the most deeply melancholic man he's ever met in his life.' I remember that worried me for weeks and weeks afterwards. It's a very distressing judgement to have delivered about you by someone who's highly intelligent and deeply into psychiatry. We all have our dark moments and I felt that he'd penetrated one of mine.

As late as the spring of 1991, apparently still having failed to come to terms with the press interest he generated, Cleese had another brush with journalism. One Sunday lunchtime he took his current girlfriend Alyce Faye Eichelberger and daughter Camilla to eat at the Café Kensington, a new restaurant a mile or so from his home, and opposite the offices of the *Daily Mail*, from which three journalists on the Nigel Dempster Diary had also come for lunch. The gossip writers noticed Cleese, but were unclear who Alyce Faye or Camilla were. One of the journalists observed to her amusement that Cleese kept changing places throughout the meal. 'Every time you looked round,' recalls Helen Minsky, 'he was in a different seat. He was very sweet to Alyce Faye, trying to feed her long chocolate tubes, which she refused. He looked unshaven and pale and we thought it would be wrong to disturb him, but that this rather nice scene might make a pleasant little paragraph.'

Back in the office, Minsky decided to confirm who Alyce Faye and Camilla were, and rang Richard Laver, PR man for Cleese's training films company Video Arts. He came back to say Cleese was hopping mad 'that the restaurant should have put the "story" out as publicity'. He told Laver to ask the Dempster people if they didn't have better things to do with their time than to invade his private life. He threatened to write to the newspaper's editor to complain, but instead he wrote a very nice letter to Minsky, saying there were thousands of people who liked to be written about, so why not focus on them instead?

Minsky replied that she thought it was perfectly reasonable for someone in his position to be the subject of an innocuous gossip column paragraph. Nothing more was heard. The next weekend Dempster himself (who is distantly related through a couple of marriages to Barbara Trentham and is certainly a well-known face) bumped into Cleese in Kensington Gardens. 'I just said, "Hello, John," and he looked at me most oddly. He didn't seem to recognize me. It was very strange.'

Away from the world of gossip columns and Hollywood stardom, in his home town of Weston-super-Mare, the respect and devotion Cleese commands from old schoolfriends is astonishing. Even those who have been out of touch with him for years (twenty-seven in one case) were anxious to seek Cleese's permission before contributing to this book. The range of past acquaintances that Cleese remains in contact with is equally impressive; Chris Pickwoad, the cricket captain at Clifton College, Bristol, and now an accountant in Canada – a wonderfully Pythonesque target – corresponds regularly, and when we spoke had just received a letter from Cleese asking him 'to send over a whole list of stuff'.

Listening to a string of Cleese's boyhood friends, I was struck by their similarity. All were gently spoken, courteous men in their fifties, the best of the breed of polite, discreet, wry Englishmen. Middle-class Weston-super-Mare in the 1950s is the most incongruous of backgrounds for a comedian, the antithesis of flashiness and theatricality. I began to see John Cleese as a kind of displaced provincial solicitor, wandering lost and bemused through the glittery theatrical world, an alien being in the psychiatric world, a confused what-am-I-doing-here? guest at royal dinner tables. I do not think he has ever quite belonged anywhere other than in those sedate, grey Somerset streets.

John Cleese doesn't get roaring drunk at smart parties, boff duchesses or take drugs, which ironically makes some regard him as dull, slightly peculiar and certainly not the cliché stuff of routine showbusiness journalism.

After two years studying John Cleese I would say that if he is dull I hope I never grow up to be interesting.

Jonathan Margolis
Mbabane, Swaziland
June 1991

Cleese Encounters

1   *A Scar is Born*

There is a spot well known to all
Where the beautiful breezes blow,
Fathers and mothers, sisters and brothers
All seem to love it so.
Faces are beaming, sweethearts are dreaming
Of love that is to be.
Music is stealing, happy are they
In the breeze of the Weston sea.

From the popular song, 'Weston', by Fred C. Brooks, 1928

Two scenes, more than sixty years apart, episodes so pre-posterously different that only a man as uniquely in tune with the absurd as John Cleese could have contrived, even in a comedy, to connect them.

One is set in 1925 in an English village church in a popular seaside resort, a time when social correctness mattered above all, when the great English institutions of pride, poverty and pianos ruled the waves that gently broke on the beach of Weston-super-Mare. Under the nose of her father, a small, pretty woman in her twenties called Muriel Cross is slipping the assistant verger an envelope to take quietly to the lodgings of a tall insurance man she is keen on, but of whom her father disapproves. The writing on the envelope, in a precise, rounded script, reads simply, 'To Mr Cleese'. The assistant verger would take the envelope to his sister's house, where Mr Cleese lived, chuckling to her as he came in, 'Here's the postman'. Everyone knew what the letters contained, but Reginald Francis Cleese would never say anything other than 'Thank you'.

Later, much later, in 1988 in a film studio, another tall, handsome Mr Cleese, the fifty-year-old son of the man to whom that discreet missive and dozens like it were addressed, kisses one of the most seductive Hollywood actresses of the day, and asks her, in lines he wrote himself, about himself, 'Wanda, do you have any idea what it's like being English?' It is the opening of an impassioned speech on the rigidness, the blushing formality of Englishness. 'You see, Wanda,' he concludes, 'we're all terrified of embarrassment. That's why we're so dead. Most of my friends are dead, you know. We have these piles of corpses to dinner.'

John Cleese had been waiting decades to write and perform such a concise manifesto of his feelings on English reticence and his upbringing in Weston-super-Mare, and the scene was to be admired and cherished all over the world – even if, in translation for more exotic audiences, his affectionate massacre of the national psyche was sometimes less than an aid to complete comprehension. ('Do you understand the English way of life? When our friends come for dinner, they are all dead,' ran the subtitles for the Japanese.)

Englishness aside, neither Reg Cleese nor Muriel Cross was the kind of passionate soul you would expect to carry on a secret and forbidden romance, let alone one that would one day have extraordinary consequences. Charles Howe, the assistant verger at that church in Uphill, outside Weston-super-Mare, to whom Muriel passed those forbidden envelopes throughout the summer of 1925, could hardly have imagined that his church friend Muriel Cross and his sister's lodger, Reg Cleese, would have an only child who would one day be regarded as the funniest man in the world, a suntanned international figure whose comedy films would in 1991 make the President of the United States roar with laughter in the middle of the Gulf War, and whose conversation and company would be sought by the heir to the throne of England. Muriel's father Marwood Joseph Cross would – eventually – have surely had to approve.

Leading his obedient (or so he thought) troupe of womenfolk and his two sons to church each Sunday, Mr Cross, who aimed to do justice to his surname, clearly saw himself as an imposing figure. He certainly imposed on his daughters, especially Muriel, then a spinster of twenty-six. When Father told Muriel to

remove his shoes and fetch his slippers, he was accustomed to
being obeyed. Like it or not, then, every Sunday she would take
the sometimes bracing mile-and-a-half walk from the family's
large home near the sea in the Victorian resort of Weston-super-
Mare to the church in the village of Uphill. There were nearer
churches in Weston itself, but Father was friendly with the rector
of St Nicholas's, Samuel Rowland-Hosbons, so he could count
on his prayers getting an especially sympathetic hearing when
they reached the celestial department that looked after estate
agents and auctioneers in Somerset at the time. Besides which,
his brood looked so impressive (and yet pious) as they processed
to church, past the pretty Donkey Field, where beach donkeys
retired to munch bluebells under a chestnut tree, past Taylor's
Tea Gardens, with its white wooden tables on the lawn and signs
for Hovis and Lyons cakes, and across the piece of green that led
up to the church.

Courting was a tricky business for a woman in genteel
Weston-super-Mare in 1925. The done thing was to keep coy
about it, while letting one's father know who the fellow was
and seeking tacit approval of him. In the case of Reg Cleese, a
timid bachelor insurance agent living on the far side of Uphill,
and Marwood Joseph Cross, despotic Victorian father of this
parish, such approval was not forthcoming. He had put his foot
down, which would, had Muriel Cross felt obliged to play the
game, have been that. Except that Muriel was quietly something
of a subversive character, a quality that, though very, very few
people ever realized it, she shared with Reg.

Reg Cleese and Muriel Cross married inconspicuously on 21
October 1926, a Thursday, in the Bristol Register Office. Reg was
thirty-two and Muriel twenty-seven. Reg by then had moved
from Uphill to the grandeur of Berkeley Square in Clifton, a
select part of Bristol. It seems that it was thanks to Marwood
Cross's continuing disapproval that the wedding was not
reported by the *Weston Mercury*, even though only two days later
Muriel's youngest sister Margery married a Mr Chalcraft, an
official of the telephone company, and the paper gave the church
ceremony a good write-up.

For a nice, well-bred couple to have married quite so surrep-
titiously in the 1920s would normally indicate pregnancy, but

there was a stately interval before John appeared. (Cleese once said of Weston: 'Life there is, of course, entirely free of sex. Occasionally people are born in Weston by parthenogenesis.') 'John's birth was a bit of a bombshell,' admits Muriel. 'We'd been married fourteen years – and there was a war on.' In fact, Cleese was born six days after their thirteenth wedding anniversary; Reg was forty-six, Muriel forty.

Although Marwood Cross is remembered as domineering, a snob and an inveterate social climber who thought the Cleeses a little below him, the new and unwanted in-laws were no less than the Crosses' equal when it came to obscurity. Reg's father, John Edwin Cheese, was the son of a baker, James Cheese, who died when Reg was five. There were reputedly churchmen far back in the Cheese line. John Edwin was not an accountant, as Reg and Muriel's marriage certificate states, but a solicitor's clerk in Bristol, who, bafflingly, bought an office block, the Scottish Widows' Fund building, at 28 Baldwin Street, Bristol, while working on its second floor for a solicitor called Ariel. (It seems by all accounts to have been a relatively eccentric office building, since Mr Ariel was not only paying rent to one of his minions, but had as his neighbour on the second floor a man called William H. Cole, who, octopus-like, worked as the Finnish, Swedish, Russian, Norwegian and Cuban consul.)

Reg Cleese's main claim to fame at that stage was that he had changed his surname from Cheese when he joined the army in 1915 to avoid an anticipated welter of jokes. Before he married, Reg made the change legal. It had worked – few people ever laughed at, or even with, Reg Cleese – and more than thirty years later the name change was to save the young John much ragging when his best friend at prep school turned out to be a boy called Butter. Given that he found cheese jokes tiresome, Reg's choice had been limited when he hit on changing the 'h' to an 'l'. The only alternative the alphabet offered was 'Creese', which, Reg might have been mildly surprised to learn back in 1915, his son would one day be known as in Japan. 'The confusing thing for me as a child,' says John, 'was that Dad always pronounced it to rhyme with cheese, while Mum pronounced it to rhyme with fleece. I remember thinking at the time that if your parents couldn't agree on how to pronounce their name, they weren't likely to agree on much else.'

John Edwin Cheese, John Cleese's grandfather, according to family legend, put his money into railways when he should have invested in brewing, so after he died in 1951, Reg's family had nothing except his £30 a week salary – a decent income, but not in any way real wealth. The family was never short of money, but never had any spare. The summer holiday was ten days in Bournemouth, and John did not go abroad until he was twenty-one. Muriel had inherited a little money which helped to pay for Cleese's private education, and, of course, the Cleeses voted Conservative, but a constant tension between maintaining social appearances and the availability of actual funds was to be a theme in the family's life. Sometimes it would take the form of excessive caution; at other times, Reg would think nothing of writing a few harmless, almost charming, white lies on official documents. It was not by accident that he had 'accountant' written as his father's occupation on his own marriage certificate rather than 'law clerk', which his parents put on his birth document; neither was it a slip that led him to describe himself as an 'insurance broker' on his marriage certificate when he was not quite that, or, later in life, on forms as a 'marine underwriter' when he was, albeit in as gentlemanly a way as possible, a travelling insurance salesman, first for the Union of Canton Insurance Company and later for the Guardian Royal Exchange. In the same vein, with reference to his own father's clerical job, Reg often indicated to the young John that there was 'a tradition of law in the family'.

Although a tinge of irony was often attached to some of his more snobbish notions, like most of his generation Reg had a clear (and, like most of his generation, exalted) vision of his family's place within the British class system, that insidious, all-pervasive obsession which occupied people's deeds but rarely their polite conversations behind the net curtains of Somerset front rooms. As John once explained, in his late twenties Reg had worked in the Far East: 'My father travelled the world selling marine insurance and living in exotic places like Calcutta, Bombay and Hong Kong. Dad pretended to be a bit grand. He had been in India during the Twenties, and shared a house with P. G. Wodehouse's brother. He told me once that they had twenty Indian servants looking after the two of them. He always retained some of that grandness.'

Yet, with the best will in the world, it is hard to underestimate the lack of impact the Cleese family had on Uphill, where young John's first months were spent at No. 6 Ellesmere Road. (Intriguingly, George Orwell placed his insurance-agent hero in *Coming Up for Air*, published a few months before Cleese's birth, in a semi in a mythical Ellesmere Road.) He was born, with a comedian's timing, in the phoney war, on 27 October 1939. He was named John Marwood Cleese, in deference to both grand-fathers: 'I come from a family with a great deal of originality and imagination,' he has said. Ellesmere Road was not *en fête* for the event. The lady who lived and still lives opposite No. 6, a Mrs Tallboys, was typical in maintaining the decent English tradition of not having a lot to do with the neighbours. 'I remem-ber passing the front gate and seeing some cards in the front room, but I never did see the baby or speak to Mrs Cleese,' she recalls. 'Reg Cleese was a dull sort of a man,' says John Rowland-Hosbons, son of the then rector of St Nicholas's. 'A bit of a stuffed shirt, but pleasant. You got the impression he was rather pleased with himself, which was odd because insurance agents in those days were rather small fry.'

The Cleeses' extravagant helping of meekness was also evident in the young John for many years. One friend who was at prep school with him was at pains to point out: 'The one thing you *have* to bear in mind at all times about John Cleese is that, particularly before he started growing tall, he was an insignifi-cant person, quite insignificant.' It is not surprising, then, that most of the villagers of Uphill today have no idea that John Cleese is one of their own. The fact has never once been men-tioned in the ten-year history of the Uphill Village Society's magazine.

Ellesmere Road was an inconsequential curl of 1930s semis. Were the street not under permanent air reconnaissance by watchful, gracefully banking seagulls, it might have been in Loughborough or Penge rather than a few yards from the sea, in a small port, where barges of coal landed from South Wales. Uphill has managed to be a continuously inhabited seaport since

the Stone Age without ever looking especially maritime. But if
the architects of Ellesmere Road and its surrounding streets had
been less determined to create a clone inland suburb and had
made them look instead like a coastal village, John Cleese might
have grown up as some vaguely marine figure with a Guernsey
sweater, a pipe and a repertoire of comic routines about sailors
and fishing. Either that, or Reg and Muriel would have gone to
live in Penge.

Even though it had just, theoretically at least, exploded into
war, the immediate world John Cleese was born into was not one
overburdened with interest. Weston is in Avon (then Somerset) on
the Bristol Channel, twenty miles from Bristol, where Cary Grant
– born Archie Leach, the name Cleese borrowed for his character
in *A Fish Called Wanda* – came from. Its buildings are mostly of the
grey local limestone, which can make them look forbidding on a
dull day, of which there were rather a lot. The *Weston Mercury &
Somerset Herald* for Saturday, 28 October 1939, which momen-
tously recorded 'Cleese, Uphill, October 27th, a son' in its Births
column, ran as its main scoop 'Indoor Bowling Club's Winter
Plans'. There were smaller articles on the issue of ration cards and
people being fined for not observing the blackout. Another
scandal-shrieking headline, 'Weston Visitor Yields to "Great
Temptation"', was disappointingly about a girl who stole £3
from a purse. A 'Weston Sums up its Season' column reported
on the roaring summer trade: '£257 In One Day From Deck
Chairs!' A humorous column remarked that an anagram of 'A.
Hitler' was 'The Liar', which, though moderately pertinent as
anagrams go, would admit to pointing only to one of Hitler's
lesser vices. Weston-super-Mare was no intellectual hothouse.

Roald Dahl, who attended John Cleese's prep school in
Weston at the time that Reg and Muriel were warily courting,
described the town: 'A slightly seedy seaside resort with a vast
sandy beach, a tremendous long pier, an esplanade running
along the sea-front, a clutter of hotels and boarding-houses, and
about ten thousand little shops selling buckets and spades and
sticks of rock and ice-creams.'

Weston-super-Mare is renowned for an over-active tide
which, unfortunately for a seaside resort, makes the sea dis-
appear twice a day, leaving a mile-long expanse of slimy mud.

Laurie Lee, who as a boy between the wars visited Weston on a choir outing, wrote of it: 'We had a world of mud to deal with. We whinnied like horses and charged up and down, every hoof-mark written behind us. If you stamped in this mud you brought it alive, the footprint began to speak, it sucked and sighed and filled with water, became a foot out of the sky. . . .' Brave attempts have been made over the years by tourist officials to pretend that the sludge is not mud at all. Warning notices on the beach between the Royal Hospital and Uphill, where many unwary motorists have become stuck, state with marvellous sniffiness: 'DANGER, SOFT SAND'. This alleged 'sand' was for many decades credited by official Weston guides with producing the resort's famous air, said to be health-giving because of its high ozone content. When, in recent years, ozone was incon-veniently discovered to be a major environmental pollutant, suitable only for keeping in layers between Earth and outer space, the same guide books have tended to play down the association.

Like most seaside resorts, however, the beach and its kitsch seasonal attractions were a universe apart from where ordinary people worked and lived. As a typical 'upwardly mobile' family, the Cleeses had for generations moved frequently, usually from rented property to rented property. Sadly, in the Reg Cleeses' case, the mobility took the form of a mannerly slide in the vague direction of downhill. It was not designed to be thus. Whether it was through Reg's restlessness, a romantic wanderlust, or an attempt at making money, John Cleese recalls upping sticks seventeen times during his youth, once suggesting that his parents moved in the hope of changing their luck, although he believes his father actually succeeded in losing a little cash on each occasion. Muriel, still in Weston, continues to be a fidgety soul; only recently, aged nearly ninety, did she move from one flat to another in her £85-a-week sheltered apartment block. John Cleese's list of childhood homes takes in, often with several houses and flats in each location, Weston-super-Mare, Brent Knoll, Burnham-on-Sea, Horrabridge, Devon, Weston-super-Mare again, Bristol, Weston, yet again, Totnes, Devon, then, by way of a change, back to Weston.

Thus it was, with consummate ease, that Reg and Muriel

whisked baby John away from Uphill at the first drone of a German aeroplane. Not too soon. Under light hypnosis, Cleese has recalled being bombed as a child. The war was unexpectedly severe in Weston. With its lighthouse a landmark, the resort was on the flightpath from Luftwaffe aerodromes in northern France to the Midland cities. The town was also thought by the Germans to be a munitions centre. ('Who says the Germans haven't got a sense of humour?' inhabitants used to say.) The first bombs fell in January 1940; 34 people were killed and 85 injured. The day after the first raid, Reg moved the family out of the rented house in Ellesmere Road and into rooms his estate agent brother-in-law Gerald Cross had found at Brent Knoll, a village eight miles south of Weston. It was a canny move, since Uphill was an apparently peaceful spot on the outskirts of Weston, so peaceful indeed that London children were evacuated there. In June 1942, 10,000 incendiaries and over 60 explosive bombs hit Weston, with 3,500 houses damaged or destroyed, 100 people killed and 400 injured. They included some evacuees. People even died in Uphill, and both the church and school roofs were blown off.

But the Cleeses, with a maiden aunt Dorothy Cheese in tow, were safe at Hillside House, a large, detached Victorian farmhouse belonging to William and Lucy Raffill. Here they lived contentedly with their own rooms and kitchen, and took their meals separately. Doug, the Raffills' twelve-year-old son, played happily with the toddler John, and a local woman in her twenties, Emma, 'did' for both the Raffills and the Cleeses. Emma, now Mrs Haines, recalls with affection: 'Mrs Cleese used to push John in a pram. He was a big pretty boy in white, with his hair in curls. Once in the garden, his mother stopped the pram by some chrysanthemums which were just starting to bud. While I chatted with Mrs Cleese, John stuffed his nose full of tiny chrysanthemum buds. We rushed him back to the house and put a clean hanky under his nose. But every time we said "Blow, John", he inhaled more and more.' About the same time – he was around two years old – John gained some notoriety in another Brent Knoll home as being precocious. 'Miss Cheese, Mrs Cleese, John and I were in the kitchen,' says Mrs Haines. 'John was sitting in his high chair. Suddenly he started choking and Mrs Cleese said "John, whatever's the matter?" John replied: "It must be a little bit of carrot I had last week."'

The idyll in the Raffills' house lasted less than a year. The rest of the war saw the Cleeses changing address at an even more ferocious pace than usual, but Reg keeping steadfastly at his work. Despite the moving around, John continued to be a protected and indulged little boy. Which was all the more reason for his enrolment at a private pre-preparatory school in Annandale Road, Burnham-on-Sea, to come as a severe shock to his fragile system. 'Cressy's' was run by Miss Cresswell, who was in her fifties, and another spinster, darkly remembered by another ex-pupil as 'Miss Horsey'. About thirty nicely brought-up children, both boys and girls, attended, divided into two classes. 'I had a very sheltered upbringing. There was never any disorder or violence. This is probably why I remember so vividly the beating I had at school when I was seven,' says Cleese. 'I still have this extraordinary memory. I was beaten on the hand because I couldn't solve a four-digit divisional sum in front of the rest of the class. It was like something out of Dickens.'

That brutal encounter was to be John's first and last beating at school. Soon, the family was back in Weston-super-Mare and John happily installed in the sunny serenity of a local prep school. As he grew up, the town began to develop as the second most important factor (next to his parents) in shaping the man, his intellect, his emotional turmoil and his extraordinary career. John Cleese's view of Weston, 'that dull, drab, draughty town', is highly ambivalent: 'I feel I carry Weston round in my head with me, both the good and the bad sides,' he explains. The good side he describes as archetypal Small Town England: 'The essential niceness. That very praiseworthy, absolutely admirable liberalism – the idea that people should be as free as possible to make choices, and that they are entitled to disagree with you if they feel like it.' This Weston is a life of politeness, consideration and ruminative activities, like gardening, reading, fishing and, above all, cricket.

The other side of the coin, which Cleese has grown to loathe, yet which turned out to be the mainspring of much of his comedy, was to do with embarrassment, respectability and a deep suspicion of anything which might be seen as intellectual. 'That's a subtle yet powerful influence which I'm still trying to escape from.'

Quiet, constricting, formal, as it seemed, a place of brown parlours with browning wall paper, brown standard lamps, sleeping dogs and etiolated pot plants, Weston was still a reasonably large town, not quite the suffocating rural outpost that John Cleese sometimes, and with some bitterness, describes. Even then, it was not villagey enough for everyone to know one another. Although Cleese is its most famous child (Jeffrey Archer, Deborah Kerr and the cartoonist who designed the famous First World War Kitchener recruiting poster are the others), a large proportion of Westonians are still only vaguely interested in John Cleese's local origin. He only started to make an impact in the town when he took to visiting his parents in his Bentley, about as grand a gesture of showing off as Weston could survive without swooning. In fact the first time he cruised into town in his new S3 model, it was still sporting L-plates. Cleese seemed so set on making a splash with the locals that before even passing his driving test he had summoned Reg up to London to accompany him back to Weston as his supervising driver.

Not that as a child Cleese was dissatisfied with Weston-super-Mare. 'You kind of felt that there was quite enough activity there for me as a boy to feel that I was living quite an interesting and varied life. Weston was a fair place, there was quite a bit going on, being a seaside resort. I don't think I felt too bored then.'

'Sometimes I hanker after the life in Weston-super-Mare,' he once admitted, perhaps out of politeness, to the *Weston Mercury*, which interviewed him amid the ponderous elegance of the seafront Grand Atlantic Hotel. 'I certainly haven't tried to forget it. Some people I know have tried to cut themselves off from their real roots. I think that's bad.' While even a cursory examination of Weston suggests that the old ladies who infest both *Monty Python* and *Fawlty Towers* are based on any of hundreds who cruise the streets of the town in squadrons, Cleese had to go through a long process of cutting himself off from his home town before he could make use of it as material for comedy. It took at least until his late twenties, but by growing out of Weston he also learned to understand it, even to be quite proud of it.

At the same time, he learned to be more philosophical about his family's stuffiness. He was discovering that it was probably as good a family and cultural heritage as a comic genius could require. By the time he was an established performer, he realized that most of his colleagues in comedy were from the same lower-middle, with pretensions to middle-middle, class. 'It's people like that who really do quite well, who succeed in changing things. They don't have a working class complex, at the same time they're not sufficiently part of the upper class to want to contribute to its values. It is funny how the whole of the *Monty Python* crew came from exactly the same stratum. I have a feeling it's a sort of floating group without any affiliations to any other class.' As the American writer Laurence Shames explained in an essay on John Cleese in *Esquire* magazine: 'Every important humorist stakes out as his turf some integral part of the craziness around him. Woody Allen has become the paradigm of a certain sort of peculiarly New York neurosis; John Belushi made himself the high priest of bicoastal burnout weirdness; and John Cleese has claimed as his material the posturings and aggravations of the English Everyman as he tries (and always fails) to avoid friction and shame in a milieu that is orderly to the point of madness.'

If one word could sum up John Cleese's upbringing, it would be 'sheltered'. The family was a tight, rather lonely, extremely loving but inward-looking little unit, driven by Reg's hard work in pursuit of an easy life, Muriel's smothering neuroticism and the unspoken nostalgic pang for better times that they had not necessarily enjoyed but felt somehow destined for. Only a current of competitiveness, prodigious intelligence and insatiable hunger for knowledge, with an undertow of humour – not insignificant as things turned out – prevented John from becoming an adult as dull, fastidious, pompous, and, occasionally, if unintentionally, as funny as Mr Pooter.

John was a quiet, studious child, a bookworm. Rather than playing rough and tumble with brothers, sisters or friends, he would laboriously make a train set on his own out of old cotton reels, transfers and stickers. He was regarded as 'delicate', something of a catch-all condition at the time for any boy not given to pulling the wings off insects. John was never allowed a bike in case he hurt himself, and never as a child even thought to ask for one. 'I know he thinks we were a bit over-protective,' admits Muriel. 'He's told me enough times about the fact he never had a bike. But there was no need to have one. His school was opposite our house. I suppose we made life very easy for him. We were both anxious for him. I suppose it was our age. We could see dangers he couldn't see.'

Later, when up at Cambridge, Cleese often told friends about this cocooning: 'When I met his parents I realized it was true,' says comedian Tim Brooke-Taylor. 'I remember his mother telling me to make sure he had a vest and a woolly jumper on. He was about twenty-four or twenty-five at the time.' Even in John's late teens, Reg and Muriel were still over-cherishing their only child. A neighbour in Totnes, Devon, where the family lived briefly when John went up to Cambridge, recalls that if John was in the garden in his shirtsleeves on a cold day, Muriel would despatch Reg, woolly jumper in hand, to his rescue. Even years after that, when John was a famous man, well capable of looking after himself, the old mother-lion instincts would still come to the fore. As late as 1976, the press was speculating on the Cheese/Cleese name change. The *Daily Express* claimed that they received a letter from Muriel – which was signed but had no address – saying: 'John Cleese was never born John Cheese. I should know . . . M. Cleese.'

The protective shield round John does not seem to have been wielded just by Reg and Muriel. In 1986 an elderly resident of Sidmouth in Devon, Mrs Puck Boulton, wrote apropos of very little to her local paper to say that the house used for the exterior shots in *Fawlty Towers*, Wooburn Grange in Buckinghamshire, had once belonged to her and her husband. The first night the show had been broadcast on television (eleven years before she wrote the letter, but nothing is rushed in Sidmouth) she had received 'at least fifteen telephone calls' from friends who recognized the building. But Mrs Boulton went on to add, 'Personally I think the programme is ghastly, especially John Cleese and his funny walks. I think he is loathsome.' A week later, Mrs Boulton received a phone call from an old lady identifying herself as 'John Cleese's aunt from Taunton'. 'A friend of hers who lived in Sidmouth had sent her the article and she was furious. She said, "He's my nephew and he's a very, very worthy man", and started saying she was going to sue me, she was going to do this, that and the other. I said, "Carry on, old dear, but you won't get very far. I'm a lawyer's wife." She slammed down the phone with a bang.'

As well as growing up socially awkward and more adept at getting on with older people than with those of his own age, John Cleese was also saddled with a feeling of being special. It all made escape from home harder for him, and when he made the break, it took a slightly vengeful form. In the eighteen months Cleese lived in New York, after Cambridge, he hardly wrote home at all.

Cleese's father was tremendously kind and indulgent, and neither parent ever chastised or criticized him: 'I think my father could have been a bit more vigorous with me,' he revealed in his book on psychotherapy, *Families and How to Survive Them*. As an adult, Cleese would find suppressed anger an endlessly fascinating subject. So gentle, and so well known as a gentle man, was Reg that Cleese felt there was no possibility of mis-understanding when asked to contribute an anecdote and a favourite song to a Bristol radio chat show on the trawl for local celebrities' Christmas memories. 'The one thing I remember about Christmas was that my father used to take me out in a boat about ten miles offshore on Christmas Day, and I used to have to swim back,' Cleese recounted with whatever is the radio equivalent of a perfectly straight face. He went on: 'Extra-ordinary. It was a ritual. Mind you, that wasn't the hard part. The difficult bit was getting out of the sack. I asked Dad many years later why he used to do this and he never explained, but I think it was because his father used to do it to him. In fact, I wrote a song called "Daddy, Please Don't Put Me in the Sack", and that's the one I would like to hear.'

(Cleese's psychoanalyst Robin Skynner, who himself had a very unassertive father in Cornwall, believes that Reg's lack of assertion was characteristic of fathers in the years after the Second World War. 'Fathers abdicated. No one knows why, but they gave up their traditional role of strict rule-maker and law enforcer. Was it a reaction to the Nazi regime, which was based on pure maleness without female qualities? Whatever the reason, the father was shoved out and he accepted it.')

Enjoyment and fun were not a major part of life with the Cleeses. Reg found it hard to do anything for his own pleasure. He would take John to football matches but never go on his own, and would make an enormous tortured production out of the simplest outing – a trait Cleese inherited until he sorted it out under Skynner's guidance. 'We'd decide to go to the cinema,' says Cleese. 'We're talking about twenty-five minutes to decide to go – and then my father would ring up to make sure the time of the programme that had been printed in the local paper was in fact correct. Mother would be worrying about whether she should make tea when we got back home or before we left. They'd both be looking out of the window to see what the weather was like; then there'd be an argument about what I should wear. It was like organizing a safari.' Yet all the time, the rudiments of the Cleese humour were there, a strictly private, family humour, unnoticed by all except the most perceptive outsider, and certainly not a performing sort of humour. Deep within the family of most showbusiness personalities, there is usually someone who performed. In the case of the Cleeses, it is only possible to point to Muriel, whom Cleese describes as 'the artistic one' by virtue of the fact that she played the piano during the First World War. 'Dad was literate in the sense that he did the *Daily Telegraph* crossword puzzle, but you wouldn't call him literary. He liked Nevil Shute best.' John's taste at twelve or so was for Rider Haggard or Conan Doyle's *Exploits of Brigadier Gerard*.

'The Arts' were non-existent in Weston except, perhaps, for the few people who would play classical music records. 'I never had the slightest idea that I would come into the business at all, and I still find it's a bit of a surprise to be in it,' Cleese said on *The Dick Cavett Show* in the USA in 1979. 'The only thing that I can attribute it to at all is that my father did have a great sense of humour, and a great sense of cliché, and a very biting wit which he hid under a rather pleasant, polite English exterior – because the English are vicious, you know, but if they're very polite with it, people often don't pick it up – and that's the only connection I can get.'

There were a number of interestingly contradictory strands in
Reg, all suggestive of a man desperate to be funny and subversive
on the quiet. Reg was a virtual interloper in the middle class,
motoring around Somerset selling insurance in his Austin 10.
He clung on to his class by speaking in the right accent ('Mum
still says "orf",' says Cleese) and reading the *Telegraph* – something John still did as late as the 1960s. Although to Cleese he
was 'a delightfully lazy man who never worked after about 2.30
p.m. in his life', at the same time Reg was reputed to sell more
life assurance than any other salesman in the county. Despite
the surface lack of tension, there was a drive in Reg, sometimes
comical, sometimes just competitive, that was distinctly
ungentlemanly.

Once, Reg was driving down a narrow, winding country lane
with John and Muriel when a driver going the other way came
very fast round a corner and hit his brakes and horn. Both parties
screeched to a halt, and the other driver leapt out in a fury and
started shouting at Reg, who simply sat smiling beatifically at
him. At the end of this tirade, Reg said in a French accent: 'Ah!
You must be ze fine old Eeenglish gentleman, no?' The driver
apparently grunted and said, 'Well, as a matter of fact I am,' and
drove off. In a restaurant in Torquay, when he couldn't get
served, Reg got the order speeded up by announcing that he
was a doctor and had an operation in fifteen minutes. Another
time, Reg Cleese wrote to *Punch* magazine because he could not
understand one of the cartoons, the kind of thing Basil Fawlty
at his most clenched-teethed outraged might well have done.
('There's a bit of my father in him. He's got my father's heavy
sarcastic wit. But I don't see much of me,' John Cleese says of
Fawlty.) Reg Cleese's was a rare type of humour, using sometimes just a droll or bizarre comment, which he handed down
to his son in the form of a thesaurus-like grasp of the outer
reaches of the English language, with absurd euphemisms, with
outrageous invective and stale banality reheated to a turn and
served up as fresh. John Cleese has been known at cricket
matches to silence experts with knowledgeable-sounding gibber-
ish. ('With this cloud cover and a bit of a green top, the seamers
should make it move around a bit for the first hour.') He has
often considered writing a script with characters who speak

entirely in clichés; 'Uncharted waters. Now, there's a pretty kettle of fish, or should I say a horse of a different colour?'

Yet it is Muriel who seems to have had a stronger influence in Cleese's life. There is a theory that most comedians have dominant mothers, and Cleese maintains that all the *Monty Python* team came from mother-centred families. Many people who knew the Cleeses think John's humour came from Muriel, even if they find it impossible to remember examples of her wit. Cleese himself does not tend to recount stories of his mother's humour, other than of the unconscious variety, such as when he asked if his dad, who was often teased about having a Jewish nose, had any Jewish blood in him. 'Well, two of his cousins *were* furriers,' he claims she replied. 'Mum also had difficulty with my first name,' he says. 'She sometimes called me Bill, who was a cousin who'd stayed with them before I was born. I think I looked a bit like him. She also called me Reg, and sometimes Roy, who was Bill's father. But I didn't mind at all. John is not a racy name.'

Muriel Cleese has certainly turned out to be a sporting nonagenarian. 'I've told her that when she dies I am not going to bury her, but have her stuffed and put in a glass case in our front hall, like Jeremy Bentham,' announced Cleese shortly before Christmas 1990. 'She is delighted. She lives in a very nice home and everybody there knows she is going to be stuffed.' In her late seventies, and no natural fan of the *Monty Python* style of humour (she disliked most *Python* sketches, but then so does Cleese), she still made an award-winning radio advertisement for *Life of Brian*. At eighty-one, Muriel was nicknamed by the *Daily Mirror* 'The Demon Whist-Driver of Weston-super-Mare', being, according to friends, virtually unbeatable. The *Mirror* went on: 'Earlier this year Mrs Cleese suffered a terrifying ordeal when she and two sprightly chums, aged seventy-three and seventy-seven, were trapped in a lift between floors in a block of flats for around half an hour and had to be rescued by firemen.' Cleese refused to comment, bar: 'All I can say is that she is alive.' The reason Cleese says less about his mother than about Reg is simply that she is still living, and as someone brought up to ensure above all that Muriel was danced attendance upon and kept on an even keel, he does not want to upset her. Yet when asked once if he subscribes to the theory that no man can ever find anyone as loving as his mother, Cleese replied tartly, 'It depends what your mother is like!' He admits he has had relationships with several versions of his mother; 'I'm more or less resigned to being attracted to a particular type, and my best chances are to find an optimistic version of it,' he told the writer John Hind.

Even when at school, the young Cleese was never far from Muriel. St Peter's Preparatory School had been established in Weston-super-Mare for sixty-six years when John arrived (with nine other new boys) on 22 September 1948, a month before his ninth birthday. Cleese, in his grey flannel shorts, shirt, blazer and cap plus a grey and blue striped tie, joined Crawford House as a £50 a term day boy. Both Crawford, and the other house, Duckworth, were divided into two sections, Butterflies and Grasshoppers. John Cleese was a Crawford Grasshopper.

St Peter's, as *the* prep school in Weston, had been the obvious choice for Reg and Muriel, but they had still studied the green-covered prospectus in detail. The school motto, *Mens Sana In Corpore Sano*, was not the most original of all time, but originality was not a prized virtue in Weston-super-Mare. The school crest bore the two crossed keys to the Pearly Gates, which may have seemed a bit premature for a prep school, but local people were hot on preparedness. The prospectus, with its curious punctuation and odd use of Capital Letters, explained how the headmaster, Geoffrey Tolson, a graduate of Queen's College, Cambridge, was 'assisted by a fully qualified Staff of Oxford and Cambridge Men'. 'Weston-super-Mare is recommended by doctors all over England for its healthy climate which is bracing but not too strong for delicate children. Almost immediately behind the School are the Kewstoke Woods in which the boys are able to go for walks and for recreation.'

St Peter's is acknowledged by most ex-pupils as a supremely kind and well-intentioned school, and Mr Tolson, 'Tolly', to have been an enormously decent and caring man. 'He was rather unusual,' says one former pupil. 'He was very tall, not willowy, but big, and very upright, as though he had been in the Guards, although he didn't seem to have been in the armed forces at all.

He was very young to be a headmaster and he was also very young to be bald. He was as bald as a coot. Mr Tolson had a little MG sports car, and Mrs Tolson was had up for speeding in it, which we all thought was very exciting. She was a very beautiful woman who looked Spanish with very dark hair, and an extremely cut-glass accent.' ('Mrs Tolson,' waxed the prospectus, 'who was a member of the scholastic profession before her marriage and is herself the daughter of a Doctor, takes personal care of the boys and superintends the household arrangements.')

Given the quality of the Tolsons' care for their boys, it is not surprising that there is real dismay in Mr Tolson's notes in the school magazine for Cleese's first three terms at St Peter's. Like the Weston-super-Mare tourist brochures of the time, the school prospectus had promised much about the healthy local air, but 1948–9 seems to have been plagued with a succession of unpleasant illnesses. Mr Tolson's notes on the period read like a journal of epidemiology. In that first Christmas term 1948, he announced that the school had been stricken down by 'the illness', some form of 'haemolytic streptococcus', and the school play was cancelled. In Easter term 1949, it was the measles that did for the play. In Summer 1949, it was a mumps epidemic and bronchial infections; hot on their heels came whooping cough.

Not every boy at St Peter's – which closed in the early 1970s to make way for a housing estate – regarded the school with affection. Roald Dahl attended it between 1925 and 1929 – before Mr Tolson's time – and devoted a third of his childhood autobiography, Boy, to it: 'St Peter's was on a hill above the town. It was a long three-storeyed stone building that looked rather like a private lunatic asylum, and in front of it lay the playing fields with their three football pitches. One-third of the building was reserved for the Headmaster and his family. The rest of it housed boys, about 150 of them altogether, if I remember rightly.'

John Cleese was never happier than when he was at St Peter's. This was remarkable since, apart from his height, which was to become a burden, he was also a day boy at a time when even boys who lived in Weston tended, eccentrically perhaps, to board. 'We boarded because our parents believed in boarding –

it was supposed to be a good experience,' says one contemporary. 'Day boys were there under sufferance. John may well, like some other day boys, have had a bit of a chip on his shoulder, as he may have been treated with mild contempt by other boys. Day boys missed out on midnight feasts and initiation ceremonies, the life-blood of a school. Boarders were the norm, and, I suppose it might have implied that your parents were not quite as well off.' The young John Cleese also managed to give the impression even to those who knew him only slightly that he was embarrassed because his parents were over-protective, and even thought his father a bit of a buffoon.

Cleese nevertheless slowly succeeded in emerging as the undisputed star pupil of St Peter's. There is in the most English of characters a curious trait of understating one's scholastic performance: Churchill, for example, according to his biographer Martin Gilbert, claimed to have left his Latin paper blank in one exam, which was simply not true. Although John Cleese once told the author Hunter Davies, 'I was very clever at my prep school, so clever that I used to have fantasies about the other boys and how they came to terms with me being so much cleverer than them,' his own account of his social reputation at St Peter's is modest. The picture he usually paints of himself at nine is of a lonely, isolated boy, meek, bad at mixing, not well-liked and prone to being bullied. He was also with great speed nicknamed Cheese, which did not help. 'I remember my father once arriving to say hello and bring me something and finding three boys sitting on top of me. He had to chase them away.' Yet the truth behind John Cleese's protestation that he was a beleaguered, uncomplaining coward, seems to be that he was extraordinarily brave.

After creating an impression of insignificance early on – a perception that for those who did not know him well was to linger – Cleese quickly established himself as a wag by developing a version of his parents' subversive humour. In the best comic tradition, by making people laugh he gained popularity and became liked. He can precisely identify the first time he raised a laugh, though not the actual joke. It was in Form IIa, in an English lesson conducted by Mr Sanger-Davies. From then on, he says: 'I used to sit at the back of the class and make silly comments on what people had said. I discovered it was a cheap and easy way of becoming popular because I was never possessed of enough courage to do outrageous things.'

One St Peter's master by the name of Mr J. A. Milligan would have seen it differently. Soon after starting at St Peter's, Cleese had begun to grow alarmingly – by the age of twelve, he towered over Mr Tolson, the headmaster. Mr Milligan, on the other hand, did not tower over anyone much. Barnabus J. Butter, one of Cleese's best friends at school, recalls how all the boys had to line up in a corridor known as The Passage, which was plastered with school pictures, noticeboards and antlered deer heads, before each meal to show that their hair was tidy and their hands were clean.

> This small master came along, about my height, and John wouldn't put his hands out. Mr Milligan said, 'Cleese, your hands.' And Cleese said: 'You know, Mr Milligan, I've been thinking about something.' 'And what is that, Cleese?' 'A milligram is a very small thing.' Milligan was furious, but it was impossible for him to take action against John because, after all, he had only said that a milligram was a very small thing. John very, very rarely got into trouble, because, while schoolboy humour was so obvious – flicking pellets and letting off stinkbombs – his was different. Sometimes we didn't understand it and sometimes the teaching staff didn't understand it. And I can often see a direct line from his humour at school through to *Monty Python*. His jokes were sophisticated, and I think sometimes he was the only person who understood them, which, perhaps, is why people have called him serious.

Butter, a prosperous farmer's son, remembers another incident of breathtaking Cleese impudence.

> We had a very good schoolmaster who, I think, was of Austrian origin and he had certain mannerisms of speech, lots of 'er' this and 'er' that, and then he got into a habit of saying things like 'naturally-speaking' and 'generally-speaking'. And we used to keep a score of how many ers, generally-speakings

and naturally-speakings he would use in a lesson. Well, on a day when Cleese and I were in different classes, there was complete uproar suddenly in the room next to the one I was in. Apparently the master had said 'prognosticatiously-speaking' to loads of applause and complete uproar. Now to leave a classroom was unthinkable, but Cleese came out of the next door room, walked down the corridor to the room I was in with another class, stuck his head round the door, completely disregarded the teacher who was taking the lesson and said: 'Prognosticatiously-speaking'. And we then understood and rose to our feet and there were two teachers who didn't have a clue what was going on.

Another friend, two years above Cleese at St Peter's, was Michael Paget.

Why he was outstanding, and I remember him well, irrespective of his later fame, was because he was a ridiculously tall boy and he lived in Weston-super-Mare. Otherwise, he was a typical English schoolboy. He was not funny. In fact he was very serious. We were just local boys. I think the adjective that one might apply to him is harmless. He struck me as intelligent, likely to be a boffin, the sort of boy who would end up as a scientist.

In the holidays we messed around, like all boys. His house, at the time, was in Clarence Road North, by Clarence Park, which is where I met his parents. I only remember going into the kitchen, and my impression was of ordinariness. His mother made little impression. I remember his father very well as a tall, rather dapper man with glasses and a moustache. He looked like John now with glasses on. He always seemed to me to wear a flat hat and be rather gentlemanly. I never knew what he did for a living. I was surprised to find out later that he was a salesman, but it explained why John didn't board. He struck me as a very ordinary man, not a character at all, except in the sense that he was the sort of character that John now takes off, albeit with a kindly eye. There seemed to be a distance between them. His house was very nicely situated and Clarence Park lent itself to playing, which is what we did. In those days boys didn't get up to the sort of mischief they do today. Play was very innocent – tree-climbing, ball games, hide and seek, exchanging funny jokes. Other boys came along sometimes. There was another day boy who lived in the Clarence Park area. I wouldn't have said that he was John's or my type at all. He had a very red face and used to smell of urine.

Despite being the author of some elegant schoolboy japes at St Peter's and having his 'Just William' life in Clarence Park, Cleese also had a secret life at home. 'For some reason, I was always drawn to comedy. I can even remember when I was about nine, staying home from school one day and writing a script – which is a very bizarre thing to do, when I look back on it.' He had been in bed with a cold, and wrote a couple of pages of dialogue in an exercise book, based on Jewell and Warriss, a contemporary radio comedy double act. He never sent the script off. Entertainment was simply not a big part of the Cleese family's life. They listened to the radio, as everyone did, would occasionally go to the Knightstone Theatre in Weston to see someone like Frankie Howerd, and were arguably quite early in getting a television, in 1952, when he was thirteen and there were still only about 1 million TV sets in Britain. But for the most part, Cleese seems almost to have been on a mission to gather material for his adult career.

He was to borrow more than just the situations and characters Weston-super-Mare gave him; he even purloined local names mercilessly. One Summer term there was a civil war in the school, the pupils siding either with a boy called Dibble or another named Wymer, and changing allegiances fairly regularly. Dibble and Wymer (now believed to be, respectively, a farmer and a coach driver in Somerset) became particular favourites of Cleese's. An early *Monty Python* sketch, by Cleese and Graham Chapman, has Eric Idle as an architect called 'Mr Wymer of Wymer and Dibble' competing with another (potty and sycophantic) architect Mr Wiggin (Cleese) for the business of building a block of flats. In another, more recent sketch in *The Meaning of Life*, Cleese plays a headmaster baffling his pupils with a plethora of silly rules, ticking off Dibble and Wymer for inattentiveness shortly before embarking upon a graphic sex education class, to the boys' extreme boredom.

Apart from an entertainment John vaguely remembers he performed aged nine with the boy next door for three or four parents, he was eleven when he made his stage debut in 'The Concert', a termly event at St Peter's, in which pupils sang, played instruments and sometimes performed sketches. Form IV's play, *A Cure for Colds*, starred Frampton and Cleese: 'Frampton's part was by far the largest,' noted the school magazine, 'and he was outstandingly the best performer; but if we remember his excellent speaking we shall also remember a superb and shattering sneeze with which Cleese shook the room.'

At Christmas 1951, having just won the Twelve and Over Writing Competition Prize, Cleese played Malvolio in *Scenes from Twelfth Night: The Tricking of Malvolio*. (*Twelfth Night* was a play, he later said, that 'should have been sent back to the author for a redraft'.) Butter says he played the part very seriously, though Cleese was quoted in 1980 as saying of this particularly glorious Christmas: 'I played in *Twelfth Night* – who's the pain in the arse in that? – Malvolio – very badly, completely without any understanding or ability; and I never had any ability as an essayist either.' Miss S. Atherstone Cox's review in the magazine read: 'Malvalio [*sic*] gave a good performance. His speech was clear, and he was an imposing figure.

'The steward's self-importance has diffused itself over all the details of his life,' Miss Atherstone Cox continued. 'One felt that he had grasped this trait, but he was not pompous. He should have "stalked" and used the length of the stage, instead of a few steps in the middle of it. He is sober, trustworthy and diligent – one would not have doubted these qualities, but self-conceit and vanity were lacking. His vanity should appear ludicrous. How he should have enjoyed censuring Sir Toby! But, for twelve years of age, can one expect more? I think not.' It wasn't until a 1980 BBC production of *The Taming of the Shrew*, in which he appeared as Petruchio, that Cleese regained any affection for Shakespeare.

Even in cricket, Cleese was using his humour to succeed and simultaneously amuse himself in his private little way. Barnabus

Butter believes he may even have perfected an early prototype of the silly walk on the cricket field.

> He used to enrage a coach who came to us – a nice old chap called Bill Andrews who was an ex-Somerset cricketer and very broad Somerset. John was so good that he could play quite the wrong shot to the right ball. He would get a very bad ball that deserved to be hit to the boundary and he would play an immensely elaborate forward defensive stroke, with his little finger sticking out. He was very tall, with great long legs down the wicket, holding the bat like a flute, and of course what he should have done was take a swipe at it and the coach used to get absolutely enraged about this because John was doing it deliberately. And then a very good ball would be bowled at him and he would take a terrific swipe at it – all arms and legs – and hit it for six. Of course, that was the right ball to play a defensive shot to.
>
> There was a sense of mischief. But any other schoolboy couldn't have done it because they weren't good enough batsmen. They would have been out. John had a sort of angular elegance, while the rest of us were still small and running about in shorts and getting in the way, quite compact and bouncy as boys are. When we were doing gym he was just different. If we were trying to get a ball into a high net, he would just pick it up and drop it in with the wave of a hand.

In other fields, Cleese continued this strange inner life, as a largely unappreciated, personal joke. He would write sports reports for the magazine of a dullness that can only have been self-parodying. In a debate on 'Capital Punishment Should be Abolished', the magazine reported: 'Cleese, summing up for the motion, gave his ideas of suitable vocational training for assassins.' He lost by a large majority. Some of Cleese's private jokes took a few years to mature. 'It is very funny to think that Mr Hickley, who used to teach at my prep school, would not allow me to do singing classes – partly because I was subversive, but mainly on sheer lack of talent. I'm sure I was the only man he ever taught who finished up singing in a Broadway musical!' In 1985, in the press biography for his film *Silverado* – itself something of a personal joke about the incongruity between England and America, with which he was by now so familiar – Cleese wrote: 'I came out of the lower middle class in England, and was brought up in a small town where everything was very respectable, and it was only thirty years later that I realized that they were all completely insane. I'd learned that kind of normal façade too, so up to about ten years ago I even thought *I* was normal. But under the façade, I've always been trying to escape from being British.'

At twelve, however, it seems that Cleese's height was shaping his personality more than misgivings about being British. He was already six foot tall and accustomed to a crow's-nest view of life, quite as different from an average perspective on the world as that of a very short man. Muriel was little more than five foot herself, and when she and her outsized son went shopping in Weston, John was aware that strangers would nudge each other. 'He grew very quickly as a boy. His clothes and his feet were a great worry. I don't think his feet are as big these days. They must have shrunk,' his mother told the *Sunday Times* in 1988, exercising the right of the indulgent mother through the ages to spend her late years attempting to embarrass her middle-aged children. Looking at his school photographs, it is possible to sympathize with young John, looming as he did over his classmates and even over Mr Tolson. The rictus pallbearer grin, which later conveyed such exquisite, comic insincerity, at this stage appeared simply that of a cheerful boy. But there is a sense of loneliness, of being a misfit, about him.

Nevertheless, the St Peter's magazine over the years is a chronicle of Cleese's rise to pre-eminence. Christmas 1949, the Form II Prize (for English); Summer 1950, 'The Sports', Long Jump: 1st Cleese, 2nd Chapman (11 ft 4 in.); High Jump: 1st Chapman, 2nd Cleese (3 ft 4 in.). The Rowland Cup was awarded to Cleese and Chapman (a sweet coincidence, this little double act!). Cleese played in a Junior cricket match – 3rd XI v. St Dunstan's. Although bowled for a duck, he bowled well. Christmas 1950, Boxing: Junior Middleweight, Cleese beat Turton; 'Cleese made good use of reach and height to hold his opponent to long-range boxing, and to prod him with lefts and rights, to which Turton scarcely managed to make any return at all.' Summer 1951, 'The

Exhibition' (a regular event wherein pupils presented handi-crafts, models, projects, etc.): 'Cleese produced a neat little note-book containing remarks about tropical fish with illustrations.' Easter 1952, Rugby: Cleese in 2nd XV; Boxing: Heavyweights (Over 12, 6 st 10 lb), Cleese beat Dibble ('Dibble made gallant efforts against an opponent who towered over him'), but Hirons beat Cleese in Final. Crawford Butterflies top of Section. Sum-mer 1952, Gardening Club: 'A new class, one for miniature gardens, was added to the programme and Cleese won first prize with a skilful arrangement of succulents, mosses and alpines.' Lawn Tennis: Cleese and Butter reached semi-final doubles. Cricket: Cleese in 1st XI, got his School Colours. July 5th match v. Walton Lodge: 'Of our batting there is little to say. It was dominated by Cleese, whose 34 included some first-rate shots and many Cleesian glides.'

Cricket, at which John was excelling – to the point of having that adjective coined after him – was proving to be the major point of contact between John and his father. Reg used to take him and Barnabus, who were eventually made captain and vice-captain respectively, to matches. Butter: 'Reg was always very avuncular, very kind to me and used to take us in his green Austin to watch cricket matches, sometimes in Weston, sometimes in Taunton, in the days when Somerset was the most entertaining team to watch, although it always lost. They were at the bottom of the championship, but there were fabulous characters in the Somerset team. We had little bags of cherries and deckchairs.' Almost exactly the same age, Jeffrey Archer was at many of the same matches. Years later, when Cleese was a member of the Lord's Taverners and going to matches at Lord's, he bumped into Archer at a Somerset game. St Peter's being regarded as for people with money, the young Jeffrey had gone to Christchurch, a state school, so did not know Cleese at the time of those sunny days out with Barnabus Butter. Yet, curi-ously, the Cleeses, whose musical flats game around Weston continued – a change of home every eighteen months had become the regular pattern – once moved out of a rented flat at 6 Eastern Mansions (known as Butt's flat after the landlord) as the Archer family moved in. For the Archers it was the fourth move. The year was 1954. Like a detail in an Archer novel, in their late forties, the two men, multimillionaires, world-renowned figures, political opponents and even clients of the same smart London art dealer, discovered that as boys they had slept in the same bed. Their mothers remain acquaintances, and still meet to share the occasional gripe about how seldom their brilliant sons visit them.

Summer 1953 was John Cleese's last term at St Peter's. Head librarian, prefect, predominant, unopposed, in fact, in every sport, he received an exhibition to Clifton College, the public school in Bristol. Yet there was a question mark over Cleese. St Peter's School had a special role in life, and John Cleese did not seem fully to aspire to it. 'I think we were all expected to be lawyers, or doctors or parsons or insurance bods or bank bods,' says Butter, who indeed became an overseas bank officer. 'But the whole thing was embedded in a class structure which I now find quite bizarre. I think we were conscious even at that age that we were supposed to be a cut above the other boys who went to the rough schools, or whatever, but it was only at later schools that it might turn into a vicious kind of snobbery. We were all expected to be that ruling middle class. We were destined for the vicarage tea party.'

In Mr Tolson's foreword to the last school magazine of Cleese's time as a pupil, he felt obliged to explain, in effect, why John Cleese was Section Captain but never Head Boy, the honour that went to Butter, even though young Barnabus believed himself to be second-rate compared to Cleese. John was, wrote Tolson, 'An able deputy, and it is he who wins the Whitting Cup for General Excellence; his exhibition at Clifton was gained as the result of the very rapid improvement which he has maintained in recent terms and which has now carried him indisputably to the top of the VIth form.' Although the school usually combined the Whitting Cup with the Gimblett Prize (the latter given 'to the boy who is considered to have exercised the best influence in the school and seems likely to uphold its tradition after he leaves it and this should be assessed quite regardless of his prowess at work or games'), they pointedly did not award it that year – i.e. to Cleese, although it wasn't put like that. It was the first year the prize had been reserved and seemed to show remarkable foresight on Tolson's part, given Cleese's future career. The mild snub was clearly Cleese's come-uppance for his cheekiness and lack of Vicarage Tea Party virtues. The writing was on the wall, for those who chose to read it. That last magazine reported: 'Lawn Tennis: Cleese and Butter lost the Doubles Final because they must take the game more seriously if they hope one day to be good at it.'

Although he later returned to teach at St Peter's and was a willing guest at a school reunion in 1982 (but then so was Roald Dahl), John Cleese's own view of the school verges on the ambivalent, though not a quarter as ambivalent as he was to be about Clifton. 'I didn't mind school, though the education was narrow. I specialized in science and maths, but I've always had an intuitive interest in anything to do with humans, whether it was history, philosophy, sociology or religion. I'm afraid I thought the religion I got at school was absolutely half-witted: the Great Headmaster in the Sky kind of idea. You know, if you followed the School Rules, which were the Ten Commandments, you'd become a prefect and go to Heaven.'

Cleese's view of the Latin master Captain Lancaster, nick-named 'Capio', was radically different from that of Roald Dahl, who pilloried a 'Captain Hardcastle' in *Boy*. 'Hardcastle' was without doubt Captain Lancaster, and he left quite a different impression on John Cleese, who remembers weeping with laughter at the age of ten when Lancaster read *Three Men in a Boat* to the class. Many ex-pupils believe that Captain Lancaster, in a slightly more amiable guise, was the Major in *Fawlty Towers*.

Another master Cleese truly adored was Gerald Bartlett, who taught him English and Maths. 'He was very important to most of the boys who either respected or worshipped him,' says one of Cleese's friends. 'He was the second master in the school and had a rather mincing gait and an effete way of speaking. He was clean-shaven, he had whiskers along his cheek bones. I don't remember him being unkind, but a little sarcastic, and occasionally he lost his temper. He had his own gang of followers, his own henchmen.'

'He awakened in me,' said John Cleese, in a *New Yorker* interview in 1988, 'a love of knowledge. Nobody else did.'

2 Chalk and Cleese

And it's not for the sake of a ribboned coat,
   Or the selfish hope of a season's fame,
But his Captain's hand on his shoulder smote –
   'Play up! play up! and play the game!'

From 'Vitae Lampada', by Sir Henry Newbolt, Old Cliftonian

Although low in officially sanctioned laughs, St Peter's Pre-paratory School, Weston-super-Mare, and the procession of addresses his family occupied in and around it provided a rich seam of absurdity for John Cleese to mine, awakening in him a vast comic potential. But it was not until he arrived, at the age of thirteen, at his Bristol public school, Clifton College, that Cleese began to find for his private sense of humour a reliably appreciative audience beyond himself and Barnabus J. Butter. The great stimulus for this stepping up of his comic output, apart from the enjoyment he took and the power he found he could exercise by making people laugh, was that John was markedly less happy at Clifton than he had been in the comforting and closeted jolliness of St Peter's.

Cleese joined North Town, one of the two day boy houses, entering the school in Form IVA. He would remain at Clifton until the VIth. Having risen from shy obscurity to becoming the most fêted twelve-year-old at St Peter's, John was once again a 'newbug' and one among 838 bright boys. He was minor and anonymous, his reduced status compounded by his awkward height and the adjoining stigma of being, yet again, a day pupil in a school largely composed of boarders. In 1953, Reg's father,

John Edwin, died, and the Cleeses moved to his house, 2 East Shrubbery, next to Redland police station in Bristol, so that John would not have to board or make the long journey from Weston-super-Mare to Clifton every day. In his first term, he had his leg pulled about his height, and was bullied – he tells a similar story to the one he relayed about his first term at St Peter's, of his father coming to the school, on this occasion to watch him play football, to find three boys sitting on his son's head.

John also did not do as well academically as he had at St Peter's. Although he was a successful sportsman at Clifton, thereby avoiding suffering, as some boys did in public schools, at the hands of sadistic sports masters, he continues even today to describe the school with a tinge of bitterness as 'Clifton Sports Academy'. He has summed up Clifton in his day as 'lumpen and unimaginative', although he frequently stresses that it was not a cruel regime.

A measure of John's initial unease when he started at Clifton is that he continued to keep in touch with his prep school more closely and with more obvious nostalgia than many might consider healthy. Children are often seized with a longing for a school they have just left, but, like those adults who find it impossible not to cling for decades to memories of their Alma Mater, the teenager Cleese seemed to take this yearning a little far. He even returned to teach at St Peter's when his entry to Cambridge University was delayed.

Not that the masters of St Peter's thought this at all worrying. Years after he left as a boy, the school magazine continued to carry nearly as many Cleese bulletins as it did when he was its star pupil. But eighteen miles away in Bristol, issue after issue of *The Cliftonian* was circulated without mention of the school's largest small boy. Conversely, in the issue for Christmas Term 1953, the St Peter's magazine whooped: 'J. M. Cleese (Clifton) has visited us at least four times during the term and came to watch both our matches against St Dunstan's. He is very happy in his new surroundings and has taken up fencing and fives. At Rugger his height has been a handicap and he has become a wing three-quarter, merely because he cannot be fitted into the scrum. He finds French very easy, but has to work at maths, since he is in the top set.' It was not until the summer of 1955, by which time Cleese was nearly sixteen, that he stopped ghosting around the corridors, although he doggedly went back to watch school matches.

The very idea of a teenager voluntarily turning up to watch school matches may perturb any veteran of the public school system, who might recall the more customary procedure of being forced on pain of detention or worse to stand on freezing touchlines to cheer their school or house. By the age of sixteen, John Cleese was becoming a recognized wit with a skill for deriding the establishment in such a way as to avoid punishment. Yet his keenness to do something as ostentatiously conformist as attending matches at his old school suggests that two other crucial sides to his complex character (other than enjoying sport) were developing fast. The first was an overwhelming earnestness. The second, a subconscious need to be reassured – a need never really confronted until Cleese underwent extensive psychotherapy in his early thirties. Cleese's early professional career is characterized by a pattern of extreme restlessness. Uncertain about where he belonged, he felt, wherever he was and whatever he was doing, that he would rather be somewhere else, and otherwise engaged. At St Peter's, the young John had found a home more permanent and intellectually sympathetic than any offered by his well-intentioned parents and their constant domestic shifting. Analysis would later encourage the adult Cleese to build up inner strengths and securities so that he was able to discover that any truly permanent home would have to exist within himself.

As Clifton College became more tolerable to Cleese, his old prep school heard less from him. Then, as if in an attempt to reconcile the two places, in 1957, Cleese, at almost eighteen, rattled off an epic letter to St Peter's which included a complete history of Clifton College. Even in the age of innocence that was England in the 1950s, one can only imagine how odd, not to say uninteresting, such a treatise on the history of someone else's school must have seemed to the chaps back in Weston-super-Mare.

Not that Clifton's history is unworthy of a short line or two. The school was founded in 1862, 'for the purpose of providing for the Sons of Gentlemen a thoroughly good and liberal Education at a moderate cost', and its substance had little changed over the years. Fagging was still part of school life, although Cleese, as a day boy, would have escaped dormitory duties, and had only to run errands for house prefects, look after their Corps uniforms, and fetch sweets for them from the 'grubber', the school tuck shop. Corporal punishment by prefects had ended, thanks to the persistence of the psychiatrist father of another ex-pupil, Roger Cooper, who left Clifton the year Cleese arrived. (Cooper later became famous as the businessman who spent a considerable part of the 1980s in prison on trumped-up charges in Iran.) The headmaster in Cleese's first year was Sir Desmond Lee, later a Cambridge don, who is acknowledged as having steered the school in a more intellectual direction after it had become a rather rowdy place. Lee was succeeded by Nicholas Hammond, a fellow of Clare College, Cambridge, who was the ninth man to occupy the post and went on, in 1962, to become Professor of Greek at Bristol University. This busy, scholarly don must have been a far cry from the eminently approachable 'Tolly' at St Peter's. Distinguished old Cliftonians include Sir Henry Newbolt, whose jingoistic poetry encapsulated the stiff-upper-lip public school ethic, and the actors Sir Michael Redgrave and Trevor Howard. Howard, like Cleese, was more inclined to play cricket than seek adolescent stardom in school drama productions.

With Reg Cleese nearing retirement, John's parents made great financial sacrifices, using up most of Muriel's inheritance, even to put their son into what he describes as 'the middle middle middle' of the public school system. His day boy fees at Clifton when he started were about half the boarding rate, and when he later won a Mathematics scholarship worth £36 per annum they were reduced to £48 per term. The fees, though not a fortune, clearly meant less to other parents than to John's. It was only at Clifton, when he mixed with boys from all over the country, that Cleese first became aware that there were people not only brighter but better off than himself. While other boys went abroad for holidays, Bournemouth continued to be the Cleese summer retreat. These disparities began to breed in him what he describes as 'a watchful detachment' to help justify the seditious attitude he was already prone to.

John did well enough in maths, Latin and chemistry, but he maintains that, apart from his cricket coach Reg Sinfield, no master ever bothered much with him: 'I had no ability whatsoever at essays or composition, which is quite funny. I always tell kids this. Because I think it's very interesting for them to discover that here's a bloke who is earning his living actually as a professional writer more than anything else. And that nobody during my twelve years at school ever discerned the slightest ability in this direction. School seems to be a wonderful way to educate yourself so that you'll know what to do with your spare time.'

Six foot 4¾ inches when he started at Clifton, Cleese found it harder than ever to be physically inconspicuous, and this added to his sense of not belonging. 'His height gave the impression he was quite uncoordinated,' says one boy who started at the same time. Cleese remembers with some pain the humiliation of being measured for his Corps uniform in his second term. He was also hurt by a master calling him 'a prominent citizen', which he took as a compliment until the master went on to get a laugh by saying he meant that Cleese stuck out.

'I wasn't very popular at school. I don't think I was actually hated. I think they felt I wasn't one of them. I was rather tall, an only child, rather mollycoddled, and I thought by being funny I could become more popular,' he says. That outsider feeling was to travel with Cleese down the years. Michael Filer, now a leading Bournemouth accountant and former Tory mayor of the town, was close to John at school. (It is significant that an extraordinary number of Cleese's Clifton contemporaries became accountants, a favoured target in *Monty Python* sketches.) Filer observes: 'John wasn't a comedian the whole time, it was just starting to come out. He was very serious and quite shy. He was a day boy and I was a boarder but we used to share a room when we went away for two-day cricket matches, and he really was very unsure of himself. He certainly wasn't the most popular boy in any crowd.'

'He seemed mildly eccentric,' recalls John Phillpott, another day boy a year younger than Cleese, who started at Clifton in the same term. Cleese and Phillpott sometimes walked part of the way home together. 'You always noticed him in the crowd because he was so tall, and his comments always seemed to be very offbeat. He was a bit of a puzzle to most of us.'

Cleese's softly-upholstered, emotionally-cramped background continually seemed to be stumbling into the foreground. 'I went to his home for meals a couple of times. His parents were very kind, and seemed rather elderly to me,' Filer recalls. For Cleese there was much more to it than the fact that his parents were manifestly old; there was a subtle kind of deprivation caused by their gentleness. 'I had a lot of problems about asserting a normal healthy aggression. I think that went on for a long time; even at Clifton when I was playing soccer I didn't like the violent side of it, and if someone kicked me, almost on a point of principle I wouldn't kick them back. It's taken me many years to get any confidence in that sort of self-assertive behaviour – like most English people I do not like scenes or rows.'

Scenes involving comedy were another matter, however, although Cleese's comic debut at Clifton was quite accidental. He was cast as Lucifer in a production of *Dr Faustus*. Things did not go quite as Marlowe is thought to have intended. At the moment Cleese made his supposedly terrifying 'tremendous entry', the entire audience fell about laughing. 'It was the one time I was really trying to avoid laughs,' he jokes now. Another such time was on a Cadet Corps summer camp at Tidworth. John Cleese was not renowned as a particularly fine boy soldier, and such military demeanour as he mustered was irrevocably punctured when, on a night exercise, he trod on a partridge, which then clung onto his khaki trousers, defying his efforts to beat it off. Cleese's yaroos and howls coupled with the partridge's indignant squawking combined to make a din sufficient to give away his patrol's position even to a stone-deaf enemy.

By the time he was thirteen, Cleese's humour was developing a systematic side. He was now writing down jokes, particularly from *The Goon Show*, which he listened to obsessively every Friday night. 'He was very keen on that, and a lot of us just didn't understand it,' recollects John Phillpott. It was by remembering how he followed the Goons in the way that other youngsters idolize football teams that Cleese understood how a later generation of teenagers (not to mention adults) became addicted to

Monty Python: 'When you do a show like that, the kids are getting a message that there are other people out there who are a bit older and who have seen a bit more of the world who also think it's pretty damn silly, and that's why they embrace those comedy shows with that enthusiasm. It's not just the comedy, it's the world view.' John was also a fan of Bilko, George Burns, the Marx Brothers and two blacked-up American impressionists on radio and later television, Amos 'n' Andy. Today, with the exception of a few more contemporary comedians, such as Woody Allen and Steve Martin, Cleese still cites those Fifties stars as his comedy heroes.

Assisted by a quick mind and a little discreet and acknowledged plagiarism from his favourite radio routines, John was able to keep up a generous supply of facetious comments in lessons, aimed at teachers he often liked but would not spare for that reason alone. One history master at school, who wrote on his report 'Cleese indulges in subversive activity at the back of the class', may have been unaware of the excitement John was stirring up in the schoolroom. The master could not pronounce his Rs, and the young Cleese foresaw delicious trouble. Eventually, the doomed man devoted a whole term to the seventeenth century, which, as Cleese had worked out, would be an absolute nightmare for anyone who couldn't pronounce 'R', what with Woyal Pwewogatives, Woundheads and Woyalists, Cwomwell, the Westowation and the Glowious Wevolution of 1688. The history master, as only schoolmasters can, managed to remain blissfully ignorant of the hilarity he was causing. One can only hope that the poor Clifton teacher somehow missed the 'Welease Woger' scene in *Life of Brian*, where a Pontius Pilate with the same affliction is mocked to his complete incomprehension by a huge crowd of Biblical extras.

Another Clifton staff member known as The Marshal and actually a retired company sergeant major called French had the job of enforcing minor discipline. One of his routines was to go round the school checking up that boys were in classes on time. Like the history master, The Marshal also remained – or contrived to remain – blithely unaware that he was being ridiculed by the tall boy from North Town House. Cleese recounts: 'Once I was late and I told him that someone had poured a pound of hot fat over me from the fourth floor window. Now, he knew this wasn't true, but he just looked at me and said . . . I can't remember what, "Don't let it happen again" or something. Coming to a school like this is bound to help a comedian.'

The staff at Clifton may have been deaf, extremely resilient or sensible and sensitive enough to let the young Cleese have his fun. Perhaps they were a little scared of this boy who, on occasion, looked and talked like a man, with an air, at least, of worldly wisdom. It seems most likely that Cleese's peculiar brand of humour was simply an irrelevance to the business of preparing boys for Oxbridge and the City. John Cleese was neither conventionally rude enough to be punished, nor conventionally academic enough to be (he felt) encouraged in any way. Public school provided Cleese with a perfect context for his early wit because it was the very people who made the rules who didn't get the jokes. He would later refine his technique and invest it with philosophical theory, citing Henri Bergson who pointed out that comedy is a social sanction against inflexible behaviour, that is, laughter comes from showing up the silliness of rigid situations by mocking them. The pomposity and regulations that infused Clifton provided, in one of history's happier accidents, an ideal training ground for a comedian looking for a target.

With hindsight, however, Cleese's image amongst the masters who remember him has become increasingly vivid and complimentary. 'An enthusiastic hard worker, funny in class,' 'A hardworking, kind student, an excellent cricketer,' 'A very quiet and sensitive person, humorous in class,' 'A very pleasant person to teach, bright and good fun,' were some of the comments garnered about Cleese in 1991, thirty-four years after he left Clifton. Apocryphal stories have even built up about Cleese's days at Clifton. He is credited, for example, with having laboriously painted footsteps from the school's life-sized statue of Field-Marshal Haig (an old boy) to the lavatories and back to his pedestal, a stunt he has certainly never confessed to. Not all ex-Clifton boys, however, recall Cleese as funny. Those not in his year or his house, or among his admirers, tended to miss the whole Cleese phenomenon. One slightly older man, now a prominent Fleet Street editor, remembers John as 'a rather dull boy'. And it is important to see that from his point of view;

imagine being at school but not knowing a tall, rather quiet, sporty boy in another year, with no great academic or other reputation. It must be perplexing in the extreme, in one's fifties, to find him being fêted internationally as a genius, and yet having no outstanding memory of him at all.

Cleese was soon, a little nervously, he admits, taking part in the twice-a-term house entertainments, some of which were plays, such as Molière's *Tartuffe*, and others revues, for one of which he once pinched some lines from Flanders and Swann. Years later, he would rework some of the sketches and characters he devised for the house entertainments into *Monty Python's Flying Circus*. By his last term, when he was eighteen, even though Cleese was still innocent enough to write charmingly tedious letters to his old prep school, the nervousness he displayed in early stage comedy attempts was giving way to a magnificent insolence. He is remembered for one routine at the very end of his school career about a retiring housemaster he particularly loathed, H. T. 'Billy' Williams. The sketch was so vicious and unexpected that it made the head of classics fall off his chair laughing. It was the first time Cleese had tasted the power of making large numbers of people laugh. 'Billy Will' taught classics, and was a small, bald, bespectacled martinet, remembered unaffectionately by one Cleese contemporary as looking like 'a wizened dwarf, a cold and distant person'.

'In the big speeches at mid-term, everybody had been saying how wonderful he was, so at the school entertainment at the end of term, I did a very wicked parody of the speeches, being as rude about my housemaster as was humanly possible and finishing up by wishing him every success in his renewed attempt at a happy marriage,' Cleese later explained in a 1988 interview in the rather different forum of *Playboy* magazine. 'There was something about that particular evening that I haven't recalled for thirty years. . . . I remember a kind of excitement, a kind of power. But there's a feeling of control in it too. I once performed at a pop concert with Terry Jones and Michael Palin in front of more than 35,000 people, and when you got a laugh, you began to see why Hitler liked his Nuremberg gigs.'

It was dressed as Hitler and ranting in his cod-German (a routine that became famous in *Python's* 'North Minehead

By-Election' skit and, later still, in the 'Germans' episode of *Fawlty Towers*) that Cleese pulled off another legendary stunt at Clifton. At an evening entertainment, he appeared on a raised platform and gathered a crowd of boys below him in the quadrangle. As he harangued them, a timid underling soldier came out of the doors behind him and tapped him on the shoulder to give him a message. He read the message and became hysterical, and started hitting and kicking the soldier, yelling and screaming at him, and shouting how people would be punished if they behaved like him, until the man fell backwards into the building. 'John dashed back into the building,' recalls Michael Filer, 'and you could hear all hell breaking loose behind the doors out of sight, and all of a sudden he came ranting and raving back with this soldier in his hands and threw him thirty feet over the balcony into the crowd. Of course it turned out to be a dummy.'

'It was very well done,' Cleese says of the event, although it had been risky. Clifton was unusual among public schools in having a Jewish house, and a Hitler comedy skit a decade after the war might have been thought a trifle offensive, although none of the Jewish boys, least of all Filer, was upset by it. Anti-semitism was simply not an issue at Clifton in the 1950s, although ten years before that it had been rife. Cleese has often since said (and as often proved) that there is no topic on earth that can't be made funny, although, on grounds of taste, he admits he has yet to lampoon cancer or national disasters.

Long and thin, Cleese was in many ways the archetypal seven-stone weakling, which makes his cricketing prowess at Clifton all the more remarkable. When he started, he was not keen on rugby, and would opt to play fives in a quiet spot behind the swimming pool, an approved and satisfying soft alternative. In 1955 he suffered a thigh strain which kept him off the cricket field for the whole of the summer, and leg injuries resulting from his incredible height would plague him all his life. Yet, encouraged by the Gloucestershire and England player Reg Sinfield whom he adored because 'he had a wonderful kind of wry humour and a kind of wisdom about him', Cleese finally made it into the Clifton College 1st XI in 1958, when he was seventeen. He describes himself as 'a slow-scoring opening bat and occasional off-spinner', adding: 'As an off-spinner I was more or less unplayable in June because for those four weeks the pitch was in line with the schoolhouse building and being 6 ft 5 in. my arm easily cleared the top of the sightscreen. So the poor old batsman was lucky if he had the faintest clue of what was coming to him.'

Cleese was, in fact, No. 10 in the batting order, often partnered by Michael Filer, the No. 11, who joined the XI at the same time and was almost as tall as Cleese. 'We used to run impossible singles, and each week we used to run each other out,' says Filer. 'We ended up with great big green marks all over our best white flannels, and each week we used to threaten to send each other the laundry bill.' Cleese was a considerable player who appeared with his team regularly in public schools matches at Lord's. The 1958 *Wisden* records him as third in both the bowling and the batting averages, the batting a particular achievement because he lacked the strength to hit the ball very far. 'It was only when I got to around eighteen that I realized I had to have a long bat because the moment I picked the bat up, I was literally slightly overbalancing towards the off-stump because I was at too great an angle to start with.'

His coup was to get Denis Compton out – twice, actually, and in July, not June! – when Clifton College played the MCC. *The Times*, a step upscale from the St Peter's school magazine, reported: 'Compton, D.C.S., c. Whitty b. Cleese 22. Confronted by Compton dancing down the wicket, Cleese decided to conspire with his wicket-keeper to have the great man stumped off a very wide one from the third ball of the next over. The wicket-keeper refused to enter into such a conspiracy, protesting that he had come to see Compton bat, "not to stump him". When an undaunted Cleese bowled his wide one, Compton was five yards out of his crease, unable to get anywhere near it and, completely by accident, the wicket-keeper brushed the bails with his glove. Cleese was wondering whether to dare to make an enquiry to the umpire when the wicket-keeper lobbed the ball back and called out: "Bad luck, old boy. You nearly had him." Cleese, disgusted that the gods had cheated him of his greatest scalp, trundled back, offered a gentle full toss and watched Sir smack it straight to Master Whitty at mid-on.' (In 1980, something similar happened when Cleese returned to Clifton to play in a charity match. He was out four times before the umpire would concede it, fearing that the crowd would go home if Cleese left the field.)

Cleese took cricket seriously, but his sense of humour did not desert him over the subject as it can some men. In one innings at Lord's, Cleese was bowled first ball and fell about laughing: 'I thought it was terribly funny that so much effort had gone into achieving so little. But as I left the pitch I saw all the outraged expressions on the faces of the old colonels.' The Denis Compton incident was, of course, not far from Cleese's mind when he wrote the line in *Fawlty Towers* that some consider to be his all-time funniest, where Basil, told by Polly that some disaster is 'not her fault', ups an hysteria-octave and demands, 'Who's fault is it then? Denis Compton's?' A fortnight after Cleese got Compton out, Clifton played Tonbridge at Lord's, and the *Times* reporter made a prescient note of the budding *Monty Python* silly walk, with a mention of 'the long-legged Cleese, who gives the quaint impression of running on stilts'.

Given the length of his legs, it is perhaps surprising that Cleese was also a good footballer, remembered by Stephen Albert, who was at Clifton and Cambridge with him as having 'the most amazing ability to dribble'. According to Michael Filer, 'Clifton is a rugby school, and John and I went to the headmaster together to ask if we could have soccer for one of the terms, which was agreed. So we played in all the first few soccer matches at Clifton. It was very amateurish. We played because we adored the game, and John was pretty good in those days. And we were assigned a master to supervise us who didn't know much about soccer. He tried to instil some "natural flair" and tactics. The day before our first ever school match, he got us into a classroom, took out the blackboard and marker and started talking tactics, especially about square balls being passed around. And John Cleese put his hand up quite simply and said to him: "Must we play with a square ball, because I find it hurts me when I head it?"' As a supporter of Bristol City, Cleese even induced one of their players to give the boys a coaching session.

The picture of John Cleese beaming from a cricket team photograph at Lord's and the stories of him as a VIth-former causing

masters and boys alike at Clifton to collapse with laughter suggest a young man enjoying total domination of his environment.
But, in other ways, Cleese was as unsettled at the end of his
time at Clifton as at the beginning. One experience there, reminiscent of how he did not quite become head boy at St Peter's,
changed his life. After his A-level term – he passed three – he
had a legitimate claim to being made a school prefect, one step
grander than house prefect. He was in the first Clifton cricket
team to have won at Lord's for ten years and had built up the
house cricket equipment stocks by judicious theft from other
houses; he ran the library and had reorganized the catalogue.
However, when he came back from the summer holiday for a
seventh term in the VIth to sit the Oxbridge exams, friends who
had got only two A-levels and done nothing for their house
became school prefects, while he was not even made a house
prefect. The snub, which he believes was the responsibility of
the hated housemaster, made him angrier than anything before
or since. 'I thought, "Right, if that is how the system works, I
want no part of it." From that time on I wore the cap of another
house and dropped out. I have never totally joined in anything
ever since.'

Although until now he had more or less absorbed it, by the
time he was eighteen, the public school ethic was definitely not
to John Cleese's taste. He felt he was not being treated as an
adult, and certainly not as a special young man. He balked at
the way the boys were inculcated with notions of house, school
and Christian spirit, and then told that lying could somehow be
part of the same ethic. Once, the school inspectors came to Clifton and one master said: 'Whatever question I ask you, put your
hand up. But if you know the answer, put your right hand
up.' He began to realize that the rule against lying was against
unnecessary lying, rather than anything to do with morality.
The only thing his confirmation into the Church of England at
sixteen confirmed for Cleese was that he did not subscribe to
organized religion. This revelation coincided with a newly discovered interest in psychology – he even declared an ambition
to become a psychoanalyst – and the school's effective taboo on
talking in any way about emotions went against the grain.
Because of his interest in psychology, Cleese decided that he

wanted to study biology, but he soon discovered that 'the biology teaching at Clifton was awful'. Nearly thirty years later, in his psychotherapy book *Families and How to Survive Them*, he asks co-author Robin Skynner what a chromosome is, to which Skynner asks: 'Didn't you do any biology?' Cleese replies: 'Yes, but the teacher was a former rugby international and he didn't know either.'

Cleese has forgiven Clifton despite its shortcomings, however, and acknowledges that the school has changed as much as he has: 'I went back to talk to the boys and I was so impressed by how alive and on the ball they were, so much more aware, so different from my generation.' The school, where fees for a boarder are now near to £10,000 a year, has also become a little more imaginative; the North Pole was the destination of a recent school trip. In May 1991, Cleese enthusiastically joined a two-day reunion at the school, at which he was the central attraction together with Roger Cooper, who had only recently come back from his imprisonment in Iran.

'The public school system is valuable in some respects,' Cleese now maintains. 'Eighty per cent of the people I know – myself included – are all ridden with self-doubt and are really very vulnerable. It's just a question of who's got the best façade.' Demonstrating just how good his façade was, and how much more deeply than any nascent psychoanalytic tendency ran in him the idea that emotions were for wimps, Cleese describes how as an adult he once stayed with a friend in Africa whose wife had just left him. 'All the time I stayed with him, I never asked him about it, or mentioned the fact, and nor did he.'

Cleese's alleged indifference as a student at Clifton lasted until he cracked the system and taught himself to do well in exams by being organized and cynical about them. He ended up in a scholarship form. 'One year I surprised everybody and came top in English and Latin. It was like Cardiff City winning the First Division.' Yet the power of the prevailing philistine culture was enough to ensure that little more was heard of English. After comfortably passing eight O-levels, Cleese took science A-levels in Mathematics, Chemistry and Physics. Reg and Muriel were pressurizing him to become an accountant, but apart from realizing by the end of Clifton that he had been bored for most of his life, John had no idea what he wanted to do. 'We were told we were going to be leaders of men. The arts were ignored. That went on until my middle years at Cambridge. When I was twenty-two I knew this fear that would grip me in the middle of a conversation about the arts. I just didn't know anything.' The idea of going to university was a new one in the Cleese family, but ever solicitous to their son's needs, the parents stumped up the money for an additional Oxbridge term. Cleese sat the exams for Cambridge University and won a place at Downing College.

Even though, sticking closely to his father's romantic assertion that there was 'a tradition of law' in the family, John had been accepted to read Law at Downing, a two-year wait was enforced. The ending of national service meant that the universities were swamped with undergraduates on postponed places, and Cleese had to find something to do with himself.

It is hard to imagine a less enterprising move for a nineteen-year-old of Cleese's calibre than to go back to teach at his old prep school, but that is exactly what he did. He knows he should have left the country, gone away to learn a language, meet girls and demote both Weston-super-Mare and the British public school ethic to the status of memory. Instead, he grew a beard and, in his own expression, he 'retired'. 'I often feel as if I wasted those two years going back to Weston. It was so unadventurous of me. I could have gone to Hong Kong for a year. But I wasn't encouraged by my parents who tended to be cautious.'

Cleese taught his pupils science, English, geography, history and some Latin, and rapidly found teaching 'an extraordinarily pleasant way of making a living. Teaching is very rewarding – in many respects more rewarding than what I'm doing now. I was nervous about being a schoolmaster with a name like mine. . . . But it turned out all right in the end. I had support from ancient Greek relations, of course. Sophocleese, Pericleese. . . . I'm sure if I hadn't become successful at what I'm doing now, I'd have been quite happy to have remained teaching. Getting up in front of a classroom is so ingrained that, even now, I could probably pass myself off as a fairly convincing schoolmaster without too much trouble.'

Even if Cleese was simply in another phase of his subliminal mission to become the funniest man in the world, at that time his huge enthusiasm for his new occupation (which combined erudition with performance, albeit before a classroom of small boys) was entirely genuine. Cleese has a wholly admirable aptitude for plundering new experiences for all they are worth. He also has a very low boredom threshold, indicated by his desire to keep moving on in later professional life. It is doubtful whether, had he returned to teaching after Cambridge, Cleese would have maintained the same fervour for the schoolroom.

Yet at St Peter's Cleese was the most dedicated of teachers. In Easter 1959, Mr John Roe, another master, wrote in the St Peter's magazine: 'Perhaps I may be allowed to put in a word of real thanks to Mr Cleese for all the hard work he has done with the XI. With a great deal of natural coaching talent and an enormous store of soccer anecdotes he has kept us alternately amazed and amused.' Rarely for a John Cleese enterprise, his football coaching at St Peter's was to little avail; his teams had a persistent habit of not winning a single game.

Perhaps because he was the wrong physique for rugby, Cleese's soccer evangelism was unstinting at St Peter's. Private schools, and particularly minor ones, would still get themselves in a state about the rugby/soccer divide at this time. Soccer was seen as not quite the game for gentlemen, and schools that allowed it considered themselves rather progressive; perhaps promoting soccer at St Peter's as he had done at Clifton was the form Cleese's small dissidence now took. In his first term, he showed two 'Films on Association Football' which, his mentor Mr Bartlett wrote, were 'frankly rather disappointing as the commentary was neither instructive nor amusing'. The pupils and masters were also treated to regular screenings of popular new films. They saw *The Lavender Hill Mob* on 26 February, which everyone loved, though few in the audience would have guessed that the unassuming schoolmaster fiddling with the projector would make an internationally acclaimed film of his own some thirty years later, employing Charles Crichton, the director of that Ealing comedy, as the director of *A Fish Called Wanda*.

Mr Cleese, 'who is never happier than when he is with the boys – and they respond to this as boys always will', appears to have been an odd young man. Maniacal teachers were to be a mainstay of his comedy – think only of the sex lesson sketch in *The Meaning of Life* or of Stimpson in *Clockwise*. Indeed, all forms of bossy schoolmasterish behaviour became a consistent Cleese target, for example, his cameo stoning official in *Life of Brian* ('Now, look, no one is to stone anyone until I blow this whistle. Is that clear?') and the Centurion in the same film who discovers Brian graffiting a grammatically incorrect rendition of 'Romans Go Home' and orders a redraft in textbook Latin. Yet, as a teacher, John Cleese seems to have been extremely straight, and something of a conformist. Christopher Kettle, the eldest of three brothers who were taught by Cleese at St Peter's, and himself now teaching English in Southampton, recalls:

> John Cleese got me through my geography Common Entrance. He was tall, bearded and saturnine in those days, with quite a sarcastic sense of humour like teachers tend to have. He was amusing because he was dry. But he was nice. He knew his stuff and nobody messed with him. He was a long way from the ground, his head was a long way up, so he had natural advantages, particularly when we were sitting down. He could be quite acerbic.
>
> Like most teachers he had certain favourites and I wasn't one of them. He was perhaps slightly distant. But there were some right characters in that common room. And there were some people who weren't above verbal bullying and that sort of thing, but I don't remember him as being particularly distinguished or otherwise in respect of bullying boys. He certainly didn't suffer fools gladly. He could be quite sharp with people, sometimes for stupidity as he might have called it. Apparently, there was a staff meeting in which the headmaster asked them to go easy on the capital punishment, which I thought was rather a good phrase.
>
> Another thing I remember about John Cleese was the genesis of the silly walk. We had a hard playing area, with a sort of edge round where people used to play with their Dinky toys, and he quite regularly used to walk out in break with a tennis ball in his pocket and then he'd take it out and start dribbling it around the playground. Everyone else in the school tried to dispossess him of it. There was a gaggle of boys

following him around and he could never be tackled. It was a most odd display, most impressive, almost mesmerizing. His legwork was quite astonishing. The only way I can express it is to say that it was as if he had six pairs of knees on each leg, and he could bend his legs in any direction. You could watch him and become quite hypnotized. Then the bell would go, and he would pick the tennis ball up again and stroll back into the common room.

It was clear that, even if he felt a nagging sense that he was wasting his time, Cleese was content teaching at St Peter's, and not just because he was staying close to the cotton-wool of home. 'I was happy there because I think it's one of the few times in my life when I had a sense of community. Naturally, I am a loner. I was very fond of some of the teachers. There was old Captain Lancaster, a First World War veteran, who knew everything there was to know about birds. I used to get up first thing on Sunday mornings and go into Kewstoke Woods with him to listen to the birds calling.' In turn, Cleese took his young charges birdwatching and even hired BBC records of birdsong for their edification.

Never mind that Captain Lancaster was a fearsome old man, with a vile temper and a habit of beating boys on the hand with a white cane. 'Capio' was an expert on something – birdsong as it happened, but it might have been anything – and, by the age of twenty, Cleese's earnestness was developing into an awed respect for any imparter of new wisdom or potential guru, a respect that would grow in later life to almost ridiculous proportions.

Even as an outsize schoolboy, Cleese was beginning to take life seriously, embarking on a quest for knowledge and working out personal theories on every imaginable subject as he went along. One such theory was on learning difficulties, as experienced by a pupil he taught at St Peter's. This poor boy's problem fascinated Cleese at twenty, and thirty years later he was still almost obsessed with it. The boy found, or seemed to find, it impossible to learn that the River Niger was in Nigeria while the River Congo was in the Belgian Congo. When he was asked which river was in which country, he consistently got it wrong, seeing no connection between the words, even when the link was pointed out repeatedly. 'I don't think I got angry, I was just kind of awed,' Cleese recalled in *Families and How to Survive Them*. He was exploring the idea that such stubbornness in children can be a form of passive rebellion.

In 1982, Cleese attended a St Peter's reunion at the Dragonara Hotel in Bristol. Roald Dahl overcame his lack of enthusiasm for the school to attend and give a talk on his pet subject of chocolate bars; Cleese was not asked to speak. In the crowd of ex-pupils, all wearing labels indicating their name and years, he did, however, seek out one old boy to tell him how he had taught him geography, and apparently had an argument over whether a certain river flowed through the Congo. 'I told you it did, and you didn't believe me *and* I was right,' Cleese was heard saying. The young man, one bystander remembers, stood to attention, terrified, and called Cleese 'Sir'.

Even nearly ten years after that, the geographically-dyslexic youth, who would by then have been in his forties, was still a favourite dinner-table conversation topic for Cleese. In a discussion about modern education standards, he was asked when he had last been in a classroom. One of the fellow diners said, 'He put on a funny voice and said, as if in exasperation with education and youth in general, "White, White. If the River Zambezi is in Zambia, what country does the River Congo flow through? And White doesn't know the answer".' 'Nobody quite followed what he was getting at,' said another puzzled member of the company.

Perhaps if John Cleese had ended up as a public school headmaster, or a solicitor, or an MP, a fixation like this would seem an endearing eccentricity. It is only in a comedian that it is regarded as too serious by half. Cleese has long suffered from the assumption that an actor interested in anything other than how *marvellous* he was in his last film must be a poseur, or at best a dilettante. It is hard to tell where the trait came from, but, by every account, Cleese has always genuinely loved knowledge for knowledge's sake, both as student and as teacher. When he casts himself in those comically bossy-boots roles, he is not deriding learning but the pedantic and sometimes insane nonsense that goes on in its place. Even if schoolmastering in a small town now strikes him as having been a waste of his time, it is still in his didactic role, whether making instructional films or writing on psychotherapy, that Cleese appears more at ease than as a comic, as a comedy writer or as a film actor. It was with some distress and exasperation that, talking about his early comedy career, Cleese admitted to Melvyn Bragg in 1986, 'We all of us reacted very strongly against any kind of didactic purpose and laughed at it, thought it was rather awful.'

Cleese has been inclined to teach in the broadest sense from a very young age, a tendency that carried him – almost – through the painful business of going out with his first girlfriends. 'It took me several years to get over that painful public-school awkwardness – you know, sitting there at dinner, trying to impress them by explaining how the stock market worked while persistently putting my elbow in the butter,' he says. Although Cleese modestly claims he knew nothing about girls even after leaving Cambridge, he had put his toe in the water back in Weston-super-Mare. In 1960, aged twenty and a little against the run of play, the earnest St Peter's teacher invited Christopher Kettle's sister Ann (who tragically died of cancer in 1977) out for a meal and to see the new Glynis Johns, John Justin and Cicely Courtneidge comedy film *Spider's Web*. Christopher Kettle recalls, 'I was eight years Ann's junior, and in one of John's classes, so I was always a little boy while she was going out dating, but I can remember her saying to me that John had taken her out, and it was very laconic the way she put it. But he never came to the house.'

The return to Weston-super-Mare to teach at St Peter's is a curious biographical detail in John Cleese's life. It was as if all the seditious activity and restrained anger that had enabled him to rock the boat so vigorously at Clifton College had been dissipated harmlessly. This unlikely teenage iconoclast who had steamrollered schoolmasters with his wit suddenly became a schoolmaster himself where he, in turn, might learn systematically to gull maverick schoolboys back into the ways of the establishment by letting them burn off their rage until, like a dark adolescent cloud that threatens a storm, it blew away. Yet the anger in Cleese had not vanished at all. All the wires were wired and the connections connected for him eventually to vent his fury like an electrical storm. The scale of Cleese's anger, not just as a writer or thinker but as a performer, the passion that was first seen in *Python* sketches like 'The Abattoir', and later in Basil Fawlty, was a first for Cleese. One hesitates to imagine how frustrated he might have been in middle age had he not erupted, but turned out to be a slightly de luxe version of Reg, living in Guildford and driving a Volvo. At twenty, John Cleese was dangerously close to becoming a solicitor, and he was to get closer.

3 Clown and Gown

Ars est celare artem.

'The art is to conceal the art' – Footlights Club motto

Follaton is a long road on a hill leading out of Totnes, a peaceful little town in Devon. Down a sloping bank from the road stands a line of rather depressing brick bungalows, squat, miserable structures with small arches of brick over their dark front doors. These arches at their highest point measure six feet three inches, which meant that John Cleese, at a shade under six foot five, had to perform a perfunctory bob of the head, like that of a busy solicitor whisking in and out of a courtroom, to avoid braining himself each time he entered or left his parents' latest home.

Cleese, a few weeks short of his twenty-first birthday, had just started his first term at Downing College, Cambridge, when the retired Reg and Muriel moved to the decidedly sleepier end of Totnes, a town so homespun and placid as to make Weston-super-Mare, with its day trippers, naughty postcards and hint of minor sleaze, seem like Montmartre by comparison.

The move to the Devon retirement bungalow must have made John feel from the beginning even less surefooted for his coming trek across the social and academic Alps of Cambridge. John Cleese was no fool and knew that university would be a dangerous place for someone lacking either style or confidence. The trite young things of the day were high on intelligence, low on discretion and sensitivity, and had yet to discover the class unconsciousness of the Sixties. There was every risk that the braying element at Cambridge would sense his lower middle class unease, and that the mild bullying Cleese had encountered when he started at school because of his height would reappear as social and intellectual intimidation. Moreover, for someone avowedly without ambition or direction, John had at least the semblance of a game-plan. As Reg drove John to Cambridge in October 1960, the young Cleese was thinking of doing as his friends at Clifton had advised him and joining the most critical and exacting dramatic arena the university offered, the Foot-lights Club.

So while his parents' main activity was now chatting over Number 16's garden fence to the neighbours, whiling away a typical English retirement, John's was what would now be called networking, making the connections in Cambridge with the comedy names that he would be associated with from now on. It is no surprise that when he went up to Cambridge, Cleese found it hard to reconcile his sophisticated and privileged new surroundings with Totnes, which he had to call home, yet where he had no friends and was increasingly aware of his parents' age and provincial outlook.

It was a tame place indeed from which to launch oneself into Cambridge and the Footlights. Mrs Frances Hicks was, with her shipyard-worker husband, the Cleeses' neighbour in Totnes. 'John was a boy that kept to himself. He didn't have much to say, and wouldn't go out of his way to speak to you. He couldn't fit in and seemed a bit out of place, him being Cambridge and us being working class. Being the only child and coming late in life – that accounts for a lot in a chap. I suppose he was all right with his Cambridge people, but us being country folk, he wouldn't say very much. At one time I looked after John for a couple of days and did his bedroom when his parents were away. He was writing something on his desk at the time. 'Course I didn't look at it, but it was sarcastic sort of stuff about Churchill. I wasn't interested in that sort of thing, but I do often wonder what happened to him.'

Mrs Ruth Tipping, who rented the Follaton house before the Cleeses bought it, remembers the family inevitably as 'very nice and very quiet'. But she laughs as she recalls John: 'He was full of life. I think he was funny – certainly compared to his parents.

John had a little airgun and would go shooting at things across the fields over the back or play football in the garden, getting into trouble for knocking plants down, just like a young teenager. He didn't seem to have any friends locally. He'd play football by himself and seemed a lonely sort of boy.'

Downing College, founded in 1800 and home in the early 1960s to around 350 eager young men, is on Regent Street, a short walk from the centre of Cambridge. It manages to look perennially half-completed, new buildings having been added on in fits and starts over the years. While some say the college resembles Sandhurst, others consider it an architectural treasure. But Downing was in one of its building-site phases when John Cleese was up, with two new blocks of rooms being erected in 1960 and 1961. Like all undergraduates at Cambridge, Cleese was nannied until he moved out into digs at the end of his first year. He was attended by a bedder, who was ostensibly employed to keep young gentlemen's rooms in order but was generally felt to be a college spy.

At Downing, undergraduates were still kept in check by a collection of rules so inane they could only have been designed by the cream of the British intelligentsia. Gowns were to be worn when taking meals in Hall, when visiting a don and while taking exams. Undergraduates could be fined 6s. 8d. for failing to wear gowns after dark – the town was policed by bowler-hatted Bulldogs, there to dispossess any wayward students of the illusion that they were now adults. Undergraduates also had to eat a set number of meals in college. They could sign out for two a week, but had to pay for any others they missed. They had to be in college by eleven o'clock at night, and if they arrived between eleven and twelve, they had to pay a 6d. fine. After that they either got late leave or sneaked in illicitly. One Fellow of Downing, who had a house in Lensfield Road which backed on to Downing, thought the rules so ridiculous that he used to leave his back door open so that undergraduates could creep in late through his garden.

John Cleese regarded Downing as a poor college, useful to him only in that he greatly admired his Law tutors. It was one of the heartiest colleges at Cambridge, with more than its fair share of Blues in everything from rugger to table tennis. People who clung to the college Junior Common Room were regarded by even the mildly hip undergraduates as the types destined for country parsonages, so, apart from playing cricket and second team soccer for Downing, Cleese had as little as possible to do with college life. In soccer he is remembered by his great friend, the film director Michael Apted, as a tricky but erratic player, while Tim Brooke-Taylor, who was at Pembroke, the college Cleese always hankered after, says he was a very bad player, who because of his complete lack of aggression would allow himself to be dispossessed of the ball rather than become involved in anything as controversial as a tackle. Apted, an Ilford boy made extremely good, introduced Cleese to supporting his local team at home, West Ham, a mild passion Cleese still keeps up.

The Master of Downing was W. K. C. Guthrie, who doubled up as University Orator, employed to give lengthy speeches in Latin at the Senate House for distinguished guests not conversant with English. In Cleese's time, the President of the Downing College Association wrote in the newsletter, 'May our college ever continue to flourish increasingly and to produce good citizens of courage and loyalties whose sound influence and responsible example will act as an antidote to the misguided dupes of "cold-war" propaganda in our midst. Personally, I have complete faith that Downing will play its part in keeping our country great – and safe.'

Cleese came to Cambridge armed with science A-levels and was to read Law, an inauspicious combination for somebody with even the vaguest ambition to join the Footlights, predictably dominated as it was by arts undergraduates. He had only really drifted into reading Law, much as at school he had passively strayed into studying Science. That happened because he was good at maths, and now he recognized that he would be a good lawyer for the same reason – that he had a superb grasp of logic and an ability to demolish bad arguments. 'I think I'm most amusing when I'm ridiculing other people's arguments – I don't think of myself as amusing ordinarily, but if I'm in an argument with someone I'm quite good at touching the weak points.' Cleese was also becoming aware of his extraordinary ability to perform gymnastics with the English language. He suspected that rational argument together with his linguistic nimbleness would make him a good barrister, although he regarded the bar as too socially elevated for him. What he had not yet realized was that the same conjunction of aptitudes could also make him a great comedian. Consequently, he suffered an acute bout of Westonian embarrassment when he approached the Footlights stand at the Societies Fair in the first week of his Cambridge career.

This annual event was held in the vast Corn Exchange in Cambridge to give freshmen a chance to decide whether they wanted to be bellringers, tiddlywinkers and so on. The Footlights people looked uninterestedly at the tall, bearded man from Downing, with his unpromising resemblance to Jimmy Hill. 'They asked me if I sang. I sang so badly that in school they made me take extra Greek just to keep me out of the choir. They then asked me if I could dance. Well, I had never danced in my life. They looked puzzled and said encouragingly, "What do you do?" I stammered and said that I tried to make people laugh, and it sounded so pathetically lame I blushed the colour of beetroot, and immediately retired in confusion to the parapsychology stall.' It took the intervention in Cleese's second term of Alan Hutchison, a close friend who knew the Footlights Treasurer, to persuade them that the bashful giant was not the gauche young oddity he appeared.

Cleese has an appealing tendency to overstate how hopeless and ill-focused were the beginnings of his comedy career. He says of his time at Cambridge: 'I don't think I used it as well as I might have because I didn't work either quite hard enough or quite slackly enough to get the best out of it.' There was much sneering at Cambridge at the time about what were called 'professional undergraduates', the go-getting people zeroing in on the entertainment business which, partly because of the recent start of commercial television, had rosy jobs available by the cartload. 'There was no more prancing about in tights. They were all after the business,' avers a Footlight doyen of the time. Over pints in the Pembroke College bar, Cleese was finding kindred spirits in people like Tim Brooke-Taylor, Graham Chapman and Bill Oddie. Cleese's impact was not initially enormous. The

Footlights President in John's first year, Peter Bellwood (now a Hollywood screenwriter), has no memory of Cleese before his first audition. But it would not be long before Cleese and his recently acquired friends dominated their new world.

The Cambridge Footlights Dramatic Club had been founded in 1883, but it was not until the late 1950s, conveniently in time for John Cleese's arrival, that it became an international mecca of comedy revue. The five-year period that started with Jonathan Miller and continued with Michael Frayn, Bamber Gascoigne, John Bird, Eleanor Bron, Peter Cook and David Frost, spawning *Beyond the Fringe* and The Establishment club, and closing with the germ of *Monty Python* in Cleese, Chapman and Eric Idle, and even *The Goodies* in Oddie, Brooke-Taylor and Graeme Garden, marked a progression from political satire to silliness, from topical ridicule to a more timeless but virtually apolitical lunacy. Post-Cleese members were to include Jonathan Lynn, Germaine Greer, Clive James, Julie Covington, Douglas Adams, Clive Anderson, Griff Rhys Jones, John Lloyd, Hugh Laurie, Emma Thompson, Sandi Toksvig, Stephen Fry and Tony Slattery.

Cleese's Footlights career started when the Treasurer asked Hutchison to write something, and he in turn asked Cleese to help. The pair collaborated on three pieces, one based on the *Daily Telegraph*'s Peter Simple column, another a send-up of Montgomery, not so loosely based on a sketch from the radio show *Saturday Night at Home*, and the third a pastiche of a news item from *Punch*. They auditioned them, in newly acquired dinner jackets, for a smoking concert, or 'smoker' – the evening entertainments that served as heats for the big revues. About twenty-five acts would audition at each session, of whom half would be chosen. Cleese and Hutchison were elected, as was Graham Chapman, a medical student at Emmanuel College, who performed a routine in which he grew a giant hand which was magnetically attracted by some outside force. Cleese and Chapman met after the audition. 'We went off and had a cup of coffee in the Kenco Coffee House, and decided to try writing together,' said Chapman. 'After that, it became a mission of John Cleese and myself to oust all singing and dancing, which we largely achieved.' The Cleese/Chapman writing partnership would endure throughout their careers as a third of *Monty Python's Flying Circus*.

Having made it into the Club, Cleese's sense of intellectual discomfort was not yet in retreat. His background, which ironically was more public school than that of many of his Footlights colleagues, was nevertheless so divorced from the arts that he was quite unable even to talk about the theatre. It really was not enough to have been to see Frankie Howerd perform in Weston, or to have taken a local girl out once to see a dud British comedy film and pronounce it OK. In the Footlights, he was suddenly associating with people steeped in the arts and professes (disingenuously, one suspects) that he rarely knew what they were talking about. 'But the one thing I did have was this sense of cliché, an awareness of the difference between real behaviour and phoney. It was my only point of reference. The way they thought was so different from the way I thought that I was really out of my depth. They would tear to shreds a film I had seen and thought jolly good and I used to get really worried. I had to get them to explain what they meant. The artistic or creative way of thinking was completely alien and I was very insecure.'

As Cleese arrived on the scene, the Footlights, under the guidance of its Secretary, David Frost, had just taken new premises in the ex-HQ of the Cambridge University Labour Club, on a first floor in Falcon Yard, a turning off Petty Curie, pungently poised above the back of MacFisheries. To get to the club (which was demolished along with Falcon Yard in 1972) you went down a dark alley and up a narrow staircase. The main room housed a piano, a lot of chairs, a television, a stage across one end and a small bar. The rooms were open at lunchtime and in the evenings from nine until late, porters and officious landladies notwithstanding. It was a real club, offering a venue for everything to satisfy an even moderately gilded youth, from parties to poetry readings and, of course, the twice-termly smokers. Footlights members could also be sure of finding a meal or having a drink after hours, often with Arts Theatre actors, who would drop in post-performance. The Footlights could be a cruelly critical environment, but Cleese points out that audiences tended to be friendly, if only for their own sakes. 'Most of the audience had a vested interest in making it a good atmosphere, because as likely as not they'd be getting up on stage later in the evening.'

The Footlights President had considerable autonomy, and he not only proposed his successor, but selected the director of the crucial May Week revue. 'May Week', with that inexorable Cambridge logic, lasts a fortnight and always takes place at the beginning of June, as soon as the examinations are over. Summer in Cambridge throws the beauty of the ancient colleges into dazzling relief, and most students spend the two weeks before they go down in a euphoric, alcoholic, decadent haze, attending plays and cabarets, boat races and college balls and interminable drinks parties held out of doors on pampered college lawns, or idling on the tree-shaded green 'Backs' lining the river Cam, while the punts float by.

There were two great issues of the day when John Cleese first started buying rounds in the Footlights bar. One was the question of whether anyone would ever live up to or surpass Peter Cook, who had been the previous year's President. *I Thought I Saw It Move*, the 1961 revue, and the first for which Cleese wrote a couple of items (but failed to get a part in) was a veiled tribute to Cook. 'Cook's influence was so thick in the air for two or three years you could cut it with a knife,' says Cleese. Trevor Nunn, also a Downing man, used to convulse Cleese and his chums simply by recounting Peter Cook sketches, sayings and exploits. 'Trevor Nunn had once paralysed me telling me about a Peter Cook sketch about a man who sat down next to somebody and told him interesting facts but got them confused. For instance, he'd say "A great six-foot Arab can live on a grain of rice for a year, isn't that interesting? You wouldn't think that a great big strapping six-foot Arab could live on a grain of rice." And he'd go on and on and then he'd say, "No, wait a moment, it's a mosquito. A mosquito can live on a grain of rice. I get them confused because in my dictionary mosquito comes next to mosque."'

The other topic of gossip and debate amongst Footlights members was the person of David Frost, the predominant rumour being that he was borrowing too heavily from Cook's unique style for his own performances, and getting too much publicity for them. Miriam Margolyes, who arrived at Cambridge at the same time as Cleese and became the leading actress of her time there, says everyone was wary of Frost, partly because he was from a different class, partly because he was 'a merchant, he was good at selling himself, he was ambitious, he wrote to agents and got them to come down and see him. I looked down on him too because I was swept along by it. I regret it now, although I don't think David is anything like as talented as John.'

Cleese admits to absorbing much of the ambient anti-trade (and implicitly anti-Frost) culture: 'It's very interesting – seeing my dad was in insurance – that somehow I picked up the snob, aristocratic attitudes towards trade and commerce.' He was to change his views dramatically; later, as co-founder of Video Arts, producers and suppliers of training films to the derided entrepreneurial class, he was to be mocked by his *Monty Python* colleagues for being overly commercial. It was a brave change of direction for a man who admits he was always inclined to go along with prevailing views. Footlights values were a powerful influence – Graham Chapman, a Leicestershire policeman's son, described the extreme elitism of the club, which 'taught all the members the kind of supreme arrogance that made Genghis Khan what he was yesterday'.

'Cambridge is a forcing ground,' explains Miriam Margolyes, 'because it is the first time in most people's lives when they are forced into either a real or unequal competition with their peers. And from having been the most outstanding member of the football team, or the debating society or the dramatic society or whatever their particular eminence at school was, they now come and find that they are not the best, the funniest, the fastest running, the cleverest, the best rower – they're actually just along with all the others and it can give rise to quite a shock. Also it's a very stratified place. It's where people are jockeying for position for the future, and it was particularly true in the world of the theatre at the time I was in the Footlights because of the success of Peter Cook. Everybody was trying to emulate that. And there was a great feeling that the smokers were about as hard a showcase as any you'd find in Hollywood.'

Like most student activities, Footlights ran by committee, a political form Cleese was both consummately good at and despised. The committee decided who would appear in the revue, while a script committee would edit material from smokers. Within a short time, Cleese was being regarded as the man most likely to inherit Peter Cook's mantle. Outwardly, at least, on stage and in meetings, the Weston-super-Mare diffidence was simply evaporating; just as he took control of his environment at Clifton, at Cambridge he was again emerging as a young man apparently in total command of his life. At a 1961 smoker, Cleese, never a great fan of the joke as a comedic form, told one of those intentionally unfunny 'screw you' gags, recalled by one fellow Footlighter thus: 'So these two Frenchmen go into a bar in Tunisia, and they notice that the bartender is a camel. The first Frenchman orders a Bloody Mary, and the second says he'll have the same. So the camel says "Fine", and mixes the drinks. The Frenchmen clink glasses and take a sip, and the first one says, "Mon Dieu, this camel makes a terrific Bloody Mary." And the second Frenchman says, "Hoots mon, what makes ye think I'm French?"'

At the beginning of his second year, Cleese moved into digs, which were ideally situated right in the middle of town, a hundred yards from the Footlights Club and a short walk from lectures at the Law School. He continued to play cricket and football for Downing, but there was little other need to go into college except to attend supervisions, pick up mail and consume his quota of college meals. Eating out was extremely cheap in Cambridge, so students in digs did not need to master the boiled egg unless they were so inclined. Cleese's domestic chore was largely that of very occasionally harvesting the abundant crop of empty milk bottles.

While days were diligently devoted to lectures and essay-writing, nights were given over to the Footlights clubroom, Cleese's newest home from home. As soon as he walked into the bar at the start of term in that second year, he found administrative greatness thrust upon him. The leading lights of his first year – Peter Bellwood, John Fortune and David Frost – had graduated; Robert Atkins was President and Cleese, responsible for membership as Registrar, was now *de facto* the most compelling character of an artistic caucus, all of whom were his friends. 'Suddenly we were the big boys,' he says.

'John was a very tall, slender, minor public school type, very much with the in-crowd,' recalls Miriam Margolyes, who was in the Company for the 1962 revue *Double Take* but, as a woman, could not become a member of the Club. 'I don't think John encouraged fawning, but the Footlights was his kingdom and he was king of it. He was always regarded as the best, the star, the original comic talent. And I think that's true.' Another performer recalls: 'Even then Cleese had a very commanding, forceful personality. He was the moving spirit. Backstage if there were any discussions going on, what Cleese said clinched it. And I do remember that when he got cross about things, he *really* got cross. You sometimes heard his voice from down a corridor.'

Margolyes continues:

There were always people around John. There was a degree of sycophancy about it. People were over-flattering, laughing at everything he did and said. I think it's inevitable in a student society that when somebody is streets ahead of the others, there's a Pied Piper element. I found it rather irritating and I didn't particularly subscribe to the total admiration of the man, although I think he was extremely funny and very original. And because of my particular position at that time in being a woman, and Jewish [the Footlights group were always telling Miriam to stop 'going on' about being Jewish] and fat and plain, I was of no interest to John and I probably resented that, and therefore we didn't really have a relationship at all. The people who became *Monty Python* didn't think I was funny and weren't interested in whether I was funny. They're not actually interested in women like that.

I can't remember women being around at all. John was very cool and always behaved in a gentlemanly way. I think that was the main difference between his lot and the Goons. The Pythons were cold. And the people that followed – the Fry/Laurie group – were not cold. But in the middle was this glacial patch called the Pythons. And about the class thing, I suspect that John, coming from that curious middle ground of the English class system, was feeling a little uncertain privately. He may have been putting on the English gentleman because he felt he wasn't quite it.

One Footlights musician of the time, the jazz saxophonist Dave Gelly, remarks that all the Footlights performers (with the odd, token exception) were 'posh' types, very fogeyish and, above all, very proud of their exclusivity. 'They just had different assumptions. They had the voice and that public school social confidence.' He describes their uniform of 'blokish sports jackets' as rather middle-aged and fuddy-duddy, although 'they were more devoted to showing off than being public school people. It was very easy to be nonconformist then. You had to do very little to be thought unconventional.

'Although it was the early Sixties, it was really the pre-Sixties generation, very much still the "'Varsity". It was the end of an era, and everything changed quite dramatically shortly afterwards with the Beatles and Rock and Roll. Politically, there were no great camps. Even the Union was regarded as a bit stuffy. The only political thing was CND which was vaguely fashionable. And there was a lot of religion. As for work, things were on a very rising curve then. The opportunities seemed to be endless, particularly in media. People were getting the most ludicrous jobs, being paid to do virtually nothing.'

'Our generation at Cambridge was the least political and most selfish until the recent generation,' affirms Margolyes. 'Some years after I left Cambridge I heard the Garden House Hotel had been burned down as a result of a riot about the Greek Colonels. And I remember thinking how impossible it would have been in our time for such a thing to have happened because the Garden House was where we went for Sunday lunch. We wouldn't have burned it down – we ate there. When the Bay of Pigs happened, our reaction in case of war was not to demonstrate but to form queues at phone boxes to ring our parents.'

Uncomfortable as it was to Cleese, class-consciousness actually played an enormous part in Footlights. Not entirely immune to the seducing elitism of Cambridge, Cleese and his co-performers were ostensibly contemptuous of the Establishment but also revelled in their fusty environment. Clive James, who went up to Pembroke College a couple of years after Cleese had left Cambridge, observed in his memoirs: 'Since I was still a radical socialist, I had no trouble analysing how the system worked. The idea was to tame the intelligent upstart by getting him addicted to privilege. The beautiful architecture had a political function.'

'I think we all had a reverse chip on our shoulders and were trying to slough off all the trappings of privilege – the public school attitude and accent,' Tim Brooke-Taylor says, telling only half the story. The Footlighters may have mocked class distinctions, but secretly, apart from the fact that their schooling made them hopeless with women, outsiders reckoned they were rather pleased to have been a part of the public school elite. 'Intelligent, charming, ex Public School (23) . . .' began Cleese's own – albeit jokey – description of himself in the programme to the 1963 Footlights revue. Public school also put Cleese and his friends in a position to act as a homoeopathic cure to some of the more vile attributes of their own people, the provincial English middle class; by being part of it, a small dose of the poison itself, they could somehow neutralize it.

Miriam Margolyes has an intriguing insight into how unpleasant the Footlights men, Cleese included, could be if you were not one of them.

I was sent to Coventry by the company during one of the revues. I come from Oxford and my mother gave an interview to the *Oxford Times*, which was my local paper, saying I had been chosen out of hundreds of girls for the part. She exaggerated out of pride and perhaps thinking it was true. When that report got back to them in Cambridge during the run, nobody would speak to me. I had a dressing room on my own because I was the only girl, and I think the only person who ever spoke to me was Nigel Brown [now a master at Abingdon School]. I never forgot that and I never forgave it. John went along with it. They'd walk straight past me in the corridor without looking at me.

It was totally disgraceful. It was sustained, deliberate cruelty. I used to cry. They kept it up for the run of the show, so it was a very unhappy experience being in it. Apart from that one episode, I never saw John being anything other than polite. He wasn't particularly funny in conversation. He just seemed a confident kind of chappie and rather above himself. To me, he was dull because I didn't like his personality which was rather unformed then. None of those men had any emotional development whatsoever. They weren't whole people. Graham Chapman and I just loathed each other, although at that time there was no suggestion of homosexuality and the group was aggressively male, all pipes and tweeds.

So male, indeed, were they, that they developed what was later to be regarded, especially in America, as a very rum penchant for dressing up as women to play their leading ladies. As an example of how not so much disregarded as invisible women were to the Footlights men, Graham Chapman baldly informed *Rolling Stone* magazine in 1979: 'There were no women actors at Cambridge, and the women we wrote were certainly not meant to be attractive, so there was no reason to actually have real breasts. We might as well do them.' Women may have been thin on the ground at Cambridge (out of twenty-one colleges, only three were for women) but it seems that Chapman was speaking as a Footlights man rather than as a homosexual when he managed to overlook not only Margolyes but her Footlights successor Jo Kendall, the one woman Cleese and Chapman seemed to accept willingly into their circle.

To be fair, Cleese at least was perfectly aware of his shortcomings at that time with women. 'Some of us, certainly myself, were almost inconceivably inexperienced so far as women were concerned. And there would have been very little point writing about women since they were from another planet as far as I was concerned.'

Perhaps the haughtiness observed in Cleese and his friends was really a reaction to their various complexes of insecurities. John was still perversely clinging to the wreckage of prep school, attending an Old Boys' dinner at the Grand Hotel in Bristol, visiting the school regularly and turning up on sports days. His insecurity took the form of the familiar restlessness, always wanting to be elsewhere, along with the familial lack of assertiveness (which instilled in him a peculiar mixture of extreme arrogance and extreme deference); for Graham Chapman, it was the fact that, totally unknown to Cleese, he was actively and enthusiastically homosexual, which made him affect an even tweedier and pipier exterior than the others.

Chapman supplied Robert Hewison's authoritative book, *Footlights!*, with a rather sad story of intellectual snobbery. Club members used to do private cabaret engagements, sometimes for a small fee, at balls and dinners. Once, Cleese and Chapman were dispatched with others to the Cambridge Allotment Society Annual Dinner. According to Chapman: 'The audience could not understand us at all, even though it was the sort of stuff that went down very well in prisons. John Cleese went right over the top, when he started emphasizing the jokes in order to explain them. It was about a bald man who had a rabbit tattooed on the top of his head. . . . Yet afterwards one of the Allotment people came up and said, "We do wish we'd had your education."'

It was easier for men than for women to be in tune with Cleese. Peter Bellwood (whom Margolyes remembers as being among the nicest of the Footlights men) explains: 'One of the things that made me feel that Cleese was one of the funniest guys I'd ever met was that he's really quite a grave, serious sort of fellow, and all of my comedian friends, primarily Peter Cook and Dudley Moore, have a certain depressive, sombre kind of quality which I suppose I possess myself – it seems to go with the territory.' Bellwood believes Cleese's preference at the time for being as deadpan on stage as he was off it was the essence of his genius. 'Alexander Mackendrick, when he was directing *The Ladykillers*, said the reason why Herbert Lom was so terrific was that at no time did he ever think he was taking part in a comedy. And there's a quality of that in Cleese's humour – he loves being straight.'

That apparent stuffiness on stage was to be naively misconstrued many times by critics before John Cleese became a fully-fledged national institution. *Varsity*, the university newspaper, decided that Cleese in his first revue in 1962 was 'a straight man swamped by funnier cast members'.

The revue was called *Double Take*, and was first performed in May Week after Cleese took his Part Ib Law exams. Then, as now, the revues were written and rehearsed earlier in the year, before the exam-swotting started. By a nice happenstance, a prototype version of *Double Take* was given a try-out the previous (Lent) term, at Bristol University, less than a mile from Cleese's last great critical success, the public lampooning of his house-master at Clifton College.

Double Take was produced (which also meant directed) by Trevor Nunn and performed by a company that included Cleese, Humphrey Barclay, Tim Brooke-Taylor, Graham Chapman and Miriam Margolyes. It was the first Footlights revue to pride itself on being devoid of any vestige of satire. As the television-viewing British public was still waiting for satire to happen in the form of *That Was The Week That Was*, which started the following year, the brand leaders in comedy were test-marketing a rudimentary form of *Monty Python's Flying Circus*, a mixture of physical humour and verbal gymnastics: in one sketch, a list of euphemisms for death was rattled off, a device that reappeared, much extended, in Cleese and Chapman's 'Dead Parrot' sketch. There was also a daringly unorthodox *Python*-style link between two sketches: 'I think we've seen all there is to see in here, and we'll go straight into the next number. . . .' The critics also noted, without seeming greatly to appreciate, the sadistic element in Chapman and Cleese's contribution.

The programme notes for *Double Take*, which opened at the Cambridge Arts Theatre on 11 June 1962, billed Cleese as: 'Bluff, slate-faced 22-year-old Registrar, he reads Law and plays soccer for Downing. He grew his beard to avoid being mistaken for Pete Murray: an enthusiast for verbal humour, he is nevertheless always prepared to stoop to slapstick, where he rates the custard pie above the banana skin. He has a laugh which is coarse and ingenuous to boot: he says he cannot sing, and keeps a locked piano in his room to prove it.' There were thirty-four sketches in the revue, of which Cleese wrote or co-wrote six and performed in seven. Parts of the show turned up in later Cleese sketches for television: his solo 'Startistics' (a send-up of an incomprehensible astronomy talk about a big star named Regella, presumably after Cleese's father) was reconstituted in *That Was The Week That Was* but performed by David Frost. A sketch on karate was reworked for *At Last the 1948 Show.*

The critic from the *Cambridge News* was fairly kind to *Double Take*, as well he might have been, considering the alternative assignment he could have been landed with for the night of 11 June. Peter Sellers, at the height of his fame, was in Cambridge to address the University Indian Society. There he told the eagerly gathered members: 'I hope you did not all think that I was going to be funny because I am a uniquely unfunny person. I usually climb into a corner and am a quiet sort of person.'

'This is a friendly show,' said the newspaper of *Double Take*. 'Eight men and a mat-haired, swivel-eyed explosion called Miriam Margolyes presenting a bouncing, painless bridge over the gap between dinner and dancing. It entertains with vigorous good humour, is raucous, intelligent, varied, witty, slick, crammed with sketches, anecdotes and songs; never stoops to parochialism or crudity; has no Ena Sharples and it effuses a hearty aura of goodwill to all men except Richard Dimbleby.' The reviewer noted Cleese's 'piece of expertise nonsense about the stars at night', but concluded that overall, 'the sting was missing'.

In the summer vacation, *Double Take* went to Oxford and the King's Lynn Festival. It was also the first Footlights revue to appear on the Edinburgh Fringe, as part of a package with Ibsen's *Brand* and Cocteau's *Intimate Relations*. As a wheeze to avoid appearing in the Ibsen, Chapman and Cleese – who both had tiny roles – arranged to do an early evening set at a coffee-club, which they could not of course leave, because they had to serve the coffee.

At the start of the Footlights summer of 1962, at the Oxford Playhouse, the *Oxford Mail*'s critic Don Chapman wrote of *Double Take*: 'Somebody's doused the Footlights. The Ghost of Peter Cook seems to have lost his way. Two numbers . . . worst of all, not so much sick as sadistic, are the work of John Cleese and Graham Chapman who are responsible for a lot of the poorer material.' He twisted the knife further by accusing Cleese of the sin of satire: '"Although It's There", with Mr Cleese as a wilfully hearty, sadistic mountaineer scaring his timid companion, while it has an element of bad taste in its writing, exploits with satirical effect the specialist jargon of rock-climbers.' To make matters even worse, the critic raved about the local girl, Miriam Margolyes, who accidentally, perhaps on purpose, had not been invited to the Footlights party in May Week. She went anyway.

Cleese became disconsolate over his less than glowing notices:

'I had thought I was terrific in that first revue but nobody said anything so I thought, well, perhaps I'm a bit less good than I thought I was,' and the next year, his last at Cambridge, he came close to not bothering to take part in the 1963 revue, *A Clump of Plinths*.

Cleese is fond of affecting a languid Reg-style idleness as a cover for deeper uncertainties, and indeed he was in a predicament in early 1963. Twenty-three and still a virgin, he had recently fallen in love for the first time, and it had become plain that the girl – he has never named her, and few of his friends were aware he was even keen on anyone – did not reciprocate. 'She didn't fall in love with me and she was well advised not to. If I'm soft now I was a wimp then,' Cleese has since said. 'No girl is interested in somebody who just adores her,' he ruefully told the *Daily Mail* in 1986, with two divorces behind him. 'My complete awkwardness with girls took a number of years to get removed. It was a slow process. I don't know if it's totally completed even now.'

Cleese confessed to George Perry, the *Sunday Times*'s distinguished film critic, that his first taste of unrequited passion shook him badly. 'I couldn't cope with it at all. I couldn't get any work done, and halfway through my second term I decided more or less not to do the revue because it didn't seem to matter. After all, I'd done it the year before when Trevor Nunn was directing. Then I remember thinking one weekend that I rather liked the blokes and that it would only be two weeks in Cambridge and we'd be finished, so I did it.'

Cleese could hardly have accused the Cambridge authorities of neglecting to warn him that this sort of thing might happen. The *Varsity Handbook* the year he went up advised: 'Remember that socially you are living in a man's world, but don't let this tempt you to forget the normal courtesies and your natural intelligence when in contact with the opposite sex. In talking to girls, do try to talk *normally* (just listen to yourself at the next sherry party).' The *Downing College Association News Letter*, in 1963, had a word to the wise on the same subject: 'Undergraduates can now invite ladies to dine in Hall with them on Saturdays. The Editor hopes that the infiltration of women into men's last refuges will go no further.' And in the same year, the *Cambridge*

Review published a survey of first-year undergraduates which concluded that 43 per cent of the freshmen had never been to a mixed party, or at the most only one a term. 'Another 57 per cent had never taken a girl out in Cambridge, whether an undergraduate, someone from the town or a visiting "steady" from home. The average number of parties attended was just over three a term for the men and five for the women.' For Cleese's part, embarrassment and confusion remained his principal reaction to women; he would still find himself enchanting girls with elaborate, lucid prescriptions for the perfect off-drive.

Interestingly, in a later interview with Roger Wilmut, author of a fine study of humour from 1960 to 1980, *From Fringe to Flying Circus*, Cleese blamed pressures of work for his contemplating missing his second revue. 'I was rather Weston-super-Mare about it all, and I took the work really quite seriously. I seriously considered not doing the revue the third year, because I was a bit behind on my work and I suddenly thought, "Well, I don't really need this revue," and it was only at the end when I thought, "Well, what the hell, it's not *that* much work, I'll do it" – and it was an appalling winter, so there was no football, so that gave me a bit more time.'

Cleese's overgrown puppy love was touchingly innocent, and he left Cambridge a virgin, a state of grace that went unaltered until almost a year after the end of his scholastic career, one winter's night in the Station Hotel in Auckland, New Zealand, when he was on tour with the university revue. He has never elaborated on the happy event.

Considering he was on stage more than some full-time actors, Cleese had been managing his academic work remarkably well. 'He was excellent, unlike me. I was a leech on him, getting him to help me,' says Tim Brooke-Taylor, who switched to Law in his second year. 'He would have made a remarkably good barrister. Those glaring eyes would have won him many a case.' Accordingly, during the spring of 1963, Cleese made, then abandoned, plans to become a lawyer. 'I don't think I could have coped very well, although I quite liked Tort and Contract.' Not surprisingly, given his Part I results, a terrific reference from his tutor John Hopkins and his lawyerly demeanour, the London firm Freshfields, solicitors to the Bank of England, offered him a place as an articled clerk at £12 a week. He accepted it, and when he later wrote to announce he would not be taking up the job, but was joining the BBC instead, it was not without regret. 'The only thing I got out of three years' training in Law at the state's expense was a ten-minute court sketch,' he joked. But, as late as 1984, he said of his aborted legal career, 'Even now, I still have this lingering craving for dusty, tweedy, English respectability. Yes, the very things I always seem to be railing against. These old emotional habits die hard. I view this as a character flaw, but there it is.' It took Cleese until 1976, when he was thirty-seven, to throw out the last of his Law books.

Cleese got a 2:1 in his Part I exams in 1962. In 1963, with his Footlights finals (as Chapman called the May Week revue) only a few days away, Cleese, along with Brooke-Taylor and Michael Apted, started his real finals – the Part II exams – with Land Law on Wednesday 22 May at 9 a.m. at the Senate House, a grand eighteenth-century building in the centre of the town, next door to the Law School. Three years of learning were crammed into six fraught days. Cleese's final exam was Criminology, which he sat at the Law School at 1.30 p.m. on Tuesday 28 May, and he came out three hours later the unwitting possessor of an above average 2:1 degree. A 2:2 was the standard degree and only one Law undergraduate at Downing that year, Laurence Collins, now a leading international lawyer, achieved a First. Cleese is typically dismissive of his own achievement: 'If you meet anyone from Cambridge who hasn't got a degree at the end of their time there, they are likely to be walking into the furniture. The hard thing is getting in.'

That Saturday, *A Clump of Plinths* opened for two weeks at the Arts Theatre in Cambridge. The show was produced by Humphrey Barclay, and the company included Cleese, Oddie, Chapman, Brooke-Taylor and David Hatch, with Jo Kendall as this year's token woman. No one thought much of the title. 'Either John Cleese liked the word Plinth and I liked Clump, or vice versa – I can't remember,' says Brooke-Taylor. 'It was a recount, actually, because the original title that came up – it was done on a secret ballot – was "You Can't Call A Show 'Cornflakes'".'

'We were all totally unshowbizzy then. Especially John Cleese,' says Barclay. 'There was a bizarre logic about his humour – a strong element of fierce nonsense running through it.' The *Clump of Plinths* programme contained a photograph of a side profile of a very handsome, clean-cut-looking Cleese, with short back and sides. His biography read: 'John Otto Cleese: Intelligent, charming, ex Public School (23), smattering French, driver, requires interesting remunerative employment July onwards. Do anything, go anywhere. (A non-lollard, and utterly trend-less, he was converted from Luddism by watches, and cannot ride a bicycle. – Ed.).'

At Cambridge, where a fashionably cranky bicycle is *de rigueur*, Cleese had taken the wise step of facing head-on the old embarrassment of not being able to ride one by making a minor gimmick of the affliction. He had also taken by then to the device of putting the satisfyingly palindromic but otherwise baffling 'Otto' in the middle of his name. 'John's middle name is Marwood,' his mother was later to tell the *Sunday Times*, 'but he never used it. It is a shame. He used to call himself Otto at one time. I don't know why. It was when he went a bit mad. My husband and I used to say he was always going a bit mad, with that *Python* programme especially, but he's done all right for himself.'

Cleese's student predilection for the name has gathered strength, rather than abated. In a scene cut from *Life of Brian*, Eric Idle plays a Jewish Nazi, leader of a crack suicide squad, called Otto. Eight years after that, Cleese was to be found enthusing in an interview in Los Angeles, 'I really love the name Otto. If I were to have another existence, I think I would come back as a rather saturnine archduke called Otto inhabiting a beautiful rococo castle somewhere outside Innsbruck.' Still later, Kevin Kline was allotted his evil role in *A Fish Called Wanda*, named, funnily enough, Otto. It remains only to point out that maybe coincidentally, maybe not, an advertisement the *Cambridge News* regularly carried on its front page in 1963 was for a Cambridge jeweller called Otto Wehrle, 'Wedding rings – plain or fancy, wide or slim, largest selection'.

A stuffy thought from the early nineteenth-century writings of William Hazlitt appeared at the front of the programme for *A Clump of Plinths* to pre-empt any sharp-pencilled critics: 'Clowns and idiots laugh on all occasions; and the common failing of wishing to be thought satirical often runs through whole families in country places, to the great annoyance of their neighbours. To be struck with incongruity in whatever comes before us does not argue great comprehension or refinement of perception, but rather a looseness or flippancy of mind and temper, which prevents the individual from connecting any two ideas steadily or consistently together.'

Hazlitt's portentous caveat might have struck a chord with Mr and Mrs Cleese, who travelled up from the West Country by train to see their Johnny in the revue, Reg having given up driving because he found the modern roads too frightening. Muriel was full of trepidation. 'I think she thought it was just a lot of students prancing around a church hall,' Cleese says, and his mother confirms: 'I felt like crawling under the seat when we went in. You know what these student plays are like. I expected it to be awful, but they all started screaming with laughter when the curtain went up, so I knew it would be all right.'

Again, there were 34 items in the programme, 5 written wholly or partly by Cleese, and 13 in which he performed. Cleese was praised by the local newspaper for his 'shrewd insight' in one sketch, and by *Varsity* for his 'portraits of the psychotic fringe of several kinds of officialdom' and for his 'paranoic interrogation' in 'Judge Not', the courtroom skit which he regarded as the only fruit of his academic labours. 'Judge Not', which Cleese wrote in 1962, was considered the best sketch in the show, and was used as its finale. In the sketch, Arnold Finch is accused of assaulting Sidney Bottle (a dwarf, played by Oddie) via the complicated route of having thrown a watering can at his pet ostrich. Cleese played prosecuting counsel Mr Bartlett (borrowing the name from his favourite master at St Peter's), who announces 'In this case, my learned friend Mr Maltravers appears for the defence, and I appear for the money,' and has to spell out everything he says to an ancient and obtuse judge. Cleese had not, after all, entirely wasted his and the taxpayers' time by studying Law; he later wrote nearly all *Monty Python* trial sketches. And Mr Bartlett got a further airing in a court scene as a prosecutor, the role Cleese invariably cast himself in.

The *Varsity* critic wrote about another sketch, 'Bigger Than

Both of Us', a pastiche of Somerset Maugham, with Cleese and Kendall as a romantic duo grappling with the end of a relationship: 'Edwardian jungle-play sentimentality is sent up from the outside – Cleese's concentration on strangling a python evokes an interest separate from the situation, whilst the actual parody is so creative that one ends up sympathizing with its real pathos, against the sending-up which one feels is tactless and irrelevant, though very funny.' Absolutely nothing is, of course, to be drawn from this quite coincidental first association in print between John Cleese and pythons, but the *Varsity* reviewer concluded by disapproving of two techniques in *A Clump of Plinths* which were to become staples of *Monty Python*: 'Too often in the first half a lack of punch-line, a striving towards one in the last lines, or a blackout instead of a fade-out, ruins a sketch with a clever line.'

Happily, disdain for *A Clump of Plinths* was far from universal. Two men from BBC sound radio Light Entertainment – Peter Titheridge and Ted Taylor – came to Cambridge that summer on their annual talent-scouting pilgrimage. Titheridge, who was distinguished by his penchant for writing memos in verse, was a great champion of gifted youth. After seeing *A Clump of Plinths*, the men from Auntie offered Cleese, Barclay and Oddie jobs as writer/producers. Cleese avers: 'It just happened that at the time someone had realized that the BBC hardly had a producer under the age of 45 and they thought: "Gosh, we've got to get some".' The BBC were offering £30 a week, almost as much as Reg Cleese was earning when he retired. Oddie declined the offer, Barclay accepted and Cleese, realizing at last that getting into showbusiness was feasible, took the job partly because it was more money than Freshfields had offered and he could wear jeans to work, and partly because his parents would be reassured. 'The BBC was very respectable and very establishment and had a pension scheme,' he said. His and Barclay's appointments were announced in ten lines in the *Daily Express*.

The news went down as well as could be expected with Reg and Muriel, who had left Totnes to return to the bright lights of Weston-super-Mare. Mrs Hicks, back at the next-door bungalow in Devon, had guessed all along that Totnes was too quiet for the Cleeses, but before they left, Muriel was a regular popper-inner who kept her neighbour informed of developments in her son's distant world. She also politely kept on writing after the return to Somerset.

'To tell the truth, I know they were very disappointed with John,' Mrs Hicks still remembers. 'Muriel was so excited when she came in here and said John had passed his exams at Cambridge. They thought he was going to be a solicitor, and then he fell in with David Frost and that was it.' Soon after the move back to Weston, Muriel, then sixty-three, wrote to Mrs Hicks:

Since being here, I have had rather a bad time – gall bladder trouble which caused me a lot of pain – however that is better now, but my other leg is now playing me up, and I am having treatment – old age seems to be setting in rather quickly much to my disgust.

We did go to Cambridge at the end of term to see the Revue, and we were all very pleased with it – very funny, John came back with us for two days, and that is all we have seen of him – he is now at the Arts Theatre in London with the show – he has given up the idea of law and has taken a job in London at the BBC starting in September with a very good salary – he seems to be more interested in this than law, so perhaps he will make more money!! – he of course got his BA degree.

4 *An Englishman Abroad*

Sexual intercourse began
In nineteen sixty-three
(Which was rather late for me) –
Between the end of the Chatterley Ban
And the Beatles' first LP.

From 'Annus Mirabilis', by Philip Larkin

'In Paris,' wrote the theatrical impresario Michael White in his autobiography *Empty Seats*, 'I had been introduced to Jean-Jacques Lebel, a surrealist-anarchist painter who dreamed up events which involved audiences with unrelated visual mixes and performances. Discussing this turn of events in Cambridge one weekend I was told about the current Footlights Club revue called *A Clump of Plinths*, which had been on for two weeks. All the major London managements had looked it over and passed – it didn't for them match *Beyond the Fringe*. I went to the last matinée and felt that I saw pure comic genius at work. It turned out that, embodied in one hilarious sketch at the finale of act one ['Judge Not', by Cleese], was the embryo of The World of Monty Python. . . . John gave a performance which made me ache with laughter. It is generous of him to say that I discovered him but this is nonsense, he was born a comedian.'

In the summer of 1963, *A Clump of Plinths* had been scheduled to go on a modest tour with the Cambridge University Theatre Company, first for a week at the Robin Hood Theatre, near

Newark, then for another week at the Rowntree Theatre, as part of the York Festival, and then finally on to the Edinburgh Fringe. Michael White threw the plans to the wind. Within a year, restyled as *Cambridge Circus*, *A Clump of Plinths* had basked in a long run in London's West End, toured the world and come happily to rest in New York. It was a stupendous achievement for the seven men and one woman in the company, but for none more so than John Cleese, who ended up staying in the USA for eighteen months and at last briskly severing the umbilical connecting him to Weston-super-Mare. He claims only to have written home to his parents once during this most crucial period of his life. 'He made things worse by worrying them unduly,' recalls Tim Brooke-Taylor. 'I remember being abroad with him when he wrote a postcard home to his mother saying he was going to take a ride on a new experimental monorail which was very safe, not to worry, it only did 250 miles an hour, though this was its maiden trip.'

Although White had intended to simplify the revue's title, it subsequently caused some confusion because neither of the London theatres where it ran was actually at Cambridge Circus. He held a party to promote the show at the Oasis swimming pool in Holborn, which was felt by Fleet Street in the innocent 1960s to be such a wacky venue for a theatrical shindig as to merit considerable newspaper publicity; the world in 1963 still had a lot to learn about the *Monty Python* method of bewildering the general public. White, who – like the BBC's Peter Titheridge who recruited Cleese from Cambridge – was in the business of spotting cultural trends early on, saw that the satirical television show *That Was The Week That Was* had firmly established itself as mass market entertainment and decided that *Cambridge Circus*'s benign comic anarchy was the next Big Thing. He found the revue 'without political barb . . . without bitterness or hurt' and described it as 'a welcome reversal of a trend which has completely lost its meaning. The cast are more interested in the "visual situation" type of humour which Buster Keaton made famous.'

Cleese and the rest of the cast moved to London, and *Cambridge Circus* opened on 10 July at the small Arts Theatre in Covent Garden. Cleese stayed temporarily at a hall of residence secretive, and it also disapproved very much of trade, which was thought to be vulgar.'

In May 1964, a few weeks after the pilots of *I'm Sorry I'll Read That Again* were broadcast, Cleese took leave from BBC Radio to tour New Zealand for six weeks with *Cambridge Circus*, an excursion arranged by Michael White. New Zealand had just been visited by the Beatles and English entertainment was the in thing. The revue was billed in advance by the New Zealanders, with an enviable ability for neatly missing the mark, as 'The Masters of Mirth'. The company left springtime in London, stopped off in Pakistan (where, according to Graham Chapman's less than reliable memory, 'John Cleese had a shower in Karachi, lost his watch, and held up the plane for an hour while he looked for it') and finally arrived in Christchurch on a cold and wet mid-winter lunchtime.

In Christchurch they stayed in a temperance hotel made of wood. Chapman describes the mildew on his bedcovers. For breakfast, the nine members of the company had to sit at tables corresponding to their room numbers although there were only two other residents, so each had, according to Cleese, whose lifelong fascination with mismanaged restaurants and hotels got a kickstart in New Zealand, 'terrible individual little tables, just like the guest house in *Psycho*. The waitress came up with this menu and it said "Porridge or Cremota". We asked "What's Cremota?" She said "Porridge". So we had the Cremota. Next was "Fruit or Prunes". "What's the fruit?" She said "Prunes". There was a choice between "Lamb or Colonial Goose" and the Colonial Goose was quite clearly lamb.'

After a night with leaky hot water bottles, they left this prototype for both *Python*'s 'Spam, spam, spam' sketch and *Fawlty Towers* and found a concrete hotel with a licence. Another story both Cleese and Chapman tell is when they were dining together in their second New Zealand hotel and Chapman ordered a three-egg omelette. The waitress brought him an omelette with three fried eggs on top. Chapman wrote: 'Even people three tables away threw up.'

'New Zealand was a hopelessly inefficient place,' Cleese later complained. 'It's all to do with standards. If you don't know what's good you can't provide it.' He and Jonathan Lynn went

belonging to St Bartholomew's Hospital, where Graham Chapman was now studying medicine. According to Chapman, Cleese was secretly squatting in the room of one 'Nick Spratt', a Cambridge graduate doctor who was away on an expedition in Greenland. 'Spratt' returned to England unexpectedly, found Cleese sleeping in his room and, ever the gentleman, spent the night in the bath. The next day, Cleese was politely asked to find alternative accommodation. He moved into a rented flat and found himself in the curious position of being, for the first time in his life, a fully paid-up bachelor, unsupervised by the army of women who had 'done' for him down the years, from Muriel, to the bedders at Downing, to Mrs Hicks next-door in Totnes, to the college-approved landladies who kept a watchful eye on him and laundered his underwear.

The London critics gave *Cambridge Circus* a mixed reception but it proved the most successful Footlights production and played for five weeks, extended from three. Bernard Levin wrote in the *Daily Mail* that the material was 'pretty thin', and asked: 'Have they got a new Jonathan Miller among them? I may as well get the answer over right away. No.' *The Times*'s Dramatic Critic disagreed, writing: 'It is the funniest show to emerge from Cambridge for a long time.' He devoted a hefty paragraph to raving about Bill Oddie, and remarked passingly on the 'gimlet-eyed Cleese' before enthusing about many of the sketches he had penned. 'The show even finds something new to say about television with an Old Testament news bulletin and weather forecast prophesying fire and brimstone here and there, plagues of locusts, and death of the first born ("Sorry about that, Egypt"). As a finale we get a trial scene ['Judge Not'] concerning a case of alleged ice-cream assault against a dwarf too small to see out of the witness box which is the funniest thing of its kind since the heyday of Beachcomber.'

After a few weeks, Michael White began to worry that the audiences for *Cambridge Circus* were too heavily composed of students and graduates, but the manager of Stoll Moss Theatres saw no such problem and offered the company a further season at the Lyric in Shaftesbury Avenue. It opened there on 14 August, and the show's fame was clearly spreading. The Queen planned to come to the show, but got pregnant (with the theatrical Prince Edward, as it turned out) and cancelled. There were more reviews. Milton Shulman called 'Judge Not' 'as funny a skit as I can remember'. *The Times* wrote:

> Its extrovert vigour, its irreverent zaniness and its fundamental geniality keep their spontaneity; the show still succeeds in looking and sounding completely new. Is it, we wonder, as so many of its predecessors were in their days, a portent? Its authors, composers and players are neither angry nor, we gather, prone to think of themselves as satirists; they are simply amused by what goes on and not infrequently capable of wit in commenting upon it. They are, too, capable at times of inspired dottiness. The question is, of course, have we been watching a new fashion in the making?

They were euphoric days, but Cleese was still a little concerned that he was not getting as much critical attention as he merited. Bill Oddie, the most musical member of the team, was receiving, Cleese estimated, 60 per cent of the reviews, Tim Brooke-Taylor a quarter, and himself perhaps 15 per cent. Again, as he had done at Cambridge when his own press reviews were not universally good, Cleese wondered if he was quite as talented as the others. Tim Brooke-Taylor disputes Cleese's calculation: 'I would completely change that order. Well, the first two places. I'll keep myself at the bottom being modest. A lot of people did think that Bill was the best. He seemed the most commercial because he could sing. But John was by far the funniest. Without any question. He was the one who was special.'

During the summer, the influential Ed Sullivan bought the American rights to *Cambridge Circus*, holding out the possibility of an appearance on Broadway. He then sold the rights to the American impresario Sol Hurok, but the cast still appeared on Sullivan's variety show when they were in the United States the following year. The London run drawing to a close, Cleese turned his attention to the small matter of starting work for BBC Radio.

In September, he did so. Although hired as a writer/producer, he did no producing. It struck him as uproarious that a state institution, part of the civil service, in effect, should employ joke writers at all. It is not hard to see the source of the inspiration for the Ministry of Silly Walks when on his first day, assigned to assist a man who had previously worked for *Gas World*, Cleese had to sign the Official Secrets Act. 'I started off working for Brian Rix and Terry Scott shows, taking jokes out of scripts that were too gaggy. I think it is truly very funny that my first job as a joke writer was to take jokes out of somebody else's script.' He composed sketches for a Christmas show for Rix and Scott, called *Yule Be Surprised*, which still embarrasses him, wrote gags for Dick Emery, a series of cross-purpose conversations at a bus stop for Emery and Deryck Guyler (all with a strange flavour of Peter Cook's 'Interesting Facts' sketch), and also wrote a show called *Not to Worry* with Cyril Fletcher and Ronnie Barker.

Cleese also contributed material to a series of *That Was The Week That Was* which ran from September to December of 1963, performed on a special radio broadcast of *Cambridge Circus* two days before the New Year, and, in April of 1964, with other ex-Footlighters co-scripted and appeared on three pilots for a new radio programme called *I'm Sorry I'll Read That Again*, produced by Peter Titheridge and David Hatch, a helter-skelter ride of gags, wordplay, sketches, songs and silly (often stupid) voices. For nearly a year, BBC Radio became Cleese's newest family habitat, and, typically, his immersion in it was total. He was fascinated by the more irritating idiosyncrasies of the establishment, and would later draw upon them for comedy routines.

'I think I'm only remembered from those days as the person who wore incredibly sloppy clothes and always had two main courses in the canteen. Radio is a very quiet world, rather like a public school common room. There's not a great deal of pressure, not very much rivalry. Nobody is ever really dismissed unless they set the building on fire.' The story running around Broadcasting House at the time was of an executive storming out of a high-level BBC meeting snarling, 'If we didn't have to make these bloody programmes, we could run this place perfectly well!' 'The trouble,' Cleese has said, 'was that, apart from a few people who actually wanted to make programmes, the place was basically run as a pleasant, gentlemanly version of the Civil Service. It was profoundly bureaucratic and therefore

at one stage to the opening of a swish new restaurant in Christ-church, where the temperature was sub-zero. Lynn ordered a bottle of red wine, which arrived at the table, to the displeasure of the two Englishmen, well-chilled. Lynn remarked that at least it was at room temperature.

When *Cambridge Circus* opened, the reception was generally encouraging, although Michael White fielded a handful of complaints from locals about the visiting Poms. 'People occasionally asked for a refund when they discovered they were not getting lions and elephants.'

From Christchurch, where the company made four radio shows, they flew to a very Scottish town called Dunedin, and stayed in the Leviathan Hotel which had tartan tooth mugs. From there they went to Timaru, a tiny town with a tinier theatre in which producer Humphrey Barclay was arranging the lighting because the show was being recorded for television by the New Zealand Broadcasting Company. This was to be the first time Cleese saw himself on television, and it was an alarming experience for a decently self-conscious Weston lad.

> I couldn't believe this creature that was using my name, because first of all he ran around like a giraffe on a hovercraft, because the top half waves in the wind in all directions but rather slowly and languidly and the bottom half doesn't have any upward or downward cushion of air. And the extraordinary thing was that I made tiny little gestures – instead of making reasonably nice, expansive gestures, I made horrid, nervous, tight gestures. And also, which was very strange, I realized that I hardly moved my lips at all when I was speaking. I had a stiff upper and lower lip. I looked like a bad ventriloquist. So I was a very strange creature which had nothing to do with me at all which *was* me. And I had to go to lie down for about two days.

While on South Island, Cleese, Chapman and Tim Brooke-Taylor went for a spin round the mountains in a single-prop four-seater Cessna. As they landed on a glacier, Cleese was sick. In Wellington, the capital, Sir Bernard Ferguson, the Governor-General, attended the show. In Auckland they performed a cab-aret in exchange for a free meal and drink, and in the Station

Hotel ('Budget Accommodation'), Cleese, six months past his twenty-fourth birthday, finally relieved himself of his virginity. In Hong Kong, on the way home, according to Graham Chapman, 'John bought another camera.' (Renowned as a gadget collector, Cleese today reportedly keeps a handful of unused compact disc Walkmans in a bedroom drawer.)

The *Cambridge Circus* team were barely back in England before, at the behest of Sol Hurok, they flew to New York. On 6 October 1964, the revue opened without first having gone on tour at the Plymouth Theater, on West 45th Street and Broadway. The reviews were quite favourable, bar the *New York Times*. 'A scene that starts tepidly,' wrote the *Times* reviewer, whom Cleese dismissed as 'a sports writer', 'turns splendidly and irresistibly mad, like the lampoon of a British sketch called "Judge Not". A bright, droll line leaps unexpectedly from a little scene that seems to be going nowhere, as in the skit of the break up of a marriage in Malaysia when the wife suddenly asks, "Did you put the leopard out?" But there are arid stretches when the energy and talent of this engaging British septet – one lass with six men – are expended on points hardly worth making. The visitors behave as if they are sure that what they are doing, singing or saying is hilarious, but what emerges seems obvious or purposeless. . . . In "Cloak and Dagger," John Cleese interviews David Hatch for a post in the secret service. They score with an inane question and answer; then they take off on a series of irrelevancies that fall flat.'

Cleese, the Westonian self-effacement outwardly replaced by a confidence altogether more Manhattan, saw things a little differently: 'We said it was going well when people started falling out of the circle. I once saw a man so out of control that he started climbing over the person sitting next to him,' he related to the *Observer*. 'And I remember when I came on one night [in 'Judge Not'] as a barrister but wearing a white fur coat and Bill Oddie decided that instead of being a dwarf in the witness box he'd be a drunk Red Indian with an Irish accent. I had to walk off because I was choking. It was a good moment.'

The middling *New York Times* review decided Sol Hurok not to publicize *Cambridge Circus*, and, the cultural gap yawning, the show closed after a brave twenty-three performances. Predictably enough, the day after it ended, a hugely complimentary and enthusiastic article by a leading critic, Walter Kerr, appeared in the *New York Herald Tribune* colour magazine. Cleese, who was finding the experience of being in New York far more interesting than being in the show, was philosophical about the failure, and anyway, within days, a new off-Broadway venue had been found for *Cambridge Circus* at the 400-seat 'Square East' Café Theater in Greenwich Village, now The Bottom Line. It was late October, just after Cleese's twenty-fifth birthday, and the theatre promised a run until after Christmas. Cleese was beginning to attract a scintilla of attention in New York, meriting already a micro-profile in one showbusiness magazine: 'John Cleese has been described as tall and broad-shouldered by some writers, while others have called him bluff and gimlet-eyed, a man who prefers to be known as Otto and lives in a light-weight cupboard. His performance as an urbane secret service chief with a terrible case of *tic douloureux* has been highly praised by British critics. . . . He lists his hobbies as photography, football, food and sleep and declares, unequivocally: "I am utterly trendless."'

The new venue, where the audience could dine as they watched, was more to Cleese's taste than the Plymouth. 'It was small and intimate, and I was able to *act*, which I always rather preferred to the projection that was necessary on stage. I was very happy there.' He had by now developed an ambivalent attitude towards acting, as indeed towards most things. 'I don't like acting very much and I have better things to do in the evening than get up and say the same words every night. Bless all the actors who do it though, I love going to the theatre,' he has since said. Even the *New York Times* was more receptive. 'John Cleese dominated some of the skits, with a talent for portraying innate cruelty in such positions as director of a zoo . . .' read an enthusiastic notice. The cast performed two sketches on an all-Brits edition of *The Ed Sullivan Show* alongside Joan Greenwood and the Animals.

And then in November, in the midst of *Cambridge Circus*'s successful Greenwich Village run, Cleese met a shy five-foot three-inch American actress five years younger than himself, with ash-blonde hair and cornflower-blue eyes. Connie Booth came from a farming community in Indianapolis, in the Midwest, but from the age of four spent her girlhood in New Rochelle, New York. Her Irish father, a Wall Street magnate, had lost a lot of money in the 1929 crash, but bounced back. Her mother was a frustrated actress, who, Connie says, 'went to college and got married. She loved theatre and wanted me to go to drama school. My family was so extraordinary and manic that I tended to be low spirited and keep a low profile.' Connie started acting at fourteen at junior high school, incongruously enough cornering the baddies market, such as the Witch in *Hansel and Gretel* and the Devil in *Everyman*. She later studied at the American Theater Wing in New York and, as the *Los Angeles Times* bluntly put it, 'began a promising career on the stage until she met and married Cleese'. She had built up a small reputation as a serious actress in the States, starting at the American Shakespeare Festival, doing occasional minor film parts, and later more Shakespeare on the West Coast, in San Diego.

Connie was working as a waitress while understudying in a Broadway show when she met John, although 'met' is overstating their brief encounter. She was waiting on tables in a Second Avenue café called The Living Room (which later became O'Lonnie's Bar), which was decorated to look like a whorehouse and was famous for having turned down the young Barbra Streisand for its cabaret because she was 'too ugly and sang too soft'. Connie wore a black leotard and fishnet stockings and had recently been warned that she would be fired if she were not more gracious to the customers.

'When John came in with some friends,' she recollects, 'I overheard him talking about The Establishment club, so in my attempt to be friendly, I asked him if he knew a friend of mine who worked there. John looked at me, said "No" and turned his back. I was devastated, because it had been a really big effort to say that. But the next time he came in he spoke to me.'

Then Cleese recognized her as the waitress who gave him extra large helpings of fruit salad, and, as she was writing out the bill, they somehow fell into conversation about Virginia Woolf. He offered Connie tickets for *Cambridge Circus* and she went along. The first item was a musical number, not Cleese's strongest suit. With Cleese knowing that the astonishingly pretty waitress was in the audience, and she having previously thought the tall Englishman 'terrific', the competition between the two to be the more embarrassed was intense. 'I remember thinking "He doesn't have it, what can I tell him?" Then he came on in a proper sketch and was brilliant. I went for dinner with him and another friend of his and I couldn't understand half they were talking about. It all seemed so brilliant and clever. He was so articulate and funny and I felt overwhelmed and intimidated. I felt out of his league – but I did make him laugh now and again.'

On their first date, he announced in the taxi that he had forgotten his money. She became alarmed and suspected he was a gold-digger, of which there had been a few before, interested in her private income and attractive apartment. Then, every inch the English gentleman, he stopped the taxi and borrowed some money from a friend. John and Connie soon became a recognized 'item'.

'John was very smitten with Connie, who was in analysis, which was perfectly normal in New York, but he was worried about how good she was, afraid that she wasn't good enough to really make it and heading for terrible disappointment,' says a close friend from the period. 'We didn't see a lot of her. She was terribly shy and concerned about herself and her development. So she wasn't what you'd call the life of the party. She had to be protected – she was kind of open to the nuisances of the world, she'd take things quite hard.'

Although she was comfortably off, Connie Booth had not had an easy first twenty years. Her upbringing was a striking antithesis to Cleese's own – her family as uncomfortably extroverted as Cleese's had been uncomfortably introverted. She told her understandably fascinated new boyfriend that, as a child, she had been 'petrified into stillness' by her parents, whose shouting matches were loud enough on one occasion for the police to turn up at their middle-class street in New York. Her timidity was born out of fear: 'At home, I just didn't make any noise. While all the dramas were going on, I was out of it, somehow. I had an older brother and a tall father and my size always bothered me. My family was given to affection and anger. . . . You could easily get smacked or spanked. Your brother might get mad, or your father hit you. That area was very familiar to me.'

For Cleese, New York was a world where the class system held no meaning and people enthusiastically discussed their feelings. In the heady spirit of this expansive, liberating existence, happy in his work, surrounded by new, open, articulate American friends, and confronted with a wonderfully pretty young girl keen and able to talk about her emotions, Cleese overcame his shyness and inhibition with women to propose to Connie Booth almost immediately. 'I failed miserably, but succeeded two years later. The first time she said things like "perhaps, possibly and I'm not sure". Mind you, I think it was the thought of making the jump from one country to another. Leaving your country and going to someone else's is much more of a cultural shock than anyone ever thinks.'

His seat at the BBC office back in London now thoroughly cold, Cleese saw no reason to leave New York in January 1965 when *Cambridge Circus* closed. America was irresistibly attractive to other young Britons like him. Peter Bellwood, the previous year's Footlights President, came to New York with *The Establishment Revue* at the same time and never went back to England.

Soon after the revue ended, Cleese landed the most unlikely theatrical role any reject from Mr Hickley's singing class at St Peter's School, Weston-super-Mare, had yet achieved. For six months he toured America with a small part in the American production of the successful British musical *Half a Sixpence*, based on H. G. Wells's novel *Kipps*. Tommy Steele played Arthur Kipps, a draper's shop assistant who comes up in the world, and is torn between a parlour maid (Polly James) and a lady of breeding, Helen Walsingham, played by the distinguished American actress Carrie Nye, wife of Dick Cavett, the wittiest of the American chat-show hosts. Cleese played Nye's brother, Young Walsingham, an English bounder who embezzles Steele's money. He remembers having thirty lines (though Nye says it was more like eight). When asked at the audition to sing 'The Star-Spangled Banner' he politely enquired: 'How does it go?' They then wondered whether he could manage his own national anthem, which he promptly got wrong. The director laughed so much that Cleese was hired even though he manifestly could not sing a note. 'I said, "What do I do about the singing?" And they said, "Well, it's only chorus stuff, so until you get the tune, for the first couple of months just mime." So that's what I did ... and after we'd been going about three months I started joining in very quietly ... on the notes I was sure of.'

Politically, to Cleese's boundless interest and delight, *Half a Sixpence* turned out to be a troubled ship. The director who hired him to mime along – at $200 a week – was replaced after three weeks by Gene Saks with whom, according to Cleese, he didn't get on. 'I don't think he liked me much and I don't think he thought I was any good, but he had terrific guts, and he came in and he brought the thing together and got it right by the time we got to Broadway.' Gene Saks disputes this: 'Cleese was very good, very right in the part, but I had no idea of his comic ability. He was a very serious young actor. I can't say to you that I saw a great talent there. I certainly don't remember that we didn't get on.'

Carrie Nye still laughs about the disorganization of the production:

It was an odd thing, because I'd never been in a musical before, and I got a script which had huge blank sections in it. They were going to get it goosed up. It didn't seem to make any sense because the Americans thought we were doing a gentle parody of a certain sort of musical, a lot like *The Boyfriend*, and the English actors, particularly Steele, kept saying: 'It's got to be real.' Then they brought in Gene Saks, who'd been mainly an actor, not a director. Gene said, 'the script is a mess' and sent for the English script, and everyone discovered it wasn't a gentle parody, it *was* the real thing. The American costumes were of the *Importance of Being Earnest* type, the English costumes were realistic. So instead of two weeks in rep, we had three months in Toronto with people being hired and fired. It was like being in a war zone.

John's character was known as Young Walsingham, but he somehow acquired a first name, and they would keep on changing it. I remember one night our 'Mama' turning and saying, 'Come, Charles,' and I said, 'Come, James,' and somebody else said, 'Come, Henry,' so the rest of the evening we had to call John Charles-James-Henry Walsingham. He had a completely straight part, absent-minded, classic English twit, henpecked by his mother. It was a perfectly serious sentimental musical.

After the first week out of town, I tried to quit and John was very consoling about that. He seemed to be having a wonderful time. He enjoyed everything. That humour that eventually wound up in *Monty Python* was there then. And he was having a whale of a time when he hung out with the gypsies [chorus line]. We had a marvellous bunch of gypsies – it was the Sixties, and there were all those wonderful dancers.

But I wasn't going out with the gypsies. I was stomping home with Charlotte Rae, who was about to be fired for not being straight enough. And John said, 'Stop going home to your hotel room and sulking. Come out with the rest of us.' And then I had a much better time. We went to any low bar that was open where we could drink and dance and leap about. And John seemed to love the politics and the carrying on and the changing of script. He took it all very well. I was tearing my hair out, but he liked all that stuff. I never saw him get angry about anything. He was enjoying life to the absolute full.

Half a Sixpence finally opened in Toronto's O'Keefe Center in February 1965, and by April was at Broadway's Broadhurst Theater. Ironically, the *New York Times*'s Howard Taubman, the man Cleese dismissed as a 'sports writer' when he failed to swoon over *Cambridge Circus*, rather liked this show. 'Do you find sentimentality repellent? *Half a Sixpence* will give you a touch of indigestion. But it will also disarm you by its unabashed commitment to sweetness and light. And its company, led by the engaging young Briton Tommy Steele, sings and dances with so much spirit that the musical numbers compensate in some measure for the stickiness of the book. . . . If your standards are not rigorous, you will be entertained by the friendly wholesome corn in *Half a Sixpence*.'

In May, during his time on Broadway, Cleese met Terry Gilliam who was associate editor of *Help!*, a national men's humour magazine edited by Harvey Kurtzman, the founder of *Mad* magazine. 'I liked him enormously, and I think that he thought that I was good at mugging, which is supposed to be a sort of compliment,' Cleese later joked about Gilliam. As Kurtzman's assistant, Gilliam was running round New York looking for people on the fringes of showbusiness to appear, for no reward other than the exposure, in fumetti, photo comic strips. They had used Woody Allen and Gloria Steinem, who were already well known, and now John Cleese who was not, but looked funny. Cleese posed for a fourteen-page strip called 'Christopher's Punctured Romance' as Christopher Barrel, a young middle-class suburban man 'with a case of ennui', who falls in love with his daughter's Barbie ('Barbee') doll. Cindy Young, a Westchester housewife, played Mrs Barrel.

'Cleese was a very shy guy,' recalls Kurtzman, in contrast to the picture Carrie Nye paints of John whooping it up on tour with leggy dancers in bars. 'We ran around Westchester for a couple of days taking the pictures. He didn't do much in the way of giving his personality away, he just withdrew into his shell, and there was no clue that he was that special. But every once in a while, we'd be sitting round, killing time, and he'd break into a funny walk.'

The interior shots were taken in one day at the home of Irene and Harry Chester. Harry, who ran an art studio, lent it to Kurtzman as a favour. It was a small, detached house, on Jewel Avenue and 174th Street, in Fresh Meadow, Queens. Irene, a housewife, remembers Cleese as 'a charming, handsome young man', who politely covered up her embarrassment at having plaid sheets for the 'bedroom scene' by insisting they looked fine.

Posing for 'Christopher's Punctured Romance' was not the only fractionally offbeat escapade Cleese got up to in New York. There was also the time he nearly became an international journalist.

In 1964, just before Thanksgiving Day, he had met a man called Everett Martin on the subway. Martin was deputy foreign editor of *Newsweek* and had seen Cleese performing with *Cambridge Circus* on Broadway. Martin recognized Cleese, complimented him on his performance, and they started chatting.

'John was terribly interested in my job,' the *Newsweek* man recalls. 'Apparently he had always wanted to be doing serious things in foreign affairs.' Connie Booth confirms this – in fact Cleese's notion of joining the diplomatic service had been one of the things that put her off the idea of marrying him. 'I thought that that would be the end, marrying a diplomat,' she later confessed.

Martin, whose marriage was breaking up at the time, invited Cleese to a Thanksgiving dinner with a bunch of *Newsweek* and *Time* journalists and researchers. Beverley de Lucia, a *Time* researcher who became a Jungian psychologist, held the party, notable in a small way for being the first time Cleese had eaten turkey – at home, Muriel had always cooked chicken at Christmas. Martin recalls:

> *Cambridge Circus* finished on Broadway and moved down to Greenwich Village, so three or four nights a week, we'd go down to the Village and watch the show and have a few drinks afterwards. Those were really wonderful days.
>
> John was tall and gangly and lean and terribly eager to learn. He wanted to talk about international affairs. One evening he brought the game Diplomacy round and we played it with several members of the cast. He beat me badly and I was a little miffed. He was gloating, triumphing over me, how he outdid me in Yugoslavia. He loved to get into very serious discussions – he had that side to him, as if there was a big unfulfilled hole in his life. He had to have his mind doing something he thought was useful. Guilt feelings about his comedy came out a lot when we were together. So when he finished with *Half a Sixpence* and decided he wanted to be a foreign correspondent, I got him a job at *Newsweek*.

Martin introduced Cleese to Bob Christopher, the International Editor, who hired him on trial. 'John came into my office and I liked him – he had that Oxbridge facility of expression,' says Christopher. 'We had a system then at *Newsweek* of "try-outs", where we would bring somebody in and pay them slave wages. It was very informal and people might do it for a while – if they had promise, for quite a while. John came in for several weeks. And he was good – he didn't bowl me over, but what he did, he did well, producing 300–400 line stories, sometimes longer, essentially processing reporting from a few other people and fusing them into stories. It does take a stylistic ability and John had that. He also had the ability to organize material intelligently.'

The *Newsweek* offices were a rabbit warren-like complex at 444 Madison Avenue. Another journalist, Angus Deming, who was then a writer in *Newsweek's* foreign department, recalls: 'John sat a few rooms away from me, in an office at the end of the corridor which we all referred to as the ejector seat. I remember a number of times seeing him sitting in there by himself, motionless at his desk looking utterly baffled. I don't recall that he ever produced a single story. He didn't mingle much. He came and went. After that I was based in London for a couple of years as correspondent for *Newsweek*, and I saw John at the BBC. We had dinner once and he talked about his brief stay at *Newsweek*, confessing rather wryly that he felt a little chagrined that it hadn't worked out and he hadn't made the grade.' Accounts of how good Cleese was as a newshound vary. He invariably claims, as he did in an interview on American television with Dick Cavett, that he was hopeless and left to avoid being sacked, but his boss Bob Christopher, who went on to become a Pulitzer Prize Committee Administrator, does not agree.

He was an average, graceful writer. I certainly would have been content to take him on. My recollection is that we had a conversation about this – I don't remember who initiated it – and I certainly did not tell him that I wanted to end the arrangement or that I wouldn't consider him for a permanent position. The memory I came away with was that he really preferred the theatrical world to journalism. And at a certain point we parted company. I liked him a lot. He was an engaging, rather diffident guy. He *was* amusing, but not side-splittingly funny. Years later I was watching *The Dick Cavett Show* and saw John was on. And all of a sudden he came out with a statement of how much he owed to me, and how I declined to hire him at *Newsweek*. I was rather startled because that's not how I remember it at all.

Christopher's children have ribbed him ever since for being the man who fired John Cleese. The Cleese journalistic style was, however, certainly singular. Everett Martin still recalls handing him a short article to work on: 'I gave John an oil spill story to write which was rather memorable. He wrote something that started: "A US sailor twiddled the wrong stopcock", and I had to call him in and give him a talk about *doubles entendres*. His pieces were heavily edited, but he was good.' The oil story actually made it, unsigned, into the magazine. It is worth reproducing as so much Cleesian style survived the strict editing process.

FRANCE: Operation Oil. Over the years the US Navy's powerful Sixth Fleet has ranged from the Pillars of Hercules at the Mediterranean's entrance to Iskenderon in Turkey, organizing marine landings (Beirut, 1958) and liberty parties with equal ease. But last week the fleet almost ran aground on a public-relations sandbar just off Cannes when a sailor accidentally spilled 2,640 gallons of fuel oil on the Riviera's doorstep.

The crisis started at 2:30 Monday afternoon when a bikinied swimmer ran howling from the Mediterranean onto Miami Beach at Cannes. Not far behind her was a black, slimy blanket floating on the surface of the water toward the sun-drenched sand. The oil slick led back to the US aircraft carrier *Shangri-La*, anchored a mile offshore. A sailor trying to pump out a water tank aboard the carrier had turned the wrong wheel and, *mon Dieu*, poured oil on Cannes' untroubled waters.

The French reaction was so anti-American it would have made President Charles de Gaulle blush. 'Yankee go home,' yelled one irate beach owner. 'It's a calamity,' cried Roger Rappenceau, secretary of the local beach owners' association. Cannes' Mayor Bernard Cornut-Gentille quickly drew up a legal complaint against the *Shangri-La* and dispatched a process server by motorboat to serve it on the 889-foot ship.

While Cannes officials grimly estimated that their beaches would be unusable during the six peak tourist weeks, the can-do Navy cleared the decks for action. Rear Adm. Robert Lee Townsend sent sparks flying: 'Mobilize the entire Sixth Fleet if you have to, but I want those beaches clean by tomorrow.'

Shangri-La Capt. Ralph Lincoln Werner immediately deployed his forces. He sent skirmishers to dig a trench and cut off the oil's line of advance, and started an airlift of clean sand from Naples to Cannes. Two hundred sailors armed with spades, buckets and even garbage cans commandeered from the neighboring towns moved into action. Air support came from helicopters which sank the floating oil by dropping 2½ tons of silicone-treated sand on it. Reconnaissance planes sent back up-to-the-minute reports on the mopping-up operation.

As dusk fell, floodlights borrowed from a Nice movie studio were set up, and fresh, clean sailors replaced tired, oil-soaked ones. Finally, after twenty hours, when the midday sun had warmed the sands, awe-struck tourists swarmed over the glistening beaches again.

'A miracle!' proclaimed Monsieur Rappenceau. '*Formidable*,' rhapsodized a tourist. The mayor's office praised Admiral Townsend's courtesy and declared that Paris newspapers had, after all, greatly exaggerated the situation. The beach owners were ecstatic. 'We were terrified,' said Mme. Vina Cornillon, 'but now the beach has never been cleaner.' One oil-smeared vacationing Frenchman exclaimed: 'The Americans often commit errors, but the means they use to repair them outstrip all imagination.'

In July, Everett Martin was dispatched on a long assignment to Vietnam. Cleese gave him a passport case as a present. With Martin gone, 'I was rather lost,' he admits. 'I needed somebody to say, "Don't say it like that", I needed a mentor, somebody to teach me. And I couldn't do it. And I was a little ashamed that I'd wasted their money. I liked Bob Christopher the editor very much, and I just wrote him a little note before I was fired.' Martin returned in September, but Cleese had already departed. The American later went on to the *Wall Street Journal* as Latin American correspondent.

Years later, Cleese continued to harbour the vestiges of a journalistic ambition, telling the *Observer* that he would like one day to edit the *Economist*: 'Think of it. Governments would topple at my will.' The *Newsweek* episode had been something of an embarrassment to him. He had convinced himself that he had finally discovered a worthwhile profession and yet, by his high standards, had failed to make the grade. For a man who prides himself on consuming and mastering new tasks and ideas, this sense of personal failure was an unusual and unwelcome experience. By 1986, however, he could see the funny side of it. 'I now know how to write for *Newsweek*,' he said in an interview with *Women's Wear Daily*. 'It's very simple. In the first sentence, you make up a quote and attribute it to a cab driver. And in the second sentence, you start "However, by the beginning of last week, it was becoming abundantly clear that . . . ."'

John Cleese was not inclined to be unemployed for long. Three days after leaving *Newsweek*, he got a part in *The Establishment Revue*, an earlier Footlights show still doing the rounds abroad. He joined the cast as they started on a national tour, which took him to Washington and twice to Chicago before returning to New York. It was in a Chicago café that a Pole read his palm for five dollars and, to Cleese's rather naive amazement, described him in a nutshell: 'Your logical side is as developed as your creative side!'

Peter Bellwood, who had performed with *The Establishment* since 1963, remembers:

Cleese put a lot of his own material in. He would play these very strange eccentrics. The reason I responded to him was because he was a total original. But it's always been my contention that the originator of that whole business was Peter Cook. Peter seems to me still to be the sort of genesis of a total school of humour, which went right back to his own school days at Radley where he created E. L. Wisty.

Cleese had similar kinds of characters. People who were completely eccentric and weird and had their hats pulled down over their ears and would accost you at bus stops and get you involved in these unbelievable flights of fancy. The one that was the most hilarious was based on this programme he'd seen on television about birds who opened tins of fruit by dropping sharp pointed stones from a great height. You basically just wanted to get away from him.

John also had a wonderful character, who was the head of the secret service and had a slight stutter, who, to applicants for the secret service, would suddenly say conspiratorially 'There's someone behind you', and when they jumped, he would scream with hysterical laughter. And he had this fantasy that the Japanese were at the bottom of the garden, trying to get over the garden wall to steal the strawberries. It was all totally insane stuff, and the audiences seemed to respond to it.

I had a wonderful time with Cleese. He took the curse off performing because he was so loony. I found it about as difficult to keep a straight face on stage with Cleese as I did when I was on stage with Peter Cook. Peter and I originated the one-leg-too-few sketch at Cambridge, where a one-legged guy is auditioning for the role of Tarzan in a movie, and I found it hard to keep a straight face then too. Cleese got very deeply into his character and he would become so completely psychotic or paranoid or whatever it was he was supposed to be. And of course, he was so tall, like a thin bird, a heron, almost. His eyes were extremely compelling. He was a handsome lad, but he had a very intense, strange look in his eye. The review that I cherish most from when we did *The Establishment* in New York was from a critic who said: 'The light of lunacy is never far from his eyes.' I love that because I was the straight man in the show and it was always my contention that the straight man could make anybody being funny much much funnier. So I treasure that. To play with John was an absolute joy because he just made you look so good and he was so weird. He was a very, very weird guy.

5   *Les Enfants du Parody*

I suppose one of the reasons why I grew up
feeling the need to cause laughter was
perpetual fear of being its unwitting object.

Clive James, *Unreliable Memoirs*, 1980

Having just turned twenty-six, John Cleese returned to England in time for Christmas 1965 to spend the holiday with his parents. David Frost, typically about to dash onto an aeroplane, had phoned him from Kennedy Airport to offer him a job on a newly conceived television programme. Frost wanted Cleese on the strength of the few sketches he had written for *That Was The Week That Was*, and Cleese wanted a job, so accepted with gratitude. He had been planning to come back anyway, wisely leaving his on-off-on affair with Connie Booth to simmer for a while.

The first edition of *The Frost Report* was broadcast at 9 p.m. on 10 March 1966. It was preceded by a party political broadcast by Harold Wilson, which, at first, seemed to be a joke. Characterized by its fusion of satire and silliness, the opening show's theme was authority. Sketches covered wine-tasting; Cleese as a schoolmaster welcoming boys back for a new term; the police (the old Footlights joke of a police station – 'Morning Super', 'Hello wonderful') and the judiciary, including a tiny courtroom sketch; an analogy between women and cars; a church sketch; an inter-school competition sketch and one on the Unknown Soldier, who turns out to be German.

Each programme pivoted on a central topic, with sketches, usually including a long one by Cleese and Chapman (who was still a medical student), and what was known as a 'CDM' — 'Continuous Developing Monologue' to Frost, Cadbury's Dairy Milk to some of the others. Cleese and Chapman called the CDM the OJARIL (Old Jokes And Ridiculously Irrelevant Links), although it was often written by the most junior writers on the show, two young Oxford graduates called Michael Palin and Terry Jones. Julie Felix also contributed a song to each programme. *The Frost Report* achieved an average audience of 12 million, peaking at 15 million.

It was with the Two-Ronnies-to-be that Cleese performed some of his most renowned early work, the three of them giving a tripartite viewpoint on a subject. The most famous of these routines was the now wonderfully dated (if only because of the hats) 'Class' sketch in which, in order of height, Cleese, Barker and Corbett stood in a row, Cleese one foot four inches taller than Corbett. Cleese, in a bowler hat and suit, glances at Barker, who is in a pork pie hat, and explains: 'I look down at him because I am upper class.' Barker, first looking up at Cleese, then down on Corbett, pronounces: 'I look up to him because he is upper class. But I look down on him because he is lower class. I am middle class.' Corbett, in a cloth cap, gets the best line: 'I know my place.' The Cleese/Barker/Corbett trio soon became known as 'David Frost's Repertory Company'.

Cleese concedes an enormous debt to David Frost for getting him on to television. 'The one man in England who knew really everything about my work and who was in a position to give me an interesting job just handed it to me . . . out of the blue. I've been very lucky professionally. Things have always dropped into my lap without my having to try.' Frost regards Cleese as 'one of the funniest men in the world', and Cleese has always preferred to distance himself from too much fashionable criticism of Frost's commercialism. ('Everything to do with television really brought out the hidden shallows in Frost,' Christopher Booker has said.) Cleese's view of Frost was more measured: 'If he had an American accent, nobody would see anything odd about him . . . his standards are very much the standards of the outside world – a success for David is what is judged successful.'

'At the end of the show,' says Cleese, 'before this huge list of names, the credits always used to say "Written by David Frost", which was really a bit naughty. *Chosen* by David Frost, fair enough!' Later on when the Pythons had their own show, they retaliated, lampooning Frost in a skit about a TV man called Timmy Williams (played by Eric Idle), who surrounds himself with an adoring gaggle of pressmen and celebrities ('super, super, super') while ignoring a suicidal friend who is trying to ask for help. The credits for 'Timmy Williams' Coffee Time' roll with: 'THEME SCRIPT BY TIMMY WILLIAMS [huge letters] . . . ENTIRELY WRITTEN BY TIMMY WILLIAMS [huge letters] . . . ADDITIONAL MATERIAL BY . . .', followed by the incredibly rapid screening of sixty names, some invented, including Brian Feldman, Paul Raymond . . . and Reginald Marwood.

But Frost retained a lot of people's respect, if only by being an employment agency and virtually a warehouse for wits and wags. He capitalized on his own talents by being a catalyst for most of that period's comedy. On *The Frost Report*, Cleese met not only Palin and Jones and the nascent Two Ronnies, but also Antony Jay (his partner-to-be in another chapter of his life, Video Arts), Sheila Steafel, Barry Cryer, Marty Feldman, Barry Took, Dick Vosburgh, David (*Rise and Fall of Reginald Perrin*) Nobbs, John Wells, Keith Waterhouse and Willis Hall. In all, there was a team of about twenty top writers. They met and rehearsed in a converted church hall in Paddington, and the shows were recorded at the Shepherd's Bush Theatre where Terry Wogan now platitudinizes three times a week.

Ronnie Barker recalled in his autobiography that, apart from himself and Ronnie Corbett, 'The others were very 'Varsity, or so it seemed to us. They didn't mean to be, they were most friendly, but they couldn't help it. John Cleese was very grand, even then – physically, I mean, looking down at the world literally from on high. Up there in the clouds, a bit withdrawn and abstracted, with that great Desperate Dan chin – I'd love to see him playing Desperate Dan!' Michael Palin confirms: 'John, even then, walked tall. He was tall. He's never been somebody

to huddle up and pretend he isn't extraordinarily tall and dominant. And he was very nice and charming. I remember he
pushed Terry Jones over a wall. We were just walking back from
Bertorelli's in Shepherd's Bush, having had a little lunch, to the
place where *Frost* was to be recorded . . . and I was just slightly
behind a line of people, Jimmy Gilbert, John and Terry, just
walking along and being terribly nice, and John just suddenly
stuck a hand out and Terry disappeared over someone's garden
wall. I thought, "this man is exceptional". Terry did a very good
fall, I have to say. A very good fall indeed.'

Impressive enough in the flesh, when the 6 ft 4¾ in. frame
of John Cleese first appeared on *The Frost Report*, a necessarily
apocryphal BBC story runs that every viewer in the land rushed
for the vertical hold on his television set. From the moment
Cleese made his British television debut, his physique caused
unlimited fascination. What he had felt to be an embarrassing
handicap when he first saw himself on the small screen in New
Zealand – his strange system of locomotion, which he likened to
a cross between a giraffe and a hovercraft – was to be powerfully
appealing to the British public, ever receptive to new opportunities to see itself parodied.

Immediately, journalists seized upon every aspect of his physical appearance, and have continued to do so. Newspaper writers
over the years have only been outdone in their excitement about
Cleese's body by academics, one of whom has even given
scholarly consideration to 'the visual gestalt of John Cleese's
body'.

To the brilliant Donald Zec of the *Daily Mirror*, Cleese, as 'The
Tallest One, with his mournful eyeballs and sepulchral smile,
could pass for a professional pall-bearer hooked on embalming
fluid, or (stand back) only here for the bier.' William Marshall
in the same newspaper observed, 'When he finds something
amusing – which isn't often – he gives off a sort of asthmatic
nightwatchman's wheeze through fiercely clenched teeth.' Lee
Langley in the *Guardian* wrote: 'His lanky, almost anonymous
figure has an amazing flexibility: in repose he gives the impression of old-fashioned grace, a Royal Flying Corps type. Then the
frenzy descends and he is gallows-humour incarnate, second
cousin to Dürer's skeletal horseman carrying the plague, all bony

elbows and knees, ghastly grin and hollow eye sockets. It is this unnerving mixture of violence and urbanity that distinguished his best *Monty Python* characters and made Basil Fawlty a unique exhibit in the comedy chamber of horrors.'

Cleese maintained an air of bemusement about all this; after all, he literally could not help it. But despite his stated yearnings to have a useful job – to join the Foreign Office, edit the *Economist* or whatever – Cleese was, sometimes ruefully, aware from an early stage that what his tiny mother and towering father had quite accidentally given him in terms of physique was as easily convertible into cash as his expensive education. He would put as much concentration into perfecting physical tricks as into wondering about his inner self or puzzling over foreign affairs. A vivid childhood memory of one young neighbour of Cleese in London at this time is of watching him through a basement kitchen window clad in a short towelling dressing gown and dipping lumps of pineapple into yoghurt, which he would then hold at arm's length above his head and attempt to drop into his mouth.

Through being in the public eye, Cleese has had to give undue thought to his physiology. Asked by the *Hollywood Reporter* what the ugliest part of his body was (Cleese has always credited American journalists with asking more interesting questions than British reporters), he had a considered answer: 'My jaw, or perhaps my thin lips. No, my *feet*. When I look at them they always remind me of one of those dinosaurs displayed in natural history museums, because they're so strange and long and bony. You know, I almost feel that in an earlier life I must have flown through the air with small animals in my beak.'

A lot of Cleese's comedy, however, emanated from only the most northerly point of his anatomy, his face. 'I'm told by my wife, who should be a reliable authority, I have an ability to convey extreme mental derangement while keeping a straight face,' he later said. 'It worked for me on television because people could see what was going on in my mind. I think the straight face came originally from fear,' he confided to the writer David Nathan in 1971. 'I really do work out what I'm thinking when I'm performing and somehow it shows.'

Frost, who formed his own film production company, had

high hopes for his outstanding protégé. Cleese spent his first summer after returning to England in Ibiza with Chapman, Tim Brooke-Taylor and a changing cast of others, including Peter Cook and Marty Feldman and his wife Lauretta, writing a film called *The Rise and Rise of Michael Rimmer*, an idea of Frost's about an efficiency expert who becomes prime minister. The film did not make it on to the screen until 1970, and then to little acclaim. Cleese discovered to his alarm that, despite having seen thousands of movies, he had not the first idea how to write one, and used this as the spur to start watching films from then on with a more professional eye. Apart from this new piece of self-discovery, the three months in the Mediterranean were enormous fun. Connie Booth came out from New York for some of the time, and Graham Chapman met David Sherlock, the man who was to be his companion – a self-styled 'Python wife' – for the twenty-four years up to Chapman's death.

'I hired a bicycle and so did John Cleese,' wrote Chapman in his autobiography. 'He couldn't ride his, but then he was only twenty-five years old. I was worried about the aesthetics of people of that age [he was actually twenty-six] who are quite capable of basking in the sun wearing only a jock-strap, and of leaving the door open when they go poohs. I realized later that he had gone to a public school, where it's obligatory to be peered at in your most intimate moments (unless you're bullying someone).' Cleese gave the impression that he was happiest lounging with Connie. Chapman, who knew him better than anyone there, observed: 'Something had changed in John. ... The pedestrian, parentally predestined solicitor changed to a cycle-riding, lobster-red, writer-performer, wearing baggy shorts, plimmies, *no* shirt, sunglasses with white plastic nose-shield, and a floppy khaki hat.' Chapman also records an incident on the beach where Feldman found the most boring man he could and introduced him to a furious Cleese, who was engrossed in the *Daily Telegraph*. Cleese swam out to sea and disappeared 'for two days', returning with the claim that he'd swum to Wembley to see England beat West Germany in the World Cup Final.

In England, during the *Frost Report* period, and his first taste of fame, Cleese lived behind a black-and-yellow front door with a heavy iron knocker in a mews house flat off Cromwell Road, in West London. He employed a char (he referred to her as that), and had the *Economist*, the *Guardian* and two pints of double milk delivered. He ate muesli for breakfast, still a strictly metropolitan taste in the Sixties, but wore pyjamas, which were already becoming distinctly fogeyish. He adored living in London. 'I love big cities, and London's a great place to spend your spare time. You can do anything here and get the best out of any world. I think I get the best both from my work and my more leisurely life at my amusing mews,' he was quoted as saying in the *TV Times* at Christmas 1966, although the words read as if they were awkwardly massaged post-delivery by the magazine's reporter into something a little more ITV than Cleese's more usual faultlessly elegant statements. He had just started appearing on commercial television in Rediffusion's *The Frost Programme*, which began on 28 September, a frenetic thrice-weekly talk show with a studio audience discussion and comic sketch inserts.

John Cleese had found an agreeable new life in London, but Weston-super-Mare still hovered in the background. One telling sketch in the *Frost Report* with the theme of 'Youth' involved an eloquent interchange written by Cleese and Chapman, between Cleese and Sheila Steafel as his mother, in which she tries to persuade him to go to Bridlington to visit Auntie Jo-Jo instead of Crete with his friends. Steafel: 'I don't know what's happened to you. You've changed since you've been to university. All you want to do is spend time with your *friends*. Or *reading*.'

The partial move to ITV alarmed and relieved Reg and Muriel Cleese in equal measure. *The Frost Programme* was not broadcast in the West Country, which led Reg to assume that John must, thankfully, now be out of work and ready to embark on a proper career. He wrote to his son suggesting he might like to try his hand in the personnel department of Marks and Spencer. John wrote back to reassure his parents that he was, in fact, still gainfully employed, and went on to explain the vagaries of the commercial network's programming policies. He added, gently exaggerating as one does to over-solicitous, aged parents, that he had unlimited work on the horizon. Reg took the message on board. In his Christmas card to Frances and Maurice Hicks in Totnes, he wrote, in a turmoil of resignation and pride:

'Johnny is coming home for Xmas – he is with the late night show with David Frost (which is shewn on ITV London district only) and is booked up for the next 18 months.'

His relatively new television career did not mean that Cleese had turned his back on radio. In tandem with *The Frost Report* and *The Frost Programme*, he was writing and performing material that was less topical and more anarchic for *I'm Sorry I'll Read That Again*, now into its second series. For *ISIRTA*, which was originally to have been called *Get Off My Foot*, Cleese may have been a disembodied voice to the audience but he was still capable of projecting a powerful physical presence. His most successful characters remained the ones who sounded like bank managers but used the language of the insane. One interview described him as 'known to addicts of *I'm Sorry I'll Read That Again* as John "Otto" Cleese, a man at one time obsessed by the ferret'.

'This is John Otto Cleese,' he would typically introduce himself. 'Our play today is *Othello, the Yorkshire Moor*, specially adapted for radio under the title *Gentian Sprunt Goes Mousepicking*.' As the series ploughed on through the Sixties, the writing passing mostly to Bill Oddie and Graeme Garden, audience participation in the form of boos and cheers was encouraged, to Cleese's distaste. 'Suddenly the audience changed – it started getting like playing at the cup final. Instead of having a nice audience that laughed, suddenly there was a football crowd atmosphere.' He did not care for the humour much, either.

The Footlights generation, which eschewed political satire as fit only for humourless intellectuals, was now developing two distinct strands of silliness – the *Python* form, which still made its audience feel intelligent, and the silly-verging-on-stupid variety, which reached its apogee in *The Goodies*, and appealed to an audience either very young or older but tending to wear anoraks and smeary spectacles. Cleese made his dissent over scripts plain, which did not make him popular with some of the team, while others used his occasional rages as material for more material. His stature and reputation had grown to the point where he was no longer prepared to 'die' embarrassingly in front of a studio audience for the sake of someone else's sub-standard lines. Such self-assertion did not come any more easily for Cleese now than it had at prep school, but the imperatives of performance as an art and a profession compelled him to throw his weight around. 'We're all shy introverts,' he explained. 'That's why we're performing. It's a barrier we have to break. You get out there on stage and you either become more introverted and die or you say I'm here so I might as well have a bash ... and break through the barrier.'

Despite the fact, evident if only from the way the British press was seeking him out, that John Cleese was rapidly becoming a rising son of the BBC, he remained unconvinced that he was best suited to this line of work. 'I've always been able to pass myself off as a professional, reliable chap who, due to a bum steer, ended up in showbusiness. It's always been part of my strength to come on respectable and then go quietly mad – or, rather, noisily mad,' he explained. 'I even have a strong feeling that I'm not a part of showbusiness. If you give me a piece of material and let me go off in a corner for a while, I can come back with something laughable. But on most occasions I'm about as funny as the average bank clerk. I've never thought I was particularly funny spontaneously, except in an argument. I don't think I'm anything like as funny as, for example, Michael Palin, who can just roll with funny stuff in the most delightful way, without it ever becoming a monologue.'

'The great shock for a small-town guy like me,' he told *Esquire* magazine in America in maturity, over twenty years later, 'is in hitting the real world and being made to realize that the people in charge are much less smart, less altruistic, less humane, than one had been brought up to believe. It's a shock I think I'm still recovering from. . . . Humour has been my way of dealing with that shock.'

But not any old humour, as he points out. While his mother 'laughs at big bosoms and arses, actually ... and Benny Hill and that kind of humour,' he has a blind spot for sexual jokes, scatological humour and innuendo. 'The wee-wee jokes, the poo-poo jokes, the fart jokes, how can they be so funny?' he rhetorically demanded of Melvyn Bragg on a 1986 edition of *The South Bank Show*. 'I mean, you can create a situation where something about that could be funny because of the context, you can always do that, but the sheer lack of discrimination with which so many people laugh at those jokes leaves me kind of breathless.'

In his mid-twenties it was not so much breathlessness but the early onset of boredom that was becoming a consistent feature of Cleese's personality. In April 1967, when the second series of *The Frost Report* began, he professed himself tired of it. As early as the start of the first series, a year previously, he predicted his ennui in the *Daily Mail*. 'I can't see myself still in showbusiness in three years' time,' he declared, maintaining that his burning interest was international politics. 'I've always wanted to feel I could be completely at ease in a very wide variety of situations. The study of politics could give one that. . . . Satire is too simple-minded. I'll end up back with politics.' (Cleese, then a Labour Party supporter, would switch allegiance to the SDP in the mid-Eighties.) By the time he was forty, this jadedness had extended to any form of employment. 'I've found that over the years the only thing that really bores me is work. For the first time I've started to think my time is limited. When I arrive at the Pearly Gates and St Peter asks me how many TV shows I've produced and I say "about 150", I don't think he is going to say: "Well, you should have made 250."'

'John Cleese decided that he wanted to stop performing for a while and stick to writing instead,' explains Ronnie Barker of this period. 'It had been worrying him, he'd look white around the gills before starting a sketch. It wouldn't have surprised me if he had stopped entirely when *The Frost Report* finished, because clearly he was not enjoying it all that much any more.' Cleese certainly had a fear of performing on television, but one suspects that he was often on intellectual autopilot when he spoke of it. Barker was not yet acclimatized to the Cleesian use of the word 'decided': 'Consistency is the consolation of the mediocre. I know perfectly well I will say different things on different days depending on what's circulating in my mind,' he has admitted. 'I seem to have this perhaps unfortunate tendency to get bored with things faster than most people. Another of my character flaws, I suppose.'

But, as ever, one last showbusiness project arrived to prevent Cleese from activating another of his 'decisions'. This programme had first been mooted – inevitably – by David Frost on a visit to his creative summer camp on Ibiza. It was to be another ITV venture, the joke in the title being that this was a show the BBC had been shelving for nineteen years. *At Last the 1948 Show* was the nearest thing to a *Monty Python* precursor. Early in 1967 at Cleese's flat, the first script meeting of *1948* took place. Frost, Tim Brooke-Taylor, Marty Feldman and Graham Chapman attended. 'By one o'clock only Marty Feldman had arrived,' wrote Marcelle Bernstein in the *Observer*. 'He did some frantic telephoning and discovered that the other three were at Tim Brooke-Taylor's flat in Portobello Road by mistake. At 3.30 he got them back to the Cleese flat. When Cleese discovered he'd locked himself out Tim said he'd climb in for a fiver. He did too. Inside, the flat has the squalor that only a bachelor can achieve: football boots, squash rackets and magazines everywhere. Cleese swept the fag-ends off the table, the newspapers under a chair, shoved a half-empty bottle of Tizer behind a smelly cheese and said that now the place was tidy he wasn't going to have it messed up. Then they all sat in a row on the couch and watched sport on telly.'

Cleese said at the time that he and Chapman had written 'some wild sketches, like the airline pilot thinking he was a bumblebee. But it wasn't until David got the four of us together on *1948* that we really started enjoying ourselves so much.' The show, to be produced by Frost, would have a leitmotif described by someone on the team as 'Ferrets, football, females – not to mention Frost'. The format was planned as a collection of unrelated sketches, which would stretch normal situations to the point of lunacy, and be linked by a dumb, pretty girl acting as if it were her show and believing she was making coherent sense of it all. Cleese and Tim Brooke-Taylor took on the task of casting the joke link-person by going on an expedition to a nightclub to look at dancing girls. Word naturally got around that the two posh gents were looking for a girl for a television show, and the embarrassed pair were soon under leggy siege. 'The lovely Aimi Macdonald', who would become a small-scale national institution, was the final choice. Cleese told a journalist, 'There will be hardly any music or singing in our show. It will consist mostly of sketches. We want to have nothing to do with satire. If we are "blue", it will not be intentional. Our main object will be to make people laugh.' (Cleese had come a long way since he confessed to a similar desire when he first tried to join Footlights, and was met by incomprehension.)

Cleese's roles in *At Last the 1948 Show* were designed to exploit the natural incongruity between his poker face and his demented actions, his authoritarian voice and his potty utterances. As a Minister for Education, he would be interviewed on television and end up splashing around in a water tank with a hake; one of a solemn panel of art critics, he would run amok and smash up antiques; as a doctor, he would tell his patient, 'Open your mouth and say "aaaaagh". Now lift up your arm, stand on one leg, pat your head and rub your stomach and jump up and down.' In one sketch, Cleese appeared as 'Otto von Nail-Scissors'; in another, he played a barmy psychiatrist.

Cleese also performed a ferret song on the show for the closing credits in white tie and tails, singing:

> I've got a ferret sticking up my nose.
> It starts wriggling when I wear my formal clothes.
> How it got there, I can't tell,
> But now it's there, it hurts like hell.
> And what is more, it radically affects my sense of smell.

The song caused Philip Purser to remark in the *Sunday Telegraph*: 'Cleese as soloist (a rather thin tenor) in the elaborate oratorio, "I've Got a Ferret Sticking Up My Nose" . . . brings to a logical conclusion several trends which have been growing more evident every year – not only that the funny man need no longer *look* funny (Cleese looks like an accountant who in his spare time is a bit fierce on the tennis court) but also that the comic's job is to remain absolutely normal in some bizarre reversal of ordinary circumstances, indeed not even to notice it. The joke about the oratorio on intranasal infestation was that it was every bit as meaningful and profound and mystical to this performer as *Messiah* is to Sir Malcolm Sargent.'

One of the best known *1948* sketches was the four tuxedoed Yorkshiremen comparing how bad they had had it as boys. Cleese characteristically got the role in which his tale of poverty topped those of all the others: 'I had to get up in the morning at ten o'clock at night half-an-hour before I went to bed, eat a lump of poison, work twenty-nine hours a day at t'mill and pay boss to let us work, come home, and each night dad used to kill us and dance about on our graves, singing.' The sketch was one of many that passed from generation to generation in a way *Goon Show* humour never quite managed to; in a 1991 edition of *Neighbours*, twenty-four years after the sketch was first seen, the teenagers of Ramsay Street were having a conversation somewhat along the same lines, in which Sharon, the plump, curly-haired sixth former, attempts to deride her friends' accounts of penury by scoffing in a broad Yorkshire accent, 'looxury'. Granted that the teenage actress did not personally write the line, and that trends do not always travel at top speed to Australia, it was still something of a cross-cultural, cross-generational coup for Cleese and his co-writers. Cleese and his circle's early radio and television shows all became cults. 'It was a bit like performing at Wembley. You only had to say something and everyone was shouting and cheering,' he says.

At Last the 1948 Show also produced the chartered accountant sketch ('Televisione Italiano Presenta: Let's Speak English') which over quarter of a century must have dissuaded hundreds of highly numerate and suitable young people from entering accountancy. In the skit, Brooke-Taylor, Feldman, Chapman and Cleese sit round a kitchen table in bowler hats and pinstripe suits. Chapman: 'I am a chartered accountant.' Brooke-Taylor: 'I am also a chartered accountant.' Feldman: 'I am a chartered accountant too.' Cleese: 'I am a gor-ill-a.'

'John Cleese has his eccentricities,' Marcelle Bernstein noted for the *Observer*. 'He swears by Roget's *Thesaurus* for inspiration when he's writing particularly nutty sketches; wants to learn soft-shoe shuffle and knows he's in a silly mood when he starts wondering what happened to a brown hat he owned years ago.' Interestingly, Bernstein suspected, without knowing the full details of how he had first become acquainted with Connie Booth, that Cleese sometimes put on being 'terribly, terribly English' as a device to deal with strange girls in restaurants.

Cleese's relationship with the late Marty Feldman was central to *1948*. Feldman, then thirty-two, was an ex-*Frost* script editor, who had written *The Army Game* for television and *Round The*

Horn for radio. He took the view that 'Comedy, like sodomy, is an unnatural act.' To Feldman, Cleese was 'the most honest man I know. A *Daily Telegraph* reader with very poor taste in clothes, he's shy and embarrassed to show affection until he knows you well; extravagantly generous, extremely gullible – oh, and he's vain too.' Cleese and Feldman developed a routine in which he would play the standard middle-class public employee and Feldman a horrific Mr Pest. 'I would be in a solicitor's office, or a railway carriage or a posh bookshop and Mr Pest would arrive, talk in a Marty nasal voice and dement me. We would finish with me driven hopelessly insane.'

A great influence on Cleese was Marty Feldman's theory of 'Internal Logic': 'He pointed out,' recalled Cleese with reverence, 'that however crazy a sketch or whatever is, you establish certain rules at the beginning. If everybody's standing in dustbins that's fine, but then if someone appears who's not standing in a dustbin you have to explain why.' Feldman may or may not have been teasing when he described Cleese as gullible, but it was a quirk that other friends observed with amusement verging on concern. He could be almost mesmerized by an intellectual rationalization for practically any phenomenon. While other people just *did*, Cleese would want to know *how* and *why* they did. Ten years later, Tim Brooke-Taylor was unnervingly candid about this characteristic in a *Sunday Times* interview. 'He's still conscious of being emotionally immature,' he said of Cleese. 'He's always been a bit over-analytical and he can be conned into things. He can fall for intellectual names and then he becomes disillusioned. He's got quite a few hangers-on and his head is turnable. He was very impressed by David Frost at one time. Frost did spot him early on and John owed a lot to him, but in the end he was being talked into things by Frost and was ultimately being used. Basically, he's a sucker in the nicest sense.' Nice was the word: at Frost's 1967 Christmas party for a hundred people, Cleese turned up dressed as Father Christmas, a role one would perhaps have expected to find the host himself playing.

On the positive side, however, while his anxiety to pounce upon and inspect any new intellectual notions he came across led to his spending some time examining dross, it also made Cleese his own sternest critic. That was the one propensity that was to make Cleese's work infinitely better than that of everyone around him. 'Of the fifty performances I have given in the past twelve months, there are only four items that I even begin to be satisfied with,' he reflected in 1967. He was convinced that if he had not been a writer, he would not have stood a chance as a performer, and that his performing skills would vanish if he ever became too confident. Neither would he ever be a comic in the sense of telling jokes – he prided himself on knowing none. His one stated aim, in 1967 at least, was to get a belly laugh, and he was finding it hard enough to do that by his own high standards. John Cleese was already living proof of the psychoanalytical maxim that it is not that little bit extra some people have that makes them successful, but that little bit *less*.

The John Cleese of the mid-to-late 1960s was a straightforward, well-off and successful young man about London, his general appeal enhanced by a dash of cultivated crankiness. He prided himself, for example, on having no interest in being fashionable, and describes how he went out in 1966 with a young 'mod' girl, wearing a baggy sports jacket and flannels. She said, with venom, 'Ugh, 1948'. 'It's nice to see girls dressing well, you understand, but I hate to see slavish copying,' he complained to the *TV Times*. 'I love the Beatles, but on the whole "with it" to me means a lot of mindless idiots being taken for a ride by some very shrewd moneymakers.'

Cleese was refreshingly unselfconscious about having made a considerable amount of money very quickly. His first car, which he bought while still a learner driver in early 1967, was a six-year-old Bentley S3 – a late but satisfying reaction to being denied a bike when he was young. His mother was as impressed as only mothers can be by his grandeur in choosing, as he has always continued to, to drive Rolls-Royces and Bentleys. Once when he picked her up at Paddington Station, she looked at his car and asked simply, 'Has it got enough petrol?' He and Connie took the Bentley, 'a vast luxurious dodgem', to Europe as soon as he could with the odd funny consequence. 'We drove through Liège, waving to the peasants like royalty. Then we ran the car under a truck and forty minutes later went back through Liège, still waving regally but being towed by a breakdown van.'

Cleese had started playing squash – extremely competitively

– and went three times a week to the Westside Health Club in Kensington. He played soccer on Sunday mornings in Hyde Park, cricket whenever he could. Not a great enthusiast for nightclubs, he would tend to take a girl out for a meal and then rush her home to watch a football match on television.

This kind of man's man existence made a party that Graham Chapman held in summer 1967 all the more startling to Cleese, who had by this time known him for nearly seven years. Chapman informed his writing partner two days before the party that he was gay, and that the get-together, less than a year after meeting David Sherlock in Ibiza, was to celebrate their Coming Out. Because of the thoughtful pre-party briefing, Chapman noted that Cleese 'wasn't surprised, but was still in a state of shock about it all, because it was totally, totally alien to him – such a thing was unthinkable and this was going to be the ruin of my life. Although he was still friendly he was completely at a loss to give his feelings.' (How different the scene was to be in 1989 when Chapman died of cancer and Cleese wept copiously in public.)

In this newly affluent period, Cleese also started to indulge what would become a passion for food, restaurants and the whole catering industry. 'Since I have had the money, I've got to love eating out in restaurants,' he told a *Daily Star* hack over a prawn curry. Later his expertise in catering made it possible for him even to overcome that great Cleese family bugaboo that he bore so valiantly for Weston-super-Mare and England: the sending back of unsatisfactory dishes in restaurants. Post-psychoanalysis, Cleese explained how he finally learned to do it and, by analogy, to exercise his ability to channel his rage: 'I just don't like sending the food back. But I've been working on this problem for years. You see, the most effective way is to be *very* polite, and not, funnily, to get angry. You say to the waiter: "Look, I'm sorry about this. I'm very embarrassed but this doesn't really taste good at all".'

Cleese also played on a joke preoccupation with cheese and fish ('John's favourite colour is fish...' said one *Monty Python* book) for large tracts of his comedy, and would tease gossip columnists that he used the ancestral name Cheese to book restaurant tables: 'When I phone an Italian restaurant, I say

I'm Signor Formaggio. If it's French I'm Monsieur Fromage. Of course, when I eat Chinese, then I say I'm Mr Creese,' he once allegedly told the *Sun*. He unleashed a flight of fancy on the subject of cheese in the direction of Penelope Gilliatt, who interviewed him for the *New Yorker*: 'The nice thing about cheese is thinking of all those people all over the world doing different things to milk. You could do a sketch about it. "Try hitting the milk with a stick," someone would say. Then an argument. "No, don't hit it, go round and round in the milk with the stick and then see what happens. Don't give up. Something unpredictable might happen."'

Just before Christmas 1967, something unpredictable did happen. At the end of the second series of *At Last the 1948 Show*, and a few weeks after explaining to the *Observer* that he had very nearly got married in New York three years previously, and had learned a lot from not doing so ('In this business more than in any other you can only improvise, you can't plan. I don't know where I'm going and I don't think it would be very bright to get myself involved until I do'), Cleese, now twenty-eight, put the Bentley up for sale for £2,000 and headed for New York for a long holiday. Cleese and Connie Booth had been conducting a transatlantic relationship, seeing each other about twice a year. 'There's one girl I take out fairly regularly,' he had coyly confessed in 1966, with obvious emphasis on the 'fairly'. Whenever they saw each other, they discussed the question of marriage.

Finally, just after Christmas in New York, Cleese had an evening in which Connie rebuffed him totally. Walking back to his hotel, he decided to break off the relationship for good. 'So he went to the phone on the street – I suppose it was one in the morning,' recalls Cleese's old *Newsweek* chum Everett Martin. 'He called her up and said: "I want you to know I'm going to accept your feelings and your thoughts and I will never call you again." So Connie said: "Wait a minute, I'll call you back." And he sat on the front steps of the brownstone she lived in for an hour and a half while she talked to her analyst on the phone. Then she let him in.' They were married quietly on 20 February 1968.

'I'm not,' John Cleese said over a decade later, after he and Connie had divorced, 'the most self-confident person in the world. With Connie it was our mutual lack of self-confidence that drew us together.'

John and Connie returned from New York in the spring of 1968. They bought a flat next to Harrods, in Basil Street, Knightsbridge, and Connie picked up a second-hand Hillman Minx for £350, since a mortgage took up most of the couple's earnings. Apart from all these happy conjugal developments, 1968 was not a notable year for Cleese.

He and Chapman wrote a film called *Rentasleuth*, working on the script with Charles Crichton, who even then, nearly twenty years before *A Fish Called Wanda* was made, was considered a venerable old man of the cinema. The film was planned for 1971 but, because of their contractual commitments to the Frost Organization, it was eventually made much later, disastrously reworked in the view of some critics by John Wells, John Fortune and Ned Sherrin, who also produced, under a name which was about as in the spirit of John Cleese as farting jokes, *Rentadick*. Cleese and Chapman refused to be associated with it and had their names removed from the credits, which finally read: 'additional material by Jim Viles and Kurt Loggerhead'. 'Viles and Loggerhead' were predictably furious when the film was shown on BBC1 in 1983 and the *Radio Times* billed the script writers as John Cleese and Graham Chapman. 'It doesn't do much for one's personal reputation,' they sniffed.

Cleese and Chapman wrote a few scripts for a Marty Feldman series on BBC2 called *Marty*, some of which, to their slight astonishment, were sent back. With Tim Brooke-Taylor and Michael Palin, they wrote and starred in a television special called *How to Irritate People*, which included a sketch suggested by an experience Palin had suffered when taking a faulty new car back to a garage, only to be told, among other excuses, that the car *was* new, after all.

A reasonably good film called *Interlude* came out in 1968, with Cleese in a straight part as a television PR man – his first film role. 'I always play the same type. All I do is caricature myself,' he had complained the year before, on the film set at Wembley, where a make-up girl built up his confidence no end by reassuring him, 'Don't worry, love, you're smashing'. While *Interlude* played with modest success in the swingingest summer of swinging London, Cleese was making *The Magic Christian*, a satirical Peter Sellers project with an extraordinary roll-call of stars (Sellers himself, Spike Milligan, Ringo Starr, Yul Brynner, Richard Attenborough, Laurence Harvey, Christopher Lee, Roman Polanski, Raquel Welch, Wilfrid Hyde-White, Terence Alexander, Clive Dunn, Hattie Jacques, John Le Mesurier and Dennis Price). Cleese got a favourable mention as a director of Sotheby's, but the film flopped.

Cleese and Chapman also collaborated on a script for Peter Sellers, never filmed, called 'Ditto', which Chapman later rewrote with David Sherlock, who still has hopes of getting it made. The 'Ibiza' film, *The Rise and Rise of Michael Rimmer*, remained an issue in this fallow 1968. When it was finally released in 1970, Cleese's small part was thought one of the funniest things in it, a pattern which occurred in two other dud films he appeared in at the time: *The Statue* ('I predict many of the big laughs will be stolen by Cleese as a psychiatrist in need of a psychiatrist,' wrote the *Sunday Mirror*) and *It's A 2'6" Above The Ground World*, later renamed *The Love Ban*, which received crushing reviews, with generous mention only for Cleese, who played a contraceptives lecturer.

It was also the year a highly uncelebrated American film producer came to visit Cleese and Chapman. To welcome him, Cleese arranged for fifteen of his cuddliest soft toys to be in their office, peering at the producer from behind pictures, out of cupboards, under chairs and through windows. Understandably, the producer left in a state of complete bafflement.

In January 1969, a comedy called *The Complete and Utter History of Britain*, written by and starring Michael Palin and Terry Jones, was shown on LWT. They applied current television documentary techniques to ancient historical events: Jones interviewing Palin as William the Conqueror in a rugby-type bath with all the lads, and so on. Palin recalls: 'I remember John ringing in what must have been about April 1969, and he said: "I've seen the *Complete and Utter History*. You won't be doing any more of those, will you? So why don't we do something together?", meaning your lot and our lot.'

6 *Calling Henri Bergson*

There are some people one would wish to offend.

Sir Hugh Carleton Greene, BBC Director-General, on *Monty Python's Flying Circus*

John Cleese claims it was all his idea. He says he put it to Barry Took, who was adviser to BBC Television's comedy department, and Took instantly agreed. Took says it was he who first approached Cleese, Graham Chapman, Terry Jones and Michael Palin. Another account has it that Cleese (on his and Chapman's behalf) approached Palin, who brought in Jones, and then they all brought in Idle and the American artist Terry Gilliam, then went to Took, who went to Michael Mills, Head of Comedy at the BBC, told him they were fed up with working for ITV, and it was Mills who took them on. Palin and Jones recall that they brought Idle in. Idle says it was he, not Cleese, who brought Gilliam in, and Took agrees.

Two things only are clear about the birth of *Monty Python's Flying Circus*: one is that nobody has the remotest idea who first thought up the show, the other that the BBC wanted John Cleese to have his own programme at all costs and would never have given the others this chance without him.

Cleese often grumbles that in the almost twenty years since *Monty Python* came off the air, he has spent more time talking about the group than he ever devoted to writing and performing with them. Cleese, Palin, Idle, Chapman, Jones and Gilliam and their new project were unlucky enough to coincide with the education boom of the 1960s and 1970s. It has never been deemed sufficient just to watch and enjoy *Monty Python*, the show described in a celebrated turn of phrase by a South American journalist as 'forged from the anvil of Hell'. The sociology generation have from the early days felt a strange compulsion to analyse *Monty Python*. 'We have Gatling Guns mounted which go off at the word Ph.D.,' says Palin of zealous students. 'Generally they are distinguished by long ponderous letters about, oh, The Role of the Narrator in early episodes of *Monty Python*.' And Cleese, although not averse to a spot of heavyweight scholasticism himself, denies that *Python* achieved anything like the 'breakthrough' in comedy it has been remembered for. 'Shows prepare the way for other shows, and sometimes shows that make genuine breakthroughs are missed,' he said at the time to David Nathan. 'Spike Milligan's *Q5* was missed. Milligan is the great God to all of us. The *Goon Show* influenced us enormously. When we first saw *Q5* we were very depressed because we thought it was what we wanted to do and Milligan was doing it brilliantly. But nobody really noticed *Q5*.'

And yet some interesting ideas do emerge from the intensely swotty contemplation of *Monty Python* in red-brick towers and minor American campuses. 'One theory to ponder,' posited John Hind, in Cleesian mode perhaps, in his 1991 book *Comic Inquisition*, 'is that the group embodied the fabric – and thus the range of emotions – of "The Family Unit"; with Cleese (of course) playing introvert father-figure, Jones as romantic nurturing mother, Palin as cheery mummy's boy, Idle as cheeky loner son, Chapman as decadent son and Gilliam as, perhaps, American cousin. Within those constraints, they took on the world (from the man on the TV to the man in the corner shop) . . . and they took on each other. But then, as they acquired families of their own, their relationship waned.'

The first meeting of the *Monty Python* team was on Sunday, 11 May 1969, after a recording of *Do Not Adjust Your Set*, a Rediffusion children's programme that Idle, Palin and Jones had devised, more to the delight of parents than their pre-teen offspring. The group met over a curry lunch at the Light of Kashmir in Fleet Road, Hampstead, and continued their discussions at Cleese's Basil Street flat. On 23 May, Barry Took arranged a meeting between the team and Michael Mills who, in a hurry, popped into the meeting room, commissioned them to write and perform a thirteen-part show, then rushed off. Their budget was £3,500 per episode.

Early proposed titles were 'Owl-Stretching Time', 'Whither Canada', 'The Toad-Elevating-Moment', 'A-Horse-A-Bucket-A-Spoon' (variously recalled as 'A Horse, A Spoon and A Bucket' and 'A Horse, A Spoon and A Basin' – Cleese's favourite), 'Sex-And-Violence', and 'Bunn, Wackett, Buzzard, Stubble and Boot' (a football team's forward line, invented by Cleese). Some of the other names Jones wrote down at one meeting included 'Arthur Megapode's Flying Circus', 'Vaseline Review', 'The Atomic Zoo', 'Cynthia Fellatio's Flying Circus', and, with those ever-present shades of Peter Cook, 'E. L. Moist's Flying Circus'.

The 'Flying Circus' notion was originally a rather middle-aged BBC bureaucrat's reference to the First World War. Took had a reputation for arrogance and stubbornness, and was likened by Michael Mills to Baron von Richthofen, the Luftwaffe ace whose squadron was known by the RAF as the 'Flying Circus'. Thus the new series became known on memos as 'Baron von Took's Flying Circus'. 'Monty Python' narrowly beat 'Gwen Dibley', a name Palin spotted in a Women's Institute journal. 'Monty Python' as a name represented to the group the idea of a shady small-time theatrical booker.

Cleese was from the first day the group leader and spokesman, although this was never officially acknowledged. It was Cleese who would negotiate with BBC officials to persuade them to allow some of the more risqué material through, Cleese whom the tabloids would ring up with their sometimes less than intellectually coherent questions. He was always polite and could be relied upon to hand out a titbit in the right sort of style for the particular newspaper over the phone. The team wrote on democratic principles, but for Cleese it was 'democracy gone mad'. According to Palin, 'John was the nearest we got to a chairman because he was, and is, very clear-thinking and also usually in rather a hurry. A combination which was perfect really, because you would want to get out by a certain time.'

But Terry Jones, a passionate, fiercely bright and anarchic Welshman, was not emotionally inclined to be subject to any form of authority. 'So,' reflects Palin, 'it was by no means a question of one person always being in the chair. I suppose you could say John and Terry represented the two ends of the spectrum, in a sense. John, if you like, was the head and Terry was the heart of *Python*.'

Monty Python liberated Cleese's humour. 'We'd all been writing for *The Frost Report* – good material, but governed by a very conventional format,' he said. 'We'd put up something that amused us and the producer would say: "Ah, but they'd never understand it in Bradford." Pythonic humour was a revolt against that.' It was also a chance for Cleese and Chapman, who still wrote together in the new grouping, to let loose the sadistic side of their humour, which held that any subject under the sun had comic potential. Cleese made a principle of not laughing at jokes, but occasionally one would set him off: '"What's black and white and crawls along the ground? A wounded nun." I thought that was hysterical. I used to laugh at that out in the street for about a fortnight every time I thought of it. Then I started making them up.' In private, Chapman was the source of a spectacularly cruel one-liner that Cleese regards as one of the funniest things he ever heard, although he admits it left an unpleasant taste. When the *Python* team arrived in Bavaria in the summer of 1971 to record a show in German, they were informed that they were to be taken to see the Dachau concentration camp – a fairly strange idea, but they let it ride. When they got to the gate there was a great commotion, and it turned out, to add embarrassment to embarrassment, that they were too late to get in. As the negotiations between the Pythons' German hosts and the keepers of the macabre historic monument escalated to shouting, Chapman yelled out: 'Tell them we're Jews!'

Cleese and Chapman, with their shared science background and abusive verbal humour, counterbalanced Palin, Jones and Gilliam, whose jokes were more visual. Idle did his own thing. Cleese's precision often irritated Chapman, who had started drinking heavily. 'When I first began working with John he really quite annoyed me, going over the same line again and again when I thought it would do half an hour before. John writes from the left-hand side of the brain, following a logical path to come to an absurd conclusion. He is not interested in jokes, but in why people behave in the way they do. There's not a lot of emotion there.'

They wrote either at Cleese's Basil Street flat or at Chapman's house in Hampstead. Sometimes, if the ideas were not flowing, they would raid the Bible or a thesaurus for verbal triggers. In keeping with Cleese's preference for comedy based on reality, ideas would often come from everyday situations. His flat next to Harrods was plagued by the nocturnal braying and car-door-slamming of Hooray Henrys; revenge came in the form of the 'Upper Class Twit Of The Year' sketch, which he claims helped him get a lot of venom out of his system. Real but bizarre occurrences were even more suitable material. In one very short but classic sketch, Palin approaches a policeman Cleese to report a theft. Cleese hesitates a crucial half-a-second and says, 'Do you want to come back to my place?' Palin simply replies, 'Yeah. All right' and the two saunter gaily away. The inspiration for this was a *Python* cameraman Stanley Speel who, while driving down Kingsway at 5 a.m. one morning, was convinced he saw two policemen holding hands. He told Marty Feldman, who told Cleese.

Cleese would write down all his and Chapman's output, as Chapman had already managed to develop a doctor's calligraphy. In spite of the orderliness of his mind, Cleese was continually losing sketches, which even long, anguished searches of the premises would not discover. Chapman suspected that the bits which vanished frequently were the very sketches which Cleese deemed needed too much reworking. 'Our sketches would consist of people coming on and abusing each other out of thesauruses,' Cleese says. 'We both would find abuse very, very funny and we loved people arguing and fighting and being rude to each other.'

They were also keen on the slightly juvenile tactic of shocking the audience, which often gave rise to a suspicion that Cleese and Chapman were writing more to impress, if that is the word, their respective mothers than the ten million viewers that *Monty Python* picked up at its peak. Cleese was greatly taken by a piece of advice handed to him at a BBC party by David Attenborough, whose nature films he watches avidly. Attenborough recommended him to be sparing in his use of shock tactics. This did not prevent Cleese and Chapman coming up with one sketch where Cleese plays a man who takes his dead mother in a sack to Chapman as an undertaker who suggests they eat her. Cleese, the bereaved, is tempted, but decides against. 'Look, tell you what,' says Chapman, 'we'll eat her. Then, if you feel guilty about it afterwards, we'll dig a grave and you can throw up in it.' The sketch proved a tough one to get through the BBC, and only appeared in a modified form. 'If you could have seen us writing it,' Cleese later said. 'It was not two calculating members of the IRA planning to destroy the world, but two young men holding their sides and shaking with laughter.' Both he and Chapman had their own complicated reasons for delighting in disturbing their mothers – Chapman's associated with his gayness, Cleese's perhaps concerned with extirpating the memory of his sheltered and repressed childhood.

They completed about three sketches a week, which took long enough for Connie to complain that her new husband was spending more time with his writing partner than with her. Connie had been astonished to find out how famous John was in England. 'I came to London and walked into the whole Python craze. I just didn't have the incentive to go out and start a new career all over again. . . . I felt very out of things. The phone never stopped and there was so much energy in the house. I was very envious.' For a couple of years, she felt miserable.

The Pythons met for about three days at the beginning of the series to discuss what they were going to write and then went off and wrote completely different things. 'I think that was because once somebody thought of an idea there was no honour in writing it,' Cleese says. During the series, they got together each week to read through material. A rule evolved that if one Python hated a sketch, it might not be used, and if two were against it, it would not be filmed. At the beginning, Python meetings were jovial affairs. As Graham Chapman later recalled: 'When we first started, it was great fun because we were all equal and there was no ego-tripping. But as the series progressed and people like John Cleese became stars in their own right, the whole team became unbalanced. Quite unexpectedly you'd find your lines had been switched at the last minute so that somebody or other had a better part. As a result, a lot of needle developed between us all. . . . The truth is, most of the time we can't stand each other. Sometimes we bloody well hate each other. We were having stand-up rows all the time. The atmosphere was awful.'

The great antler-lock was between Cleese and Terry Jones. For Cleese, 'Jonesey' was a romantic, while he was a classicist: 'Terry is Welsh and is kind of passionate and I'm sort of repressed and logical.' Jones agreed at least on that: 'I think John is very much the Anglo-Saxon in his reaction to things and his outlook on life. And I'm much more the Celt in that I just have this more emotional reaction to everything first. . . . I think I only threw a chair at John once.' The strains of those fraught powwows were still apparent twenty-two years on; at a literary festival in Hay-on-Wye in May 1991, Palin and Jones, answering questions at a comedy writing session, were asked by a lady in pink what it was like to work with John Cleese. 'Who's he? Oh, the tall one. He makes *very* nice coffee,' they giggled.

The very fact of Cleese being an embryo businessman and small 'c' conservative created a tension with his co-Pythons that, while probably helping to make their comedy more effective, meant that he was not particularly close to the others. Cleese confessed to being a 'compulsive perfectionist' who found writing 'like pushing a car out of a ditch' and location-work screamingly dull. One Python said at the time, 'John doesn't want to get up at dawn and catch a train to some Godforsaken spot just so he can be filmed doing silly things for a silly sketch that lasts a couple of minutes on the screen.' Cleese could be charming and generous, particularly with women, but colleagues often also thought him self-centred, stubborn and disloyal. 'There was a lot of anger in all of us,' Cleese says of the team, 'and a fair amount of paranoia in the group. And plenty of envy, a lot of envy, because we never talked about anything that any of us did outside the group, a kind of taboo.'

Cleese was determined and manipulative in meetings. 'John used to get most of his stuff in,' recalls an insider who was fascinated by Cleese's mastery of a supposedly democratic committee. 'John sometimes sat quietly in meetings and he might lean over very friendly and earnestly to you and say, "What do you think about it all?" And you knew he damn well didn't care what you thought. Someone might be very enthusiastic about something and he could just block it by saying, "I haven't got time to think about that, I've more important things to do." When they performed their material to each other, John was very generous in his laughter at other people's stuff. But sometimes he would laugh incredibly loudly, and I was never really sure if he didn't do it to get his own stuff in.'

There were also unavoidable yet creative disharmonies in the production process. Ian McNaughton (described by Chapman as 'a tousle-haired loopy Scottish person'), who had been the director of Q5, took on Monty Python. If Terry Jones was passionate Welsh rugby to Cleese's sedate English cricket, Cleese and McNaughton, an amiable, sandalled type, were like Gentleman's Relish and Haggis. Cleese tends to turn up the froideur at the first sign of over-geniality, a habit Chapman noted: 'The meticulous orderly side of John Cleese's nature – the side that counts how many O, A and S levels and what sort of a degree a person has got, as in some way definitive of that person's all-round ability – was uncomfortable with some of Ian's character traits, particularly Ian's friendliness which made John freeze and resort to schoolmasterly sarcasm.'

One film editor with a long history of working with Cleese reveres him but also advises colleagues how to handle him. 'Don't, for God's sake, go up and say "Hi John, how are you?" because he'll turn round and pretend he doesn't know you. Wait till he says hello to you and then he'll be as friendly as you like. He plays games all the time. But if I was sitting in a chair, he'd come up from behind and slap my face and ruffle my hair, messing me about while I was trying to do something sensible. And you couldn't do the same to him because he would kill you with some sort of look, gesture or remark. I've seen waiters in restaurants who've tried to be funny and he just says, "Oh yes?" and they die on the spot.'

After the first series of Monty Python, Cleese, inevitably, as the de facto leader and self-confessed enthusiast of change for change's sake, tried to vary the writing partnerships, mainly because he wanted to work with Michael Palin, whom he adored. Consequently, Palin and Cleese wrote the 'North Minehead By-Election' (an 'A. Hitler' standing for election in a Weston-super-Mare-type seaside resort, a favourite sketch of Cleese's), while Idle and Cleese wrote the 'Sir George Head' mountaineering sketch about an expedition leader handicapped by double vision. The new pairings did not last long, to Cleese's regret.

Donald Zec of the *Daily Mirror* gained a special insight into the Python thought process when he ingeniously arranged a lunch for Cleese, Ronnie Corbett and Peter Cook, whom he considered to be the three funniest men in England at that time. There was a lot of silly banter, mainly from Cook. Cleese said he rarely received fan letters from anyone over the age of eighteen. Then: '"I like the word 'Neasden'"', John Cleese said morosely, which idiot interjection paralysed all conversation for a moment. "That's how we work on *Monty Python*," he added, to fill the vacuum. "Take any old word and see where it takes us. Or we play around with odd ideas like The Sex Life of a Traffic Warden or How to Defend Yourself Against a Man Armed With a Redcurrant."'

The first *Monty Python* was broadcast on BBC1 on Sunday, 5 October 1969. The show featured, among other things, a sketch with a sports-type commentary on the progress of Picasso competing in a Tour of Britain cycle race while painting an abstract, and Terry Jones as Arthur Ewing and his musical mice. Cleese's first appearance was not as a middle-class Englishman, but as a cod Frenchman in a beret and striped shirt discussing with a similarly clad Michael Palin the phenomenon of flying sheep. Even one of Cleese's best friends from his Cambridge days, Humphrey Barclay, then a budding television producer, professed himself baffled by the show. The BBC's publicity department, given the task of explaining their new venture to eager if not totally comprehending journalists, tried its best. 'It's nutty humour and a couple of generations away from satire,' a spokesman was quoted as saying, to the annoyance of the Pythons, the fateful day before episode one was broadcast.

As was usual, the team recorded the show before a studio

audience, which was something Cleese would later regret, having realized that studio audiences were in no way representative of (and often harder to please than) the much broader television public. In the dressing-rooms before the show, Cleese said to Palin, 'Do you realize, Michael, we may be about to be the first people in history to record a half-hour comedy show to complete silence?' In the event, the laughing started within seconds, when the first aeronautical sheep were seen roosting in trees.

Precisely whose laughter it was is debatable. The BBC issued tickets for shows free to anyone wanting just that – a ticket to a show, and any show as long as it was television. Audiences therefore tended to be coach-party gatherings mostly of elderly ladies mustered from the farthest-flung provinces. On occasion the studio reaction could be pretty muted, the only sounds being the raucous cackles of Connie Booth and Terry Jones's brother, loyally rolling in the aisles.

Although the forward-thinking BBC Director-General, Sir Hugh Carleton Greene, had been largely responsible behind the scenes for getting *Python* on the air at all (Michael Mills's boss Tom Sloane, the Head of Light Entertainment, loathed the show), the BBC regions were not so easily won over and were inclined to substitute their own 'opt-out' programmes at the least provocation. One friend of Cleese settled down to watch an early edition of *Monty Python* in his hotel room in Newcastle. Well used already to the programme's propensity for pulling surprises, he nearly fell off his bed with mirth at this particular evening's offering. Missing out even Sousa's 'Liberty Bell' marching music, the familiar 'It's' introductory sequence and the opening titles, the show started with a chap wandering round a city, droning on boringly about its historical monuments. After some twenty minutes of this, and marvelling at the iconoclastic cheek of Cleese and his team for having the nerve to break with tradition to this extent, he realized that he had been watching a regional opt-out on ancient monuments in Newcastle. It is easy to see why, for Cleese, the nicest thing anybody ever said about *Monty Python* was that they could never watch the news afterwards without laughing.

Caricaturing the authority figure – which is to say, himself minus the comic muse – was Cleese's explicit role in the new programme. He was well aware that had he not been funny, he would have been a solicitor. He could play members of the establishment with ease because he had the training, the accent and the bearing, but insists that he chose to play them because the more pompous characters were, the funnier it was when they did silly things. The combination of a weak father and an authoritarian school added a political justification he certainly felt strongly at the time – that all authority was misplaced.

To the public and to people working with him on sets, the dividing line between the poker-faced man-behind-a-desk announcing 'And now for something completely different' and the real John Cleese was never quite clear. Was he for real? The respectable veneer made it possible for Cleese to get away with more than other comics, and he seems to have enjoyed the exhibitionism of showbusiness, such as when he once went into a bank during filming, dressed as Attila the Hun, pretending to have forgotten he was in costume and affecting to wonder why everybody was staring at him. Yet he always maintained for the wardrobe manageress's benefit that he disliked wearing costumes, even puffing himself up so that he could petulantly complain that outfits did not fit. In on-set photographs, Cleese looks uneasy and solicitorish in his costumes, adding all the more to the studied image of the authority figure doing really silly things against his better judgement.

It was the juxtaposition of bossy narrow-mindedness and wild, anarchic action – often combined by the Pythons in mad army officers – that fed Cleese's ever growing fascination with the theoretical analysis of comedy, and especially with the writings on comedy of Henri Bergson, the French philosopher who was best known for his influence in developing the 'stream of consciousness' novel. Bergson was like the mother lode to John Cleese. The nub of his theory was that laughter is the price the public exacts from people whose behaviour has become mechanical, rigid and inflexible; this explained everything – poor Mr Milligan, the clean hands inspector at St Peter's School, whom Cleese ragged so wickedly at the age of twelve, the lunatic *Monty Python* colonel stopping sketches because they are 'too silly', the frustrated Mr Stimpson in *Clockwise*, and of course Basil Fawlty. If Bergson had not been perfectly capable of forming his own theories, Cleese would eventually have promulgated them for him.

British comedy of the Benny Hill, Jimmy Tarbuck tradition made its fun of milkmen and plumbers. The more sophisticated comics, like Hancock, Peter Cook and Marty Feldman, concentrated on lunatics and obsessives. For Cleese, a child of the 1940s and 1950s, but finding his audience at the end of the anti-authoritarian 1960s, the source of humour was the police, the army, cabinet ministers, merchant bankers, accountants, clergymen; they could be doling out rules and making fools of themselves, or trying to maintain their dignity against the insolence of a cheese shop man devoid of cheese or a pet shop proprietor trying to avoid giving a refund on a dead parrot. In both the cheese shop and the pet shop, it was the customer played by Cleese whom the audience, in accordance with Bergson, laughed at – although it is possible to imagine a retired colonel in Gloucestershire, accidentally tuning into *Monty Python*, bucking the trend and sympathizing with Cleese's checkmated genteelman.

Cleese, who, when he was tired of pushing forward the frontiers of comedy, quietly spent the *Monty Python* period also writing episodes of *Doctor in the House*, and *Doctor at Large* for London Weekend Television (and the money), was still tentative about quoting Bergson too loudly. Britain loves an intellectual about as much as Italy thrills to a tone-deaf diva. For the moment Cleese buttered his bread on both sides by using Bergson both as an icon and as a suitable case for Python treatment, or at least a prop for sketches. In one, Cleese played a Michael Miles quizmaster, who asks a contestant old lady, played by Terry Jones, 'What great opponent of Cartesian dualism resists the reduction of psychological phenomena to physical states?' She answers 'Henri Bergson', although she also replies 'Henri Bergson' to the question: 'What swims in the sea and gets caught in nets?'

The rampant intellectualism that was only starting to show itself publicly in Cleese had several uses for him. He has always regarded himself as a writer first and an actor second – it is his tragedy in some ways (though not financial ones) that he is so good as an actor. When he was invited on to chat shows and an audience expected him to start wisecracking, he seemed to delight in getting serious about life, at pains to point out that he really wasn't funny at all without a script. All at once, this tendency established him as a delightfully contradictory character, cocked a snook at the British distaste for any sniff of braininess and impressed serious-minded people out there who might mistakenly assume that John Cleese was just another comedian. 'I heard about an Oxford don,' he said on BBC *Woman's Hour* in 1971. 'He'd never seen *Monty Python* before. But he was watching one in which suddenly in the middle of a quiz programme – myself playing a sadistic quizmaster and Terry Jones playing a little sort of take-your-pick type woman – Terry Jones started going on and on about Bergson, the French philosopher, and at that point I understand that the Oxford don actually fell on one knee, which is a lovely thought.'

The great authority figure gone wrong that he played, and the character that Cleese feels has rather let him down, is of course Mr Teabags of the Ministry of Silly Walks. The sketch was written by Palin and Jones, from an idea by Chapman about government departments with silly names and duties. Cleese had characteristically wanted to do a sketch about a Ministry of Anger, when he and Chapman spotted a man struggling up the steep hill on which Chapman lived. The passer-by progressed with a strange backward slant, and Chapman enthused about creating a Ministry of Silly Walks. They had another sketch to complete, however, and phoned Palin and Jones to ask them – or make them, as Chapman recalled – write the sketch. Although he grew to detest the sketch, Cleese typically put immense work into performing it. 'When they go on about the Ministry of Silly Walks, people assume that I made it up ten minutes before I did it. Whereas, in fact, I practised the movement for a week and slowly worked out whether I should take, say, three paces before I did the big high kick, or five paces, or whatever. I choreographed it very, very painstakingly.'

But Cleese felt dogged by what he saw as the foolishness of the Silly Walks sketch from the moment it went out in September 1970. Although it contained lashings of Marty Feldman's 'internal logic' – even the tealady at the Ministry had a silly walk – it was painful for a man who prided himself on his ability as a wordsmith to be remembered throughout his career for a couple of minutes of exaggerated goose-stepping in a largely visual sketch which he had not even written.

As early as the end of 1970, Cleese was showing signs of being grievously embarrassed by silly walks mania. He was invited to visit Oxford University to help raise money for Biafra with a sponsored Silly Walk. An ex-pupil of his from St Peter's, Christopher Kettle, recalls: 'The event had been coupled with an attempt to found a Monty Python Appreciation Society at Oxford, which had held one meeting in which every motion was voted out for not being silly enough. Cleese led the sponsored silly walk of about 100 people rattling spam tins up the High Street. He led it with an air of quiet dignity as if he really wished to be disassociated from the whole thing. As far as I can remember, he didn't do the silly walk at all. He left it to his minions.'

Cleese broke down public reaction to the silly walk into four equally mortifying categories. Some people would smile and say something like, 'How's the Ministry this morning?' Others would demand he do a silly walk on the spot. Van drivers would bawl across the road, 'Oi Monty, let's 'ave yer funny walk then.' But the most helpful would accost him and burble that their four-year-old son adored his funny walk because it was just his sense of humour. 'That was such a terribly ordinary sketch,' Cleese sighs. 'I hate talking about it. Nice sensible people ask sensible questions about the origins of *Monty Python* and I almost scream as I hear myself being nice to them and coming out with the same old answers.'

But Cleese's aversion to the silly walk has not hampered him from reluctantly repeating the moves over the years, particularly when seeking publicity for a new project. Just as he has never been dramatically opposed in bachelor days to using his exceeding Englishness to impress girls – especially pretty American ones – there is record of Cleese being apparently less than self-conscious about playing Mr Teabags of the Ministry. Duytch Pojowa, an attractive female friend of David Sherlock in Los Angeles, was backstage when the Pythons performed live at the Hollywood Bowl in 1980, the series of shows at which Cleese met his second wife, Barbara Trentham. Ms Pojowa was sitting on a packing crate during the performance, and recalls: 'John Cleese was practising his silly walk, absolutely dead straight. He just said, "Don't mind me, I have to do this." I had to stuff things in my mouth to stop cracking up completely.' He pioneered a variation on this in the USA during the publicity campaign for *A Fish Called Wanda* in 1988. Cleese found himself on the Donahue show being asked to perform the walk. Eventually, he popped backstage for an instant, and returned to polite applause, announcing that he had just done it as asked.

Noblesse really did oblige briefly at the October 1989 SDP Conference in Blackpool. It was three weeks after the IRA had bombed the Royal Marines School of Music at Deal, and the Marines bandsmen were staying at the Savoy Hotel, on the front at Blackpool, where they were due to perform. The band was lined up in the hotel lobby, instruments at the ready to welcome their commander-in-chief, when Cleese happened to step out of the lift. According to John Herdman, then the hotel manager, the bandsmen spotted him and, as of one, struck up 'Liberty Bell', the *Monty Python* theme tune. Hardly able to ignore this, Cleese graciously silly-walked for three or four steps, smiled politely and continued about his business.

Commercial or any other exploitation of the silly walk by others is another matter, however. In 1977, a sculptor, Nicholas Monro, wanted to contribute a statue of Cleese silly-walking to an exhibition called 'Genius of Britain', sponsored by John Player, to coincide with the Royal Silver Jubilee celebrations. Cleese's solicitors sent a strong letter refusing to let such a sculpture be used. Monro immortalized Max Wall instead. Cleese was equally furious when the advertisement for his 1982 film *Privates on Parade* capitalized on a tiny silly walks sequence he did for the credits. Cleese has yet to remonstrate with Jacques Tati, however, for wilfully observing that he had the funniest legs in the world. Nor did he see any apparent contradiction in giving the silly walk a brief airing in *Fawlty Towers*, when Basil, who has received a nasty knock on the head, imitates Hitler to the embarrassment of his German customers.

By the time the team started on the third series of *Monty Python* in late 1971, Cleese was again getting bored. He felt the sketches were becoming repetitive and rehashing old material. He thought they were tending to use shock tactics too indiscriminately. He was also beginning to diverge from the rest of the team's kneejerk anti-censorship reaction to requests from high up in the BBC that items be dropped or softened. He took the unfashionable view that the BBC may have been wrong from time to time in restraining *Monty Python*, but all in all had been very fair.

Cleese's interests were also starting to widen. His adored daughter Cynthia had been born in February 1971, to the delight of 'Gran and Grandpa' as Reg, who was suffering breathing trouble, and Muriel liked to be known. In 1971, Cleese and his co-Pythons had made an instructional film for the Labour Party, but the following January Cleese helped to found Video Arts, his hugely successful company turning out business and industrial training films. This venture considerably alienated him from his Python colleagues, to a man left-wing Sixties bohemians who, ignoring the fact that Cleese was still a member of the Labour Party, thought him a 'crypto-fascist' for his belief that commerce might occasionally be a good thing. (The Thatcher years and the development of the 'yuppie' in the 1980s eventually left Cleese seeming more in tune with the times than the other Pythons. Terry Jones still touchingly held in the late 1980s that he was an anarchist.)

Cleese was appearing as a guest on *Desert Island Discs*, being installed as a rector of St Andrews University (a position that he assumed with great grace and seriousness), receiving offers to appear in television commercials and dining with Princess Margaret, albeit with some embarrassment, as he did so midway between filming a sketch in which he ran through a forest dressed as an eight-foot version of the princess and the sketch being broadcast. On top of all these significant developments in his life, by the start of the third series of *Monty Python*, he was coming close to joining a weekly psychotherapy group. On the whole, it can have been of little surprise to the other members of the Python team that he eventually abandoned ship. Ironically enough, he was beginning to find it all a mite too silly.

Conversely, with the exception of Michael Palin, whom the team often regarded as too normal by half, the Pythons were finding John Cleese too sensible. 'I know that I was unpopular, although they were nice to me basically face-to-face, and I knew they got pissed off and said rude things about me behind my back a bit when I said I wanted to drop out of the group for television purposes. But I think most of that rancour was really isolated to late '73, which is a pretty short period of time.' The Pythons who were the most hostile to his attitude, according to Cleese, were Jones and Chapman, the two who felt the least able to make a living without the programme. The third series of *Monty Python* lost momentum as it went along, although it did include the cheese shop sketch near the beginning.

There was an extraordinary incident during one filming session involving Graham Chapman's pipe. Verbally and psychologically, Cleese had developed into a renowned pugilist, but although he had the potential for physical violence – he was described by colleagues as being enthusiastic perhaps beyond the bounds of duty if a sequence required beating somebody up – he was and is almost Gandhi-like in his dislike of physical force. On this occasion, because he had pinched Chapman's pipe as a joke, his friend kneed him in the groin, the first time Cleese had been assaulted in any way since being bullied at school.

'My pipe is my prop,' complained Chapman rather movingly. 'Take it away and I'm lost. Cleese knows this, but he still took it and when I found out, I was furious. I rugby-tackled him in a television studio and when he fell on the ground, I sat on him and wouldn't let him get up. I think he was quite hurt. But I was hurt too. It's just another example of the strain we were all under.'

Cleese remembered the incident as happening on location in Yorkshire. 'I was just teasing, but I've never seen anyone get so anxious so rapidly,' he recounted to John Hind. 'I suddenly realized that it had a symbolic value for him that I'd never even guessed at. So I swiftly said "Here it is" and he kneed me hard in the groin. Fortunately he marginally missed what he'd been aiming at, but it was a very alarming experience. And when he retold the story months later he got it completely garbled and claimed he chased me across the floor of a studio, rugby-tackled me and sat on my head, which was some very strange public-school fantasy.' Interestingly, being wrestled to the ground and having your head sat on by your peers is something that Cleese said happened to him both at St Peter's and at Clifton College – and on both occasions claims he was discovered in this unsatisfactory position by his father.

In January 1973, at the end of the showing of the third series of *Python*, Cleese gave an interview in which he explained why the team had decided to rest *Python* for a year (he did not even hint that he was thinking of leaving the series): 'The shows now going out were recorded last May, and as the months passed, we noticed a greater tightening-up in control over what we could say or do, and what political comment could be made.' The restrictions had been put on the show, he went on, because of Mary Whitehouse, who with her supporters had been sedulously complaining to the BBC about any item they disliked on *Monty Python*. The BBC had been obliged to react to this because viewers who liked the show had failed to phone in. 'My guess,' concluded Cleese, 'is that they [the BBC] would have been interested if we had wanted to do another series. We know that some people think we are just funny. Others think we are showing sedition and acting much too violently. Yet this is only in the lunatic tradition of the *Goon Show*. We were censored over drugs and a cartoon involving nudes.'

At this stage, Cleese had not yet told the other Pythons that he intended to stop doing the television shows. In the spring of 1973, the team went to Dallas, Texas, for a weekend to help raise funds for the local Public Broadcasting System television station, KERA, whose manager was planning to pioneer *Monty Python* in the USA. It was a well-spent weekend. A year later, albeit some time behind Yugoslavia and the Lebanon, the shows went out in Dallas. By the end of 1975, *Monty Python* was the most successful series in PBS history, and *Newsweek* magazine proclaimed the outbreak of Pythonmania in the USA. Elvis Presley endlessly watched *Monty Python* recordings in his last days.

In the spring of 1973 the Pythons also embarked on a British stage tour, notable for including Cleese's first experience of being hounded by a groupie – as he related appropriately in *Playboy* magazine – at the stage door of the Hippodrome Theatre in Bristol. 'It was the only time I'd ever had someone wait for me with carnal intent. It's rather ironic that she was the only woman I'd ever met who was larger than I was. I'm 6'5" and weigh 210 pounds, and she made me feel positively dainty.' The stage tour had another significant use for Cleese, the first conscious discovery of how bad virtually all British hotels were, further feeding his fascination for them. He had yet to stay at the mecca of inhospitality, the Torquay establishment which provided the final inspiration for *Fawlty Towers*, but a St Andrews hotel he arrived at with the writer Alan Coren in 1974 played a great and little credited part in the development of the idea Cleese and Connie Booth were already thinking of. 'Alan and I arrived about 9.30 p.m. at the Old Course Hotel. About five stars when it was built and down to about two and a half now. We got our cases out of the back of the hired car, watched by the porter inside in the warm. When we got in he gave us a beady look and said "Have ye booked?" in quite an aggressive way. I was quite pissed off and replied "No. Are you very busy?" It turned out Alan and I were the only two people there that night. Six floors, empty . . . .' (Happily since then the hotel has undergone a substantial refurbishment and now boasts at least four stars.)

It was on a plane flying towards Canada for another tour in the summer of 1973 that Cleese announced he would not do any more *Python* television shows. He did not want to be dependent on one thing any longer. He could not understand why the others were not bored, he said. He suggested – perhaps to make them feel better – that the problem was that they were more extrovert than he, and consequently so long as they were getting applause they could carry on, but he was an introvert and could not. Cleese was also not at all sure about the kind of youthful mass hysteria *Python* was generating. 'There were records and books and T-shirts and a whole spinoff industry which I never really understood: people talked about "supporting" *Python* as though we were a football team. Pompous though this may sound, laughter affirms membership of a group, and that group may need something to hold on to: one of the worst things in the world is to be in a room where everyone else is laughing and you're not – you feel threatened and very angry.'

The news that Cleese was dropping out of *Monty Python* was not unexpected by the others, but cast a pall across the tour. In fact Cleese enjoyed the first Canadian venue in Toronto, a small theatre where, as he had done when *Cambridge Circus* moved off Broadway, he could act without having to project operatically. The crowds at performances across Canada got progressively vaster and more noisily crazy about *Python* sketches. Cleese was predictably less than happy with football-fan-type audiences, who greeted every sketch as an old favourite which they could reel off by heart.

It was six years later, significantly at a time when the old enmities between the *Python* rivals had long lost their momentum and were replaced by considerable affection, that Cleese broke with his past a little, relaxed, and almost gushed on *The Dick Cavett Show* in the USA: 'I do love the parrot sketch. It was the one thing each night on stage I was able to look forward to. And it was very nice because the *Python* audiences are very strange, and I remember doing it at Drury Lane one night with Michael – I really love performing with Michael, he's a really wonderful guy to be with, the timing is terrific, and we often broke up on stage. And I remember I broke up and got my face straight, and I suddenly realized I had no idea where I was, none at all. And it being the relaxed occasion that it was, I turned to the front row and I said, "What's the next line?" And about four of them gave it to me. So I said the line, and that got a laugh.' He was outstandingly mellow in 1979, when this interview was broadcast. Back in England, speaking about the *Monty Python* writing process (in the wake of *Life of Brian*) with quite alarming fondness, he said: 'Waves of joy and delight flood over us when we're writing. We don't laugh much, but we just wallow in the fact that we have been around long enough to know good writing when we see it.'

But that was then. At the end of the intermittently rancorous 1973 Canadian tour, on the west coast at Vancouver, Cleese went back alone to England while the other five, resolved to carry on as *Monty Python* somehow without Cleese, flew to Hollywood to appear on *The Johnny Carson Show*, where they proceeded utterly to baffle their American audience. Apart from his being fed up with *Monty Python* and wanting to go home, Cleese had been arguing against doing the Carson show all along. He felt it would be an alien environment for the team, and so it was

– although he has appeared in his own right on Carson since then.

Connie had bought a canary, a companion of sorts for two-year-old Cynthia and the family's Siamese cats, Vanilla and Nez, while John was away. The growing menagerie gave all the outward signs of domestic bliss, although beneath the surface things were far from ideal at home. Connie's career, which had so worried Cleese even when she was in New York before their marriage, continued to be of concern. Since she came to London, Connie Booth had had trouble getting work, even after concentrating hard on modifying her American accent. She still only occasionally got a part when one cropped up for an American woman. 'For years,' she once tellingly admitted, 'I felt like the daughter of a famous father.' (Many years later, Cynthia was to comment that John Cleese likes to father his wives.) Cleese was also becoming prone to debilitating bouts of low-grade flu.

Monty Python, he said, drove him 'potty', and he first ascribed his unease to the struggle to produce the enormous amount of comedy that he did. Only later, as a result of group therapy, did he discover the deeper-seated reasons. For the moment, he worked hard at making life in her adopted city pleasing for Connie. They took a lot of holidays in the sun – Sardinia, Morocco, Rhodes – recapturing some of the fun and laziness of Ibiza seven years before. They moved into a Holland Park modern townhouse development in Woodsford Square, where Connie occupied herself for some of the time by ordering structural alterations which she would conveniently forget to mention to Cleese, other than with a throwaway, 'It's being changed'. He would also moan good-naturedly about Connie 'moving everything', no doubt from where he had left it to fester. A visitor at the time remembers him searching in exasperation for coffee filter papers and, opening the fridge as a last resort, hissing, 'My wife's American so everything goes in the fridge: spare chairs . . . .'

Cleese had no clear idea what he was going to do now. He talked, as he always does in his periods of restlessness, of writing a novel. On his birthday in October 1973, the *Daily Express*, unaware that Cleese announces his retirement almost every month, reported that he had 'taken a sabbatical year from acting to write. And he has become so immersed that he tends to leave his telephone receiver off the hook when under pressure.' He wanted to write intensively to throw off once and for all the Mr Teabags image of being a funny man. He would duly install himself at the top of the Woodsford Square house for six hours at a time with supplies of coffee and cigarettes, then lie down for an hour. Leaving the phone dangling was not practical, and, before long, he changed his phone number so that only a few friends could reach him.

Having some influence with the *Monty Python* team, Cleese had during the Python heyday got his wife some parts in the series. In the 'Lumberjack' sketch, she appeared as Michael Palin's doting girlfriend, and in another programme played a pretty boxer from Birmingham, with a white muslin dress and a bow in her hair, taking on Ken Clean-Air Systems (Cleese), a lobotomized pro from Reigate who, rather distressingly, knocks the stuffing and much else out of her in round one. In one of the German editions of the show, Cleese and Connie performed the first sketch they had written together – a medieval fairy tale called 'Happy Valley, or, The Princess With Wooden Teeth' – which they also used in the Pythons' Drury Lane stage show in 1974.

Their biggest pre-Fawlty collaboration was not a *Monty Python* project, however, but a charming 41-minute film, *Romance with a Double Bass*. The screenplay was adapted, by Cleese, Connie and an associate, from a Chekhov short story about Smychkov (Cleese), a humble musician hired to play at the engagement party of Princess Constance (Booth). Smychkov, who appears adorned with a moustache later worn by Basil Fawlty, takes a dip in a river before the concert, but his clothes are stolen. The Princess also happens to go for a swim and is stranded by the same thief. She then shelters in the nude in Smychkov's double-bass case, while he tries to smuggle her back indoors. The highlight is naturally the sight of Cleese and Connie cavorting around in the nude, each tossing a lifetime of inhibitions into the lake in Wiltshire where they made the film in 1974. Both Cleese and Connie Booth always had an affection for *Romance with a Double Bass*. In March 1976, not long before they separated, they were spotted sitting in a Notting Hill Gate cinema munching popcorn and watching their own film unnoticed by the rest of the audience.

Shortly before they headed West to make *Romance*, Connie gave an interview to the *Daily Telegraph*, and spoke about John. 'He's very unpredictable. He was very spoilt by his mother, and he never knows where anything is. Tonight he was running around the house shouting: "Where's my vest? Where's my shirt?" John is infuriatingly good at invective.' Cleese affirmed this. 'I take pleasure in attack. I love writing sarcastic letters to people, especially to the pompous officials. I put silly things on cheques, such as "Pay the Postmaster General in the sincerest hope that the Telephone Service will soon show a marked improvement the sum of £60."' Cleese also admitted he used his sarcasm during domestic quarrels: 'But then I laugh at it.'

'Well,' Connie commented, 'it drives me wild.'

The period after Cleese split with the *Python* 'troupe' (as the Americans called the team) was another period of reorientation, a repeat of when he came back to England after marrying Connie. He and Connie were now experimenting with living separately under the same roof, the tolerability quota of one depressed creative person per marriage having been exceeded for too long. Although painful, it was an extremely civilized arrangement, helped by the fact that they liked each other, laughed at the same things, had no financial strains (the Video Arts films were doing well) and, best of all, had a great joint project in hand, *Fawlty Towers*, the dream of the ultimate perfect script that had Cleese, and soon the two of them, steaming mani-acally away upstairs in the house in early 1974. As well as achieving by working on *Fawlty Towers* something close to the professional perfection he sought, group therapy and marriage guidance sessions were also opening up a new world of fascination – for Cleese at least, both an emotional and an intellectual trip. It was ironic that one of the remaining *Python* team, who were struggling against the odds to put together a sub-standard fourth series, when asked what he thought Cleese was up to replied: 'Probably making a boring film about Industry.'

Ever the man of vast appetites and capacities, Cleese managed to combine writing at full tilt, being psychotherapized and splitting up with his wife with some diverse and rather rum showbusiness activities. Appearing several times on *Sez Les*, Les Dawson's ailing ITV show, for example, was probably not what Clifton College or Downing College quite expected of their distinguished old boy, which may in turn be why he went to all the trouble of going to Leeds week after week to do it. The sketches were fairly standard *Frost Report/Python* stuff – Cleese, as a chartered accountant, trying to inject some adventure into his job by scaling the outside of his building, with guns and karate chops; Cleese and Dawson doing officer/lower rank routines. 'We're old friends and so dissimilar in looks that we're bound to get on,' Dawson explained to fans of both himself and Cleese puzzled by the unexpected alliance.

At the same time, Cleese made a film at St Andrews University as the first programme of a Thames series *A Place in History*. The university, of which he had been so proud to be rector for three years (many VIPs accepted the title but did little to live up to it), was for him 'a very friendly university – I much preferred it to my days in Cambridge'. He explained his new serious role as being perfectly congruous with his reputation as a wit. David Frost, he argued, made the transition from comedy to serious interviews. 'I can't see why people wouldn't take me seriously as well. It's good for me to get my foot in on another aspect of TV. I've always envied Alan Whicker. I told him so.'

In between appearing on *Sez Les*, Cleese worked with determination at sloughing off his funnyman image. The Highgate home of Peter Lovell-Davis, later Lord Lovell-Davis, was a radical media/political/showbusiness meeting place in the Sixties and Seventies. Lovell-Davis, who was ennobled in the Marcia Falkender honours list, coined the 'Let's Go With Labour' slogan that helped Harold Wilson win the 1964 election. John Cleese, who said at the time, 'I still vote Labour and I don't mind about 83 per cent of what I earn going back in tax at the moment, I'm not complaining,' was now a regular visitor to the Lovell-Davises, as were people as diverse as

Denis Norden, Harry Evans (then editor of the *Sunday Times*), Mavis Nicholson and Professor Leslie Bethell, a left-wing academic specializing in Brazilian history and politics at London University.

The Lovell-Davises were renowned for Boxing Day parties at which a ferocious punch containing ice cream along with the sterner ingredients was served. It was at their 1973 party that Bethell and his journalist wife Val met Cleese, without Connie in the first instance. The Bethells and the Cleeses became good friends. Val Bethell recalls:

> He was a very serious, shy, reserved man. I remember him once coming to a birthday party at my house in Islington and actually remaining quite unnoticed in a corner of the sofa. A very withdrawn, uncertain sort of person, ordinarily dressed, but not shabby. I associate him with rather well-worn, V-necked sweaters.
>
> He never dominated occasions. One had to seek him out. Of course the people he liked talking to were people involved in his line of business. He talked shop with them and felt much happier doing that, but he felt increasingly conscious of the need to get away from being a showbusiness person, because he took his intellectual aspirations terribly, terribly seriously. I think one of the reasons that he got on so well with my husband was that Cleese had this tremendous ambition to write a history of the world. We used to come away and Les used to say, 'Christ, isn't it a shame, here am I, an historian, hating it, and there's this man who's an amazingly gifted comic talent and he wants to be an historian.'

Cleese and the professor, who stood ten inches shorter, also used to hatch plans to go to West Ham football matches together. At Cambridge, his friend Michael Apted had seduced Cleese away from supporting Bristol City and into the eccentric attractions of the East End club, which was renowned, just like the beloved Somerset cricket team of Cleese's youth, for playing beautiful, textbook football and losing heavily. Cleese and Bethell never actually got to West Ham's shabby Upton Park ground – a considerable journey across London for both of them – but discussed their matches at length.

Cleese's seriousness played very well in this new world he was exploring. Dinners at the round tables of the stripped-pine London intelligentsia tended to be racked with doubt and worry and agonizing, so John's rack level was only marginally above the ambient misery. In the entire six years she knew Cleese, Val Bethell can only once recall him being even remotely funny, describing Mr Hickley who taught the boys at St Peter's to dance. In the West Country, it's common to add an L to the end of every significant word, so, Cleese recounted, the master told the boys he was going to teach them the Rumbal and the Tangol.

In the midst of all this personal expansion, Cleese still had a living to earn; and a second Python film, *Monty Python and the Holy Grail*, which was mooted by Palin and co. in 1974, seemed to Cleese a perfect way *not* to make some money. Cleese had been all enthusiasm for the first Python film, *And Now For Something Completely Different* in 1970. He saw it as a fairly easy way to increase a moderate BBC income from the television series (£410 an edition) and a method of getting *Monty Python* known in America by bypassing television company censors. The film, a string of re-shot sketches, went into profit in Britain but flopped in America. Cleese was closer than any of the team to the man who put up the money for the film, Victor Lownes, owner of that bizarre Sixties hangout the Playboy Club, where (and it seems quite astonishing today) young women dressed as rabbits tended to the alcoholic and gambling needs of dinner-jacketed, middle-aged men. Although the fluffy-tailed delights of the club were not at all Cleese, he found Lownes congenial company at his Bunny-infested Berkshire mansion, Stocks, as did many prominent men of the time. The friendship still endures.

As a money-making venture, the Lownes film was not very exciting. Each Python saw £1,400 for five weeks' filming in Totteridge, north London. At the prospect of making *Holy Grail*, a medieval tale to be filmed in Scotland, Cleese was the least enthusiastic of the team, being by now temperamentally averse to all three of the unenticing prospects the project held out –

namely, sitting around on film sets, being in cold, wet places and not making a lot of money. But how could he tell them he made more from seven episodes of *Sez Les* than the £2,000 (plus eventual share of the profits) he was being offered for making an entire film? Rather gamely, he went along with the project: 'It would be purgatory if they weren't such a nice crowd to work with.'

To Cleese's surprise, *Holy Grail*, made for £229,000, was a huge success shown from America to Russia and had reaped $50 million by 1983. Nevertheless, in the making at the fourteenth-century Doune Castle, Perthshire, it lived down to all his expectations. It was, he said, possibly using hyperbole, 'the most miserable experience outside a concentration camp. Everyone got ratty during the first week of filming through working such incredibly long hours. Then I hurt my shoulder carrying an actor on my shoulder for six rehearsals and fourteen takes with the camera.' Cleese played the Black Knight, Sir Lancelot the Brave, the French Knight (who throws insults like 'Your mother was a hamster') and Tim the Enchanter. He told a reporter on the set that the film was 'the usual garrulous rubbish'.

The launch party for *Holy Grail* was the scene of some cathartic but unpleasant mudslinging among the Pythons, reminiscent of the break-up of the Beatles. Michael Palin, uncharacteristically pugnacious, told a reporter above the hubbub and merry chinking of glasses: 'Now he has come back to us and said we should all get together again to tour America and boost the series, which is about to be shown there. Presumably he wants to do the tour for money. But we have said "No".' Cleese, who had by now moved out of the marital home and was living in a West End flat with a four-poster bed, responded: 'It is malicious to suggest that I am money-mad. I have no yearning to own a yacht or a Greek island. Certainly money is one of the reasons for me wanting to do the American tour and also for me wishing to go it alone. If I signed for another *Python* TV series here it would mean nine months' work at East Acton and Shepherd's Bush while we write, rehearse it and record it, with the perk of two weeks in Bradford or somewhere filming. I find the prospect of New York and San Francisco more pleasing. I do want to work for my own future. That may sound selfish but it is surely the aim of most men.'

The Pythons were fixated on the idea that Cleese was mad about money. Perhaps as a result of his American connections, he was prone to being more frank about the subject than polite middle-class English people, and especially polite middle-class English Sixties left-wing people. He was financially aware. 'It's really nice that these shows do get shown on PBS,' he told Dick Cavett. 'Every time *Monty Python* goes out in New York I make two whole pounds. So for a series, I can go out and have a really good dinner.' On the other hand, he said at one time, 'I prefer to work in Britain where the money isn't good. In this country one has 100 per cent artistic control. American television offered me a five-year contract to do thirty-nine shows a year for them – big money, but laughable. I turned it down.'

A year after that fraught period with the Pythons, Cleese was performing with them again, in a three-week run of a stage show in New York. Professionally, all was well; he was kissed by Leonard Bernstein, another of his heroes. But now it was his personal life, the marriage to Connie in limbo, that was coming to a head. A few days after the Python run started in New York, Cleese was named as BBC television personality of the year for *Fawlty Towers*, and Connie collected the award on his behalf in London, before flying to New York to see him.

Cleese had meanwhile got in touch with his old *Newsweek* friend Everett Martin, who was now on the *Wall Street Journal*. After the show one night, he had dinner with Martin and his children.

> He said he was through with *Monty Python* and was writing a history of England. My son said, 'It must be awful to have people expecting you to be funny all the time.' And John just threw his arms around him, saying: 'It's the worst cross I bear.' He told us about a time he tried to buy some thread in Harrods. He went inside and everyone started laughing. He stamped his foot and finally stormed out and had to be calmed down. He also told me about him lying on the floor and stretching to line up his body – he seemed to take up any

theory he could. And before he went on stage, he said he beat up his hotel room, smashing the pillows and hitting his fists on the bed.

Then we had lunch at my New York apartment with Connie, who had just come over. And, as I understand it, they went back to the hotel and Connie said she was leaving *him*. I never saw John again. I think he felt crushed, awkward and humiliated.

7 *Commercial Breaks*

I find it rather easy to portray a businessman.
Being bland, rather cruel and incompetent
comes naturally to me.

John Cleese, 1987

'In England,' John Cleese once explained to an American
journalist, 'it isn't vulgar to have money, only to get it.' And
it is the making of money that Cleese, by way of his willingness
to advertise products and his involvement in business training
films, has popularized and, it sometimes seems, almost sanc-
tified.

Cleese's commercial ventures are a perfect case of the message
being secondary to the medium. His respectable, conservative
appearance and voice, no matter how much we all know them
to be a parody of what they seem, give his message authority; at
the same time, being a comedian, and particularly one associated
with intelligent, youthful, even moderately right-on comedy,
endows what he says with complete honesty.

To a lot of his friends imbued with the anti-business attitude
of the 1960s, the idea of flogging his honesty to the highest
bidder was marginally dishonest in itself, but when he first realized what he could make by, let us say, renting out small chunks
of his soul, Cleese ceased to worry about what other people
thought. John Cleese, more than many people, is proof of the

axiom that money does not buy happiness, but can help you suffer in comfort.

'I've always had a vulgar commercial streak in me, and I discovered that the scale of remuneration in advertising was quite insane. When I realized it was insane, I decided I would accept it as it was. I decided I would get my foot in the door and I began doing voice-overs,' he says. He was staying at L'Ermitage Hotel in Los Angeles when his agent phoned to tell him Sony were offering nearly £100,000 for an exclusive advertising contract. 'I rolled off the couch laughing. It was hysterically funny money.'

His persona in the radio advertisements was 'a silly-assed, slightly pompous Englishman . . . but being very up-front about doing a commercial. You know, "I'm frightfully sorry this is another Sony commercial. . . ." By laying it on the line, you've broken a barrier with the audience.'

In making the television adverts that followed, Cleese showed from the outset the same diligence as he does in his comedy work – as well he might, since he gets paid more than he could hope to earn for the same amount of work from showbusiness. On an early Sony advert, he spent hours in a television studio with a piece of ham between his teeth trying to get his cat to 'talk' to him. In a 1989 British Telecom Talking Pages commercial, Cleese, playing a husband whose pipes burst on a Bank Holiday, slowly drowns as the room fills with water. The room set was built into a large tank, with the water heated to 80 degrees, and between shots, Cleese kept dousing himself with jugs of water to keep his hair and face wet. He refused to wear a wet suit for the sake of authenticity, although his clothes were silicone-coated.

Another Sony commercial demonstrated brilliantly how his image had become ingrained in the public mind, how Cleese, like only Charlie Chaplin and possibly Laurel and Hardy, was instantly recognizable even in symbolic representation. The commercial starred a demented Anglepoise lamp, long, stalky and able to get into impossible positions. Almost before the Cleese voice-over began, the manically contorting light fitting in conjunction with the Sony logo made it clear precisely who was promoting the product.

In September 1976, when Cleese made his first British television advertisement, there came an incident which with great
push and shove by the newspapers just about staggered into
life as an 'embarrassment' story. Cleese's debut was in a car
insurance TV commercial for General Accident, and no sooner
had it gone out than he had a quite specific accident all of his
own, while driving his brown convertible Rolls-Royce on the
A30 near Salisbury. Amazingly, shock horror, it turned out that
the insurance salesman's son wasn't covered by General Accident, and had no idea who his insurers were. John Barclay, a
director of the agency who made the award-winning advert,
swerved instinctively when the *Sunday Mirror* rang him up. 'The
Rolls is not John's car. His wife owns it. If he had a car, he would
no doubt insure it with General Accident.'

There was a *frisson* of real embarrassment for Sony after
Cleese's contract expired. In 1983, the London estate agents
Jones Lang Wootton imaginatively hired Cleese to advertise an
office block to let in Covent Garden. He created a tape and sent
it on their behalf to over 100 prospective clients. The heads of
the agency were reportedly not amused when they heard the
tape on which Cleese says: 'Bloody estate agents. I wouldn't
believe anything any agent told me. They would describe a blaz-
ing abattoir in a swamp as desirable. Let's hope that Messrs
Jones, Lang and Wootton – all three of them – will be found on
Monday morning hanging from the very desirable Blackfriars
Bridge. It won't be foul play. It will be fair play.' He went on to
dismiss Covent Garden as 'full of nancy boy restaurateurs' and
to parody his Sony commercials, assuring listeners that JLW
were good eggs really: 'Sony are not the only frightfully nice
people and they better wake up to it too – the conceited little
slit-eyed buggers.' Although Sony had given Cleese permission
to take the rise out of them, a spokesman (who doubtless had
the unenviable task of reporting back to Tokyo) wailed, 'I'm a
bit taken aback by that description of us. I don't understand it.
I don't think John Cleese has ever met anybody Japanese from
our company.'

Cleese was just having fun. So powerful a selling tool was he
that he could say whatever he wanted and still get work. An
advertising industry joke in Britain was that there would soon

be an award for the best use of John Cleese. 'The nice thing is I can go off and do some perfectly cheerful commercial for a few days, put that in the bank, and then run off and do things I'm interested in which you don't get paid for at all,' he chuckled on a local radio interview with Phil Easton of Orchard FM on a visit to Taunton, back in the West Country. The solid Somerset people in the audience would have been the first to appreciate his delight at being able to exploit smart Londoners so satisfyingly. 'This is one of the great laws of the world: the more trivial whatever I do is, the more I get paid for it. It's insane.'

Adapting to each market he makes commercials for, Cleese has made adverts for upscale products only in Britain and the USA, while elsewhere (almost as a joke, it seems) he is happy with less prestigious accounts. Chocolate bars, beer, pretzels, fish fingers in Australia, Lowney's Peanut Butter Cups in Canada, the Danish Shoe Council, Norwegian mayonnaise and the Dutch Post Office. . . . 'I've done commercials I would pay for you not to see,' he likes to say.

The Americans have always been admiring of Cleese's commercials. His first in the USA was a series of radio adverts for Callard & Bowser. In the first – a 'taster' – he advertised the product in the best tradition of English reticence, never mentioning it by name, just the firm's thistle trademark. 'It is frightfully popular among the more educated classes here in England', it is 'not as sweet as regular candy' and has a 'characteristic thistle as a trademark'. The advert was taken off air because of a Federal Communications Commission rule that commercial sponsors must identify themselves.

Back home, Cleese used his advertising skills voluntarily for a two-and-a-half-minute corporate image commercial, designed to make the public feel better about the escalating BBC licence fee. Cleese played Joe Public, and the advert was a variation on his 'What have the Romans ever given us?' tirade in *Life of Brian*. 'Diabolical. What's the BBC ever given us for 58 quid?' he complained, then each of a gaggle of stars mentioned some bounteous marvel of the corporation. Barry Norman had to say no more than the one word 'Films', but he did it so woodenly that Cleese shouted 'Been practising a lot, have we, Barry?' The set was surrounded by BBC bureaucrats trying to put visiting journalists straight by explaining that it was not an advertise-ment but a 'trailer' or a 'promotional film'. Cleese put paid some-what to the illusion by shouting before the taping began, 'This way for the commercial!'

In this instance, Cleese was retreading an old *Monty Python* idea (from *Life of Brian*) in the interests of the BBC. But, in accordance with his philosophy of exploiting the advertisers who need him so badly, he is not averse to presenting old wine in new bottles. In another British Telecom Talking Pages advert in 1989 he recycled an even older Python joke to the extent that it did not quite work. On location at the Devil's Punchbowl in Surrey, Cleese played a woolly-hatted six-year-old on a family outing with his arguing aged parents. First he zooms around imitating a plane, then gallops like a horse. But when his dad breaks the key in the car door lock, Cleese flies to a phone box and calls Talking Pages in a respectable, adult voice, then canters back to the car. His parents are surprised when a locksmith arrives, whereupon Cleese reminds them, 'But mother, I am fifty-two years old and a High Court Judge.' It was an excellent line, at least for the few people who did not remember the *Monty Python* sketch in which a bowler-hatted Cleese is chin-chucked and oochy-cooched by two dear old ladies, one of whom exclaims: 'Look at him laughing . . . ooh, he's a chirpy little fellow,' and asks the other, 'Does he talk? Does he talk, eh? Cleese irately replies: 'Of course I talk. I'm the Minister for Overseas Development.'

More often, however, Cleese commercials have been comi-cally innovative, as if, despite his best endeavours, he finds it hard not to give his best. In the summer of 1989, the one-time oversized ugly duckling of Weston-super-Mare played a hunky beachboy type in a Schweppes commercial, part of a £200,000 two-year contract from the drinks company. The very idea of Cleese as bronzed macho man was enough to get a laugh. Back as himself, he also made an advert for Schweppes that parodied subliminal advertising, with Cleese complaining about it, while the Schweppes name appeared everywhere, from the bottom of his shoes to being spoken by a moose's head.

At Christmas 1990, Cleese extended his mercantile repertoire to posing for magazine advertisements. He was photographed for an American Express campaign, part of a series of famous people (which included Judi Dench, John Alderton and Pauline Collins, and Gary Lineker). In the Amex campaign, he appeared as a bat (hanging elongatedly upside down from a tree in Windsor Great Park) and as a seductive, if slightly hairy-legged, young lady in a little red dress, Cleese's first spot of transvestism in many a year. The latter photos were taken in Eaton Square. The outfit was accompanied by all-red accessories: ostrich feather hat, long satin gloves, satin high-heeled shoes (specially cobbled in his size 13), a little handbag, pearl ear-rings and necklace, blonde wig, bright red lipstick, and two long-haired Pekineses, one of which naturally bit his leg during the session. The dress was made to Cleese's instructions – he wanted something Bardotish and tailored – and he had another version in fake leopard skin on stand-by.

Two days in front of the American photographer Annie Leibovitz's camera earned a useful £15,000. Cleese insisted that 'the photographs should be as silly as possible'. 'I have never appeared in a press or magazine advertisement before – to the best of my knowledge – and I don't want readers to get the impression that I'm doing anything even one-tenth serious,' he said. Before the bat idea emerged, he had wanted to appear dressed as a giant chicken at Wimbledon. Then Ogilvy & Mather, the advertising agency, suggested he might pose naked in a gentlemen's club, covering his bum with The Card. But then the IRA bombed the Carlton Club on the week it was to be shot. Cleese then suggested as a compromise that he might valuably be hung upside down from the goal posts at Wembley. In the final picture, he was suspended by a wire as he had been from a window in *A Fish Called Wanda*. Hoisted up by a sixty-foot crane, he proceeded to dangle there for over an hour, with safety mattresses below.

Cosmically lucrative though it has been, Cleese's love affair with business and commerce is highly misleading in two important respects. It bred the idea that he was in love with money, whereas it would be fairer to say he is interested in money because it provides convenience and comfort, which he is certainly in love with. 'I just don't need all the money that I have,' he has often said. 'Margaret Thatcher once asked why it is that when an Englishman makes two million pounds he retires, while a German or an American will go and make twenty million. As far as I'm concerned, that's the *problem* with Germans and Americans. I have far more respect for someone who will use his wealth to buy himself time to do things like reading books or listening to music than I have for someone who simply wants to accumulate more money.' Very quietly, Cleese gives money to charities and on a small scale even commissions scripts from writers he knows: 'Most of them don't come to anything, but that's fine because one of the few altruistic feelings that one ever has is the occasional sense that something should be in the old-fashioned sense patronized.'

Cleese's commercial success has also led to the universal assumption that he is a talented businessman, whereas in fact (and fortuitously) the millions he has made in the business world have involved him in doing little more than he does normally, writing and acting. It has not escaped Cleese that someone in another profession, say a surgeon, would count himself extremely lucky to make millions in, say, showbusiness, by doing nothing but surgery. Business ideas Cleese has that involve more than writing and acting tend, not very surprisingly, not to come to fruition. In 1976 he considered opening a restaurant called 'Basil's' with a Savoy-trained restaurateur, Andrew Leeman. They formed a company and were looking at a Knightsbridge site; Leeman told the *Daily Express*, 'He's always eating in restaurants and knows a lot about the customer side. We intend to create a feeling of effortless superiority with very simple and incredibly good food. The whole look will be low-key ... of non-pretty elegance.'

Where Cleese differs from the majority of his colleagues in the arts is not by having a special talent for making money, but simply by appreciating it more than is common. *Fawlty Towers*, as he points out, was something of a loss leader, earning him £1,000 for an episode that took six weeks to make. It was income from commercials and Video Arts that made *Fawlty Towers* possible; he has said he would have had to sell his house had it not been for his commercial ventures. To those who accuse him of selling out, he argues that most of the great names in the history of the arts, Shakespeare included, have been obsessed with money. 'Money has never been of the slightest concern to me – all I'm interested in is "Do I have enough?" I've spent all these years making myself secure financially. I seem to be damn determined to have a totally secure financial base,' he told Michael Schrage of the *Washington Post*, who concluded: 'He is really obsessed with the stuff, a Jack Benny with a BBC accent.'

As he is inclined to do with most subjects, Cleese has rigorously examined his attitude to money and come to the conclusion that the most important commodity it buys is time – time to read, study, or, as he likes to say when he slips into his slightly phoney languid mode ('The one thing I really don't like is work'), do nothing at all. So often does Cleese tell people that he hates work that Graham Chapman, when asked once what he would do with a million pounds, replied that he would give it to John Cleese so he wouldn't have to work tomorrow. Endearingly, Cleese has never been prone to moaning even momentarily about British income tax rates, which have caused many comics to lose their sense of humour. He adopts in place of complaint an appealing bemusement: 'I never feel that I earn money. I feel I'm a kind of post office – money passes to me, remains briefly in my bank, before it's handed over to the Government.'

As far as possessions go, he is fond of retelling a parable about Gurdjieff, the Armenian philosopher-mystic, the comforting, all-purpose conclusion of which is that it is all right to have possessions as long as they don't matter too much. 'I don't really know how much I am worth,' Cleese says. 'I know it is sufficient to enable me to run a Rolls without needing to look beneath the bonnet.' When, thanks to revenue from *A Fish Called Wanda* and the sale of Video Arts, he became very rich in 1989 – to the tune of around £17 million – he said he would give much of it to ecological and psychiatric charities, and intended only to buy a swimming pool.

Although he makes apologies for being what one psychiatrist acquaintance calls 'a total breadhead', Cleese is still at pains to dissociate himself from the image of having become some besuited businessman. 'I've no head for business at all,' he frequently claims, pointing out that Video Arts, which made him considerably more money than showbusiness activities, was run by his partners. And yet Video Arts is the most comprehensive expression Cleese has produced of his deeply held desire to teach by using comedy. Helping to educate business and government employees to be happier and more productive is the one achievement he feels he will be able to boast of if he ever was to talk his way through the Pearly Gates.

Video Arts was formed in December 1971 by Cleese, Antony Jay (co-author of *Yes, Minister*, ex-editor of *Tonight*, and *Panorama* pioneer who was knighted in 1988), Peter Robinson (*This Week* director, and producer of some thirty documentaries for ITV) and Michael Peacock (former controller of BBC and managing director of London Weekend Television). The idea originated from Jay, an intellectual who came into showbusiness with a first in Classics from Cambridge. Cleese and Jay met in 1966 as scriptwriters for *The Frost Report*. Jay admired Cleese because he could make people laugh, and Cleese respected Jay because he was bright. 'We both recognized a kindred spirit,' recalls Jay. 'We were interested in comedy as something more than making people laugh, that it was making them laugh about something.' He immediately saw Cleese's didactic bent as a sign of the schoolmaster in his tall friend coming out. It was not a trait that everyone Cleese encountered enjoyed. The journalist Christopher Wilson has observed, 'Cleese believes in taking those in his company out for a brisk intellectual walk. You sense his *need* to be setting an example to those around him and it's slightly uncomfortable.'

By 1970, when Jay asked Cleese if he wanted to get involved in training films, Jay had already written two books – *Management and Machiavelli* and *Corporation Man* – which were international best-sellers. All the founders of Video Arts made an initial investment of £1,000. Dr Robert Reid, an ex-editor of BBC's *Horizon* and head of BBC science and features, joined two years later as a partner (he committed suicide in August 1990). Looking for evidence of where businesses were getting things wrong, Cleese asked friends about their own experiences. David Dimbleby told him about a gas man coming to his flat to mend an Ascot heater which had exploded. The repairman said to him, apparently without a hint of a joke, 'You've been using this, haven't you?' This line, applied to a kitchen gadget, starred in the first Video

Arts film, *Who Sold You This Then?*, which was made in 1972 for
£4,000, paid for itself in three months and is still a high earner.
Directed at sales staff, the film featured Cleese as five different
service men, starting with engineer Charlie Jenkins appearing
from underneath a car to ask the eponymous question. Charlie
then goes on to demonstrate the whole range of British service
industry virtues that have lost his company 214 customers in
the last year.

Who Sold You This Then? was Cleese's first serious work after
his father died back in Weston-super-Mare, aged seventy-eight.
Reg Cleese had been suffering breathing difficulties for over a
year, and Cleese had taken a weekday off in July 1972 to drive
down to Somerset, really to see him, but ostensibly to judge the
traditional Modern Venus bathing beauties competition on the
sea front in Weston. His fellow judge was John Rowland-
Hosbons, son of the rector of the church in Uphill from which
John's mother Muriel dispatched, via a young verger, illicit
love letters to Reg in his digs. A photograph of Cleese
ponderously contemplating the outstretched leg of the competition winner, Miss Deirdre Greenland from Machen, near New-
port, appeared in the *Bristol Evening Post* the next day, a sad
coincidence as it turned out, because Reg died the evening of
the competition.

Video Arts made ten films in its first year, mostly about customer relations and selling. 'But after a while,' recalled Cleese,
'we discovered that management needed training films too, and
the company took a quantum leap forward.' Making Video Arts
films alongside *Monty Python*, Cleese was entranced by having
what satisfied him as a serious purpose at last. Typically, he
spent enormous amounts of time making sure his scripts were
absolutely clear.

His *Monty Python* colleagues remained deeply unimpressed by
their leader's Big New Thing. He later told the *Financial Times*:
'I got a lot of teasing and chiding from my *Python* friends who,
I think, had a fairly primitive, student-based view of what business or industry were about – that it was the first resort of the
crypto-fascist. Anybody who cared would be a doctor or a social
worker – or a comedy writer. Whereas anyone who was running

a factory was obviously out to impress people.' The anti-mercantile views of people in the arts continue to frustrate and gall Cleese. In October 1990, on a US lecture tour, in which he addressed Harvard Business School and groups of businessmen on the subject – or subjects – of 'bureaucracy and creativity', Cleese pronounced, 'The dichotomy is utterly false. You need creativity to create and market a product. Creativity is defined much too narrowly. I think people have confused it with being bohemian.'

From the beginning at Video Arts, Cleese took the trouble to go in person to show their films to business people, and willingly let the new culture in which he was immersing himself, or at least taking a dip, influence his approach to *Monty Python*. He developed a particular disdain for meetings, a feeling he claims to have succeeded in grafting on to the rest of the *Python* team. Cleese and meetings had started not getting on back at Cambridge in the Footlights committee, and his experience as Rector of St Andrews from 1971 to 1974, particularly chairing the University Court, helped him develop an even stronger dislike of the things. 'It's very difficult, when you are only twenty-nine and known as a television comic, to tell a professor of logic he is getting off the point. Meetings are an executive itch. They know they can do nothing about a particular problem, so they have a meeting instead.'

The VA film *Meetings, Bloody Meetings* was about a workaholic executive who brings work home every night because he spends all day in meetings. He tells his wife: 'If it wasn't for the sleep we got at meetings, we'd never be able to work this late.' 'I suddenly realized,' said Cleese about what led to the film,

> that there is no point getting together just because you always have a meeting. I got very stroppy with the *Python* group and said, 'Look, I really don't want to come in until I know what we're discussing, and why we're discussing it, and whether we need a decision.' Everybody thought I was being very awkward, but they now really rather like it, because we do get through meetings in about a third of the time and cancel the ones that we don't need.

A lot of the *Python* team had the kind of left-wing views in which business was regarded as negative activity. People think in a rather confused way. I was never against business but I was against certain ways of carrying on business. The main thing is people's attitudes to authority. I always felt that authority was not necessarily a bad thing. I now think it can be an absolutely excellent thing. I'm interested in making fun of authority that's exercised badly.

The technique Cleese developed for training films was always well defined. He maintains that comedy at its best is 'education, pure and simple – trying to tell someone something about themselves, about their lives and about the world. It's absolutely no good just writing a straight script and then sticking half a dozen jokes in, because people would just remember the jokes and forget the teaching points.' However, if you can get the humour and the jokes to arise out of the training points themselves, then there's no problem. Once there *was* a problem, when the company decided to do a straight film. 'I said, "Oh, do please let me be in it, I've never done anything straight." And my fellow director said, "No way. If you walk on to the screen, people are going to expect you to be funny and this will throw the balance of the film."'

The old problem of being expected to be funny wherever he went still tormented Cleese; 'I've only begun to realize slowly how highly introverted I am. I'm perfectly happy to socialize, but I don't like being a public person. It has brought me a lot, but I would much rather not be recognized in the street. Viewers who watched me in *Python* thought I was completely mad. And those who liked *Fawlty Towers* assumed I was like Basil. The business people who see these [Video Arts] films regard me as almost a normal person,' he said with relief. Cleese certainly adopts a brisk persona – perhaps that of a busy middle-manager, perhaps of an irritable schoolmaster – when he is dealing with business matters. He once ticked off the journalist Sandra Parsons for the shortcomings of her newspaper's telephonists. 'Look, before we begin, can I just say that you really ought to do something about your switchboard? It really is vital, you know, because the switchboard is your first contact with the company and you form an instant impression from them. I rang just now and they just sort of mumbled and when I asked for your extension there was silence. . . . I had no idea whether I was being put through or not. In my experience, it all comes down to lack of training.'

Cleese and Jay wrote all the scripts for the training films together – with titles such as *It's All Right, It's Only a Customer, The Competitive Spirit, In Two Minds, Awkward Customers, More Awkward Customers, I'll Think About It* and *How Not to Exhibit Yourself.* Cleese's favourite, in which he plays Elizabeth I, Field-Marshal Montgomery, Winston Churchill and Brutus, was *Decisions, Decisions*, about an executive who has bungled a corporate relocation and is standing on a window ledge. His secretary asks if he will jump. He says, 'I might . . . on the other hand. . . .'

Video Arts became a valuable source of work for dozens of well-respected British actors, bringing Cleese, unusually for an actor, considerable powers of patronage. James Bolam, June Whitfield, Bill Maynard, Una Stubbs, Bill Owen, Bernard Cribbins, Dinsdale Landen, Tim Brooke-Taylor, the Two Ronnies, Rowan Atkinson, Nerys Hughes, John Bird and Penelope Keith were a small selection of the performers; writers hired included Denis Norden, Barry Took, David Nobbs (*Reginald Perrin*), Bob Larbey (*A Fine Romance*), Jack Rosenthal, Graeme Garden and Jonathan Lynn. In a field not blessed with talent of Cleese proportions, it was no surprise that Video Arts won sackloads of awards, and the films attracted praise on an almost religious scale in America where among the early buyers were IBM, Gulf Oil, 3M, General Motors and Hilton Hotels. 'I will testify that these films work,' proclaimed boss after boss at a Boston meeting Cleese addressed, a convention he said had much of the atmosphere of a revivalist rally.

By 1981, Video Arts boasted 47 films, over 17,000 customers in 24 countries and 49 awards. Within three years, the award count was 120, and Video Arts was selling and hiring films to 24,000 British companies (including the Post Office, the Inland Revenue and gas and electricity boards). The films cost between £40,000 and £60,000 to make and were completed on hectic schedules. In one film, *So You Want to be a Success at Selling?*, with Geoffrey Palmer, Nigel Hawthorne and Derek Fowlds, Cleese completed thirty-five different scenes in one day. In 1982, Video Arts even won a Queen's Award to Industry for Exports. Mrs Thatcher held a reception on 20 April for the winners. Cleese was absent, but brimming over with delight at the recognition. 'I'm very proud. With all these bloody silly showbiz awards around nowadays there are really only three left worth having – the CH, the OM and this one. I should mop up that lot in a couple of years. I certainly wouldn't want any old OBE. They're like school prizedays where you go up and get patted on the head for being a good boy.

'Deep down,' he continued, 'most comics are a bit worried that they are a bit of a luxury and not quite useful. I feel that at last I've done something useful.' The company's export performance was extraordinary, and it was clear that John Cleese was the product country after country wanted. The Soviet Ministry of Health bought *The Unorganized Manager*. ('Let's hope the Central Committee don't get hold of the film. If they do, we are in real trouble,' Cleese joked.) Over 6,000 video cassettes were ordered by Volkswagen for its Brazilian dealers. 'John looks particularly convincing speaking Portuguese,' commented a Video Arts spokesperson. The Saudi Arabian government bought *Understanding Business* and the Zambian administration sent off for a series of cassettes on *Caring for Your Customers*. But when the Soviets bought one VA film, *Managing Problem People*, the point was lost because they failed to see what was supposed to be wrong with Rulebound Reggie, the character Cleese played – indeed, he seemed an excellent candidate for the politburo.

In October 1989, on the advice of merchant bankers, Cleese and his four partners sold Video Arts for £50 million, from which he pocketed £7 million. 'It's going to mean that I don't need to work. I shall then do the things which really interest me,' he announced, agreeing to continue to contribute to Video Arts as a writer, publicist and performer for the next three years. The company now employed eighty full-time staff in London and twelve in Chicago.

If the original idea of Cleese making a little extra money by doing some small-scale training films on the side had outgrown itself, that was nothing compared to the events of the following autumn, when Cleese ended up co-starring in a film for a charity on business and the environment with HRH Prince Charles, who had volunteered to play himself. Meeting royalty was nothing new for Cleese, who since the early 1970s had dined very occasionally with the royal family, but the relationship between a supposedly iconoclastic comedian and the apex of the class system is bound to be complicated – for the comic's credibility, at least. Cleese was furious when the press once accused him of 'fawning' over Princess Margaret at a race meeting. 'Of course, as a Weston-super-Mare lad, I am not that used to brushing shoulders with royalty and I am sure my demeanour lacked the effortless grace, charm and refinement of, say, the average Fleet Street gossip columnist,' he griped.

Prince Charles said before filming: 'You should never act with children, animals or members of the Royal Family as I am sure John Cleese will find out to his cost.' *Grime Goes Green: Your Business and the Environment* has Cleese playing Mr Grime, an environmentally unsound managing director, preparing for a visit from HRH to unveil a plaque. Mr Grime mistakes two environmental advisers for the Palace advance team, and these two start pointing out various environmental sins, reducing Grime to a gibbering wreck. Meanwhile, HRH is patiently reading a newspaper in reception. When the receptionist tells Grime his visitor from the Palace has arrived, Grime, suspecting another trap, says: 'Oh, another one from the Palace, eh? Well, I suppose you'll be wanting to see the drains then. Let me guess – you're the Royal Sanitary Inspector, eh? Well, I've had it with you lot. . . .' Charles lowers the paper and steals a few lines of hopelessly embarrassing subject-changing from Basil Fawlty: '. . . Uh, um, nice colour. Fabulous. . . .' 'You know, Mr Grime,' says HRH, 'this is not a conspiracy and none of this would have happened if the lead had come from you.' Then Charles delivers a short speech on making the workplace green, concluding: 'If everybody's going to wait for a royal visit before they clean up their act, we'll never get anywhere.' Grime, not completely convinced: 'Of course I've heard of the Greenhouse Effect. But you're not telling me that every time I spray my armpits a tomato ripens in Minnesota.'

Prince Charles was judged by the fawn-free press to be an

absolutely dreadful actor, very stilted and uneasy. One news-paper came up with the marvellous headline, 'Upper Class Wit of the Year'. Cleese, on the other hand, found a form of praise that was polite while meticulously steering clear of either fawn-ing or gushing. 'If there is a revolution he is not going to be short of work. It's almost impertinent to say this in a way, but he is very funny, in that the remarks that he makes off the cuff are genuinely amusing. And I think that's quite a surprise to people.'

Having a film made by Video Arts was the Prince's idea. The original script, by the writer of *To the Manor Born*, cunningly included in its last scene a royal personage, described as an HRH lookalike. The outcome when the Prince was sent the script can hardly have surprised Cleese, although he put up a good show of amazed gratitude. 'He was, if I may say so, a delight to work with,' Cleese enthused soon afterwards in a Christmas Day inter-view. 'He's an extraordinarily kind man and considering that everyone is nervous when you meet someone who's royal, the degree to which he put the whole set at their ease was extraordi-nary. And after he'd finished shooting and we still had a couple of hours to do, I remember he left and everybody said "Was that it? Was it as easy as that?", and we all had to have a coffee before we could get on with it again.'

Cleese's involvement in something as apparently prosaic as business training films did not only outgrow itself socially (to the extent of his working, even in a contrived way, with the future king of England) and financially, but, more importantly to Cleese, it helped his personal development. Cleese's views on what he *really* wants to be change regularly, but he is consistent on one point – that he has never wanted to be just one thing. 'I think it's always a shame in life that there is so much specializ-ation,' he has said.

There is something wonderful about those people in the eigh-teenth century like Vanbrugh – an architect who wrote plays. . . . Maybe it's more fun to do six different things pretty well than do one of them superbly well. It's a much more interesting life. I would always go for that.

I don't think my *Python* stuff trained me for much except

comedy writing. Arthur Koestler, when he went to Reykjavik to cover the chess between Fischer and Spassky, said the trouble with playing chess is that the only thing it makes you do better is playing chess. My dissatisfaction with comedy writing is I don't feel it has developed me more. It's just taught me how to write comedy, which is a very nice way of earning a living, and making sure the bank manager is happy – and thank you very much, God, for that.

By 1990, comedy, psychology, psychoanalysis, philosophy and business had all coalesced for Cleese into something that was beginning to satisfy him as some kind of explanation for, you might say, the meaning of life.

He was, and remains, as Michael Palin has said, always exceptionally busy and so involved in so many areas that he rarely has much time for anyone, but he was using disciplines he had learned from one activity to help in another. Thus he habitually consults psychologists when he writes training films and made great efforts to treat the cast of *A Fish Called Wanda* like a family. Discussing humour, he reaches for philosophy; considering philosophy, he talks about business management. 'You and I could talk about the meaning of life, or education, or marriage, and we could be laughing a lot, and it doesn't mean that what we're talking about isn't serious,' he explained to one American journalist.

In some ways similar to Prince Charles, Cleese manages to display a fascination with almost anything he sees or is told, an interest that is all the more irritating for being genuine. After a visit to Marks and Spencer, he enthused, 'I found it very interesting sitting down with a couple of smashing very bright girls who taught everybody how to sell across the counter. They were terrific and what they told me about psychology in two hours was solid gold.' Before an interview with Victor Davis, the doyen of British showbusiness writers, Davis happened to mention the low price of cars in the USA compared with Britain; Cleese seemed quite overawed to learn even about something so humdrum. 'I didn't *realize* that the difference was so great,' he gasped. It was as if Davis, instead of indulging in some pleasant smalltalk, had just elucidated a great universal truth. It is that kind of politeness, bordering, to those who do not understand him, almost on the absurd, that makes journalists cleave to Cleese. Performing stars more often ignore or patronize the showbusiness writers on whom they rely for their image, and, in many ways, their livelihood.

The essentials of his views on management also have a strangely Prince Charles ring about them. 'I think what matters is the atmosphere in which you function, whether you're a child in a family or an employee or an executive in a company. Research into healthy families has shown that they discuss things very freely. They talk things out. They are supportive. The encouraging thing, it seems to me, is the way that there is now a real sense in management that you get the best results by treating people as people.'

Cleese certainly inspires great loyalty in the staff at his own office, round the corner from his house in Holland Park. The office, a former carpet shop, is thinly disguised as an art gallery, and the first loyal act his secretaries have to perfect is going through the gallery pretence. The place does not have planning permission as an office, but by displaying the odd painting at some ridiculous price, Cleese just about gets round the local planning department. Cleese's staff tend to stay with him for many years, and, although they have to sign a confidentiality agreement (as do staff at the Python company, Prominent Features), are highly protective of his privacy. Joan Pakenham-Walsh, his secretary for several years, affectionately describes working for the man behind two Video Arts films about boss/secretary relations: 'Telephones are thrown here with monotonous regularity, and he sometimes uses words which appear in no dictionary yet written. Although he is very easy to work for, he does have the habit of disappearing when you are in the middle of telling him something.' He said of her, 'It is nag, nag, nag, the whole time. She scolds me unmercifully. She spends most of the day watching racing on my television, but these upper-class types with hyphens in their names are always like that.'

It is no surprise that people who have worked for Cleese, even those who find him too demanding, attest not only that they are given Video Arts tapes to watch but that he practises what he preaches. 'The one time I really wanted to shout at Tony [Jay],' says Cleese, 'was when he said that any chairman worth his salt knows exactly what decision he wants on every point on the agenda before the meeting starts. I can't go along with that philosophy, that you know it all and can't learn from anyone.'

John Cleese teaches because it is a way of learning. It was a telling Freudian slip, based on a happy linguistic fluke, that led him to inform an interviewer from *The Face* magazine: 'Work seems to be only valuable to me if I sense that I am earning . . . I mean learning.'

8 *Fiddly Twats*

The essence of comedy is the subtle
counterpoint between what is thought proper
and what actually happens.

Philip Mason, *The English Gentleman: The Rise and Fall of an Ideal*

One night in 1973, Professor Leslie Bethell, the eminent London University historian, and his journalist wife, Valerie, were at a dinner party at John Cleese and Connie Booth's Holland Park house. Cleese, still at the peak of his *Monty Python* fame, and Booth spent much of the evening talking about an idea they had thought up for a comedy show. The Bethells listened with interest, but when they got home, they felt sad about what their friends had been discussing. 'We said, "It's a shame, isn't it? *Python* was so good, but this is never going to take off."

'He sold it in a way that actually made it sound as if it would be a real bummer,' recalls Val Bethell. 'It was all very matter-of-fact, about this hotel, and, you know, the guy isn't very good at it and he hates doing it and he upsets the guests and there's this American waitress . . . hopeless stuff. We went to another party later with Bill Oddie and Tim Rice and their wives, and John and Connie. We had been specifically asked because of my husband's interest in Latin America so that Tim Rice could try out this idea *he* was working on. He was waxing lyrical about this musical he was going to do about Evita Peron. Of course, we thought that was an absolute bummer too. I seem to remember Les wondering if Fidel Castro might make a better musical.'

Most attempts at absolute perfection in anything end in disaster. In showbusiness, the syndrome is at its most virulent; it is hard to think of a single hugely awaited and hyped play, film, actor or television series that has not fallen gloriously and most often deservedly flat on its face. John Cleese's attempt post-*Python* to produce the definitive television sitcom, seamless, faultless, impossible to surpass, would probably have come to an equally sticky end had he and Connie Booth not kept their desire to reach comedy perfection largely private. Each episode took over a month to write and went through ten drafts. Cleese tried to make each first version good enough for a Thames Television sitcom, the second for Granada, and so on until he eventually produced a script good enough for BBC2 – and better than any other sitcom. Many years after *Fawlty Towers*, he was honest enough to admit to his much younger colleague Stephen Fry that he believed he had mastered the comedy sketch as an art form. Fry, an admirer, says the admission nonetheless left him speechless.

'We have deliberately gone as far as possible from *Python*,' Cleese said before the first *Fawlty* (the Lord Melbury episode) was broadcast on 20 September 1975. 'There seemed no point in doing sketches which could never compare with *Python*. It will disappoint *Python* addicts, but I hope it opens a new area of comedy on its own.' As it was, *Fawlty Towers* slipped on to BBC2 without much hoo-hah. It is now recognized widely as simply the sitcom by which all others are judged. Michael Frayn regards it as the most amusing script ever written, while others go further and define it, if without total scientific precision, as the funniest 'thing' ever. Recognition of *Fawlty Towers* is international. In 1990, after the memorial service in Piccadilly for the film director Michael Powell, Martin Scorsese shared a cab back to the British Film Institute with Bernard Tavernier, the French director known for *Sunday in the Country* and *Life and Nothing But*. The two celebrated directors discovered they shared a passion for *Fawlty Towers*. Scorsese's favourite bit, he said, was Basil trying not to mention the war in front of the Germans ('So tasteless, it's hilarious'). Tavernier's, predictably perhaps for a Frenchman, was gastronomic: Basil telling the American who ordered a Waldorf salad that they are 'out of Waldorfs'.

Amazingly, *Fawlty Towers*, even with the expertise of *Python* producer John Howard Davies, still almost foundered. The early reviews were mixed. The *Daily Mirror* headline after the second episode, the one about Basil getting a cowboy builder in to do some repairs to the hotel, was 'Long John Short on Jokes'. ('The Builders' had always been problematic; the Sunday it was taped, Cleese was alarmed to find studio audience reaction muted in the extreme. It ruined his timing, until he discovered that a large part of the audience comprised a group of tourists from Iceland.) The first series of *Fawlty Towers* ended on 24 October 1975 'to a deathly hush of indifference', according to one report. It was not until the series was repeated in January that Fawlty mania began.

It was all, or nearly all, thanks to a Mr Donald Sinclair, a retired naval officer and the proprietor of the Gleneagles, a quite attractive modern hotel overlooking a pretty cove in Torquay. Cleese, Booth and the Pythons had once stayed at the Gleneagles during the filming of some *Python* sketches. In the very few hours they were at the hotel before escaping for the more routine comforts of the five-star Imperial, the whole company was struck (almost literally) by the astonishingly graceless Mr Sinclair. The Pythons claimed he reprimanded a guest for using his cutlery like an American (the guest was American); he threw Eric Idle's football gear bag out of the hotel and hid it behind the wall by the swimming pool, claiming it was probably a bomb; he refused to let the bar be open unless he was around because he mistrusted the staff, even the faithful Spanish waiter, called Pepe. 'When we arrived back at 12.30 a.m., having watched the night's filming, he just stood and looked at us with the same look of self-righteous resentment and tacit accusation that I've not seen since my father waited up for me fifteen years ago,' Michael Palin remembers. 'Graham tentatively asked for a brandy; the idea was dismissed out of hand.' Cleese asked him on one occasion, 'Could you call me a taxi, please?'

'I beg your pardon?' said Mr Sinclair.

'Could you call me a taxi, please?'

'A taxi?'

'Yes.'

He gave a great sigh. 'I suppose so.'

'The owner was,' recalls Cleese, 'the most wonderfully rude man I've ever met.' The relationship between Mr and Mrs Sinclair, who retired to Florida, had similarities to Basil and Sybil's, she running him and him running the hotel, but at the Gleneagles, Mrs Sinclair was large and her husband was small.

The wonderful paradox for Cleese about the Sinclairs was one that had struck him before about British institutions charged with providing a public service of any kind: guests were to Mr Sinclair a massive inconvenience, foisted upon him by cruel gods malevolently bent upon preventing him from managing his hotel smoothly.

It did not take long for a version of Mr and Mrs Sinclair to find their way into a John Cleese script. Their first trial appearance was in an episode he wrote for *Doctor in the House*. 'No Ill Feelings' was shown in May 1971. Roy Kinnear, as a Mr Davidson who insists on being the life and soul of the party, turns up in a hotel where Dr Michael Upton (Barry Evans) is staying. The grumpy hotelier, played by Timothy Bateson, was the Fawlty prototype. Humphrey Barclay, Cleese's old Cambridge friend who was the producer, advised Cleese that there was a series in the hotelier and his wife.

Nearly three years later, John and Connie (their marriage under some strain by now, but the two of them determined to write together) were looking for an idea. Realizing that there was no point in trying to better *Monty Python*, within an hour they hit on reviving the hotel concept. They even went to Torquay to do some more research, but found the Sinclairs had sold up and gone to live abroad with a daughter. But they hardly needed more evidence of the gruesomeness of British hotels – Cleese had been collecting examples of bad service for many years, such as the Oxford hotel where his morning call came two hours early, at dawn. He complained, and was duly rewarded, just as he got back to sleep, with another call from reception apologizing for waking him up the first time.

To be fair to British hotels, some of the raw material for *Fawlty Towers* came from foreign establishments. The New York restaurant where Cleese once asked if they had mineral water, and was told 'Not as such', played its part, as did the hotel in New Zealand he encountered on the tour of *Cambridge Circus*, and the

Oasis, an extraordinarily rude hotel in Gabes, Tunisia, where, shortly before the second series of *Fawlty Towers*, the Python team stayed for the making of *Life of Brian*.

Basil Fawlty, on the other hand, was an entirely English creation. Proper restaurateurs are a subject of abiding interest to Cleese. He is enchanted by their ability to glide discreetly round a room as if on castors, by their politeness, humour, discretion and immaculate dress. Basil Fawlty, on the other hand, with his shabby cardigans and gauche manner, accurately exemplified a certain type of English hotelier and restaurateur, a bitter breed of men who can be spotted in every seaside town, with their implicit air of having fallen into innkeeping after a semi-successful career in something involving less on the service side, like debt collecting or possibly abattoir management. Basils always try to serve food dressed in gardening clothes, glare at even well-behaved children, count it a matter of professional pride to inform guests that the dish they want is 'off', and, for real satisfaction, like to say smugly that they do not take credit cards.

Cleese also took inspiration by way of the Communist Party of Great Britain. During the filming of *Monty Python and the Holy Grail* in Scotland in 1974, Julian Doyle, a film editor who had a major role in the *Python* films and was a member of the party, told Cleese about an odd elderly couple who were the CP subscription collectors in Tufnell Park and Camden Town. Doyle still wonders why he bothered to tell Cleese about the couple, as there was nothing particularly notable about them – except for their archaic names, Basil and Sybil.

Such is the innate contrariness of the British public that, to a limited extent, Basil Fawlty became a hero. Cod Fawlty Towers hotels sprang up in Torquay and Tenerife, while a guesthouse owner in Sidmouth, Devon, not only called his establishment Fawlty Towers but in 1985 changed his name, Stuart Hughes, to Basil Fawlty by deed poll. Unfortunately, Mr Hughes/Fawlty spoiled the effect by rather misjudging the spin on Cleese and Booth's creation. For some reason he painted the outside of his terraced guesthouse in Union Jack colours, and although he dutifully obliged the *Sun* newspaper on day one of business by pretending to throw a guest out on to the pavement in his pyjamas for coming down late to breakfast, he remained a pleasant, witty and well-mannered man. 'I wouldn't normally be rude to my customers,' this apology for a Fawlty told the local newspaper, 'but most of them seem to want it.' In May 1991, by way of a postscript, 'Stuart Hughes Basil Fawlty', as a local election candidate, was elected to East Devon District Council as a member of the Raving Loony Green Giant People's Party, a breakaway group from Lord Sutch's official Raving Loonies.

Cleese and Booth co-wrote *Fawlty Towers,* and Cleese was from the start anxious to emphasize the importance of Connie's contribution to the script. They had collaborated only infrequently before: on *Romance with a Double Bass,* and on a sketch for the German *Python* show, a fairy tale in which a Prince, armed only with the *Guardian,* had to fight off 200 horsemen. The revived partnership for *Fawlty Towers* was 'a great combination', Cleese said with a studied glibness; 'she dictates, I type.'

As one might imagine, the business of a husband and wife writing the finest television comedy of all time while undergoing psychotherapy and counselling because their marriage is falling apart was a little more complicated than that. They wrote the second series of *Fawlty Towers* four years after the first, when they were fully separated, but, according to Booth, she and Cleese did not live together at any time during the writing of the first either, her husband having moved into a rented house round the corner from Woodsford Square. Ironically, they spent far more time together and got on better when they worked as partners than when they were conventionally married. For the first time in their marriage, Booth felt the intellectual closeness to Cleese that she used to observe and envy when he was writing with Graham Chapman. The marriage had not been one marked by big arguments, but working together they could argue healthily, and the sense they had of holding each other back would diminish.

Cleese and Booth spent weeks on the plot, slowly working it out on huge sheets of drum paper, scribbling ideas here and there. They took pride in trying not to let the audience guess what was going to happen next, and made a point of never starting on dialogue until the plot was devised. Cleese found his wife invaluable for portraying the women. She would point out, for instance, that Sybil would never say a line that he had just written. But this was not Booth's only role. 'She's enormously fertile with funny ideas,' Cleese explained. 'Only Michael Palin compares with her for funny ideas. I'm good at the carpentry, saying, "let's shift that line up, move that section down a bit." I take a script along obvious lines, moving towards farce, but Connie stops me from doing the obvious. She says Basil works best when he's unpredictable.'

'You wouldn't believe the technical detail to which I worked on those shows,' Cleese says of the 'carpentry' phase. 'During the course of a week, I would decide that during someone else's speech, I should look at him three times. And that the first look would be done one way, and the second another, and the third yet another. It was that technical. And you keep doing it until it feels right in your gut.' Dialogue came easily once the plot was so carefully constructed. Sometimes Cleese and Booth would laugh until tears ran down their faces.

Not all their friends quite understood the nature of the unexpected John and Connie writing partnership. After their first experimental split in 1974, Val Bethell (who was also in the process of a divorce) went out for dinner a few times with Cleese, and her husband with Connie Booth. At no time did Cleese mention the break-up of his marriage, despite the obvious anomaly that he and Connie were writing *Fawlty Towers* together. 'He never discussed the issue, other than to say how good she was,' said Val. 'He always said she had a considerable writing talent, but to us it was quite hard to work out how they functioned as a writing pair. Connie was tremendously nice, and he felt bad about the break-up. You felt he was extremely aware that he was very successful, very talented, very powerful and was leaving someone far less able to cope with life and make a success of it than he was. I'm sure that he therefore made great efforts to help her get some lift-off without him.'

Highly introverted, though with a deliciously cruel sense of humour and a good deal of wilfulness hidden within her, Connie still felt painfully aware that Cleese was socially the more adept, an academic and a writer with ten years' experience, while she was an American actress and former waitress. She took the fact that her part in *Fawlty*, as Polly, was as a waitress rather badly at times. She loathed waiting on table, had met her husband when she was a waitress, and was now getting her big break on British television as one. But it was keeping her end up in the writing partnership that was most important now, and this she managed.

> There were some bad times for me because John was a more experienced writer. When he suggested we should try writing together it was like ... discipling clay. He became the 'senior partner'. But we worked well together. It was something incredibly private between us. We'd talk about ideas and then we'd often spend quite a lot of time just being quiet. . . . If I'd been a published writer to start with, I might not have been so willing to let John dominate the relationship. John is a very strong personality – that was a greater problem in our marriage than in the writing. With my writing I could make John laugh, so he respected me and left me alone. . . . The nice thing about writing *Fawlty* was a man and a woman working together; if they get on it lends a quality you don't get with two men or two women. We laughed at the same things and our senses were very much alike.

Each episode of *Fawlty Towers* was camera-rehearsed and taped in one twelve-hour Sunday marathon. Cleese did not enjoy those Sundays. 'I act in the thing only to keep someone else from screwing up the script. I'd be happiest if someone would invent a machine to plug my head into a videotape machine,' he commented grimly at the time. He would sometimes relax away from the seven-room set by his favourite method of lying on the floor for five minutes. The cast spent a week rehearsing – 'Two too few days to get it slick' – did a camera line-up on Sunday mornings, a 'stagger-through' and a dress rehearsal run-through in the afternoon, and the actual taping before a live audience ended at around 10 p.m. Though rushed, the production was far more intricate and exacting than is common in situation comedy. Each episode averaged over 400 camera shots, which means a cut every four seconds – about twice the normal number for a BBC comedy programme and enough, says Cleese, to make American television performers blanch.

There was little filming outside the studio, although one location incident during the fifth episode almost put an early end to the series. In 'Gourmet Night' the chef gets drunk, and Basil has to fetch the food from the restaurant of a friend, André, in his seven-year-old Austin 1100 estate. Cameraman Stanley Speel recalls, 'John had to drive along a main street somewhere near Acton in this small car, folded up like a praying mantis behind the steering wheel. I was lying on my back on the front seat with my head down by his feet with the camera looking up at him. And in the back seat was the sound recordist and the director. And as we were driving along, suddenly an arm shot out into the middle of the frame, grabbed the steering wheel and swerved the car to one side, and a voice said, "For Christ's sake, we were going straight into an oncoming car." And John Cleese's answer to that was: "I've never had driving lessons."' There were two mishaps in the studio, both involving considerable discomfort to Andrew Sachs. In one, Cleese, who always mischievously put his all (or a good part of it) into scenes entailing violence, had to hit Manuel on the head with a saucepan, did it fractionally too hard and left poor Sachs feeling woozy for two days. On another occasion, Sachs was burned when the pan fire in the 'Germans' episode got out of control. They carried on shooting as Sachs's jacket started smoking, but when the cameras stopped he found he needed hospital treatment and burns on an arm dressed every day for three weeks.

The same car Cleese nearly crashed in 'Gourmet Night' starred in what for many people is their favourite part of any *Fawlty* episode – the moment when Basil attempts to thrash it with a tree branch for conking out with most of the Gourmet Night menu on board. The instant Cleese most treasures – indeed what he regards as the best single scene he has ever written – was also in 'Gourmet Night', when Basil, with a dining room full of hungry, angry customers in attendance, rips open a giant blancmange with his bare hands in the desperate hope that a missing Duck Surprise might somehow be lurking inside it. 'My favourite moment is when he takes the lid off, puts the lid back on as if it might help the blancmange to go away, but when he picks it up he actually looks in the blancmange, he puts his fingers down it, just in case there is a duck underneath it.' 'Gourmet Night' was distributed by Video Arts as a catering training film, after the London Hilton decided to hire the episode for a special screening at the New London Theatre in November. British Holiday Inns also use the film.

The *most* famous *Fawlty Towers* moment, of course, was the one cherished by Martin Scorsese – the scene in which Basil, with memories of television's *Colditz* racing around in his concussed mind, abuses a group of German guests. Cleese still bridles slightly at people's reaction to that episode, much as he has his doubts over the old *Monty Python* silly walks routine, which he surprisingly re-enacted for a few seconds during his tirade against the Germans. 'I'm always a bit confused. Some people interpret it as a racist laugh, but I see it very much in the opposite direction – it's aimed at Basil *I* think. . . . My aim wasn't to make fun of Germans, it was just about Basil being concussed. It was experimenting with him going completely over the top. From thereon embarrassment lies.'

Viewers soon developed their favourites from among the characters in *Fawlty Towers*, and their choices typically fascinated Cleese. 'Manuel was the best loved character in the show,' he discovered when he asked around. 'Next came the Major followed by Basil, Polly and Sybil in that order. Their popularity was in inverse proportion to the amount of control they had over their lives.' Children, he found, particularly identified with Andrew Sachs's put-upon Manuel, reflecting as he did their own complete lack of self-determination. Prunella Scales's Sybil, on the other hand, provoked the least sympathy because she was clearly running the hotel. 'It tells us a lot about how people respond to other people, that it's helplessness that really makes us feel good about them, and if they can look after themselves we don't like them,' Cleese says.

Given Basil Fawlty's balding middle-aged look, his fusty clothes and old-style *Daily Telegraph* attitudes, it is easily forgotten that in the first series of *Fawlty Towers*, John Cleese was only just thirty-five years old. In order to look ten years or more older, he ensured that he was heavily made up in the first series, though did not bother for the second; the gaunt, crow's-footed, dark-eyed appearance he achieved led to some speculation on his emotional state. On a visit to Weston-super-Mare (he went frequently – his daughter Cynthia's love of riding extended to donkey trips on the beach at Weston) Muriel was relieved to see how much better he was looking than on the television.

There has been a lot of fatuous journalism about Cleese over the years, and many examples, as reporters search for evidence that he is barking mad or a manic depressive, of the axiom that a journalist is a man who possesses himself of a fantasy and lures the truth towards it. One topic, however, is likely to continue to exercise enquirers in years to come. The question is, to what extent *is* John Cleese Basil Fawlty?

John Howard Davies, the show's first producer and a former child prodigy actor, warned Cleese at the outset, 'You do realize that everyone will now think you're like Basil?' Cleese professed surprise at this, and for a long while parried the suggestion that there could be anything of the crazed anger of Basil in him. Indeed, it is a sensitive area. As late as 1989 he won 'substantial' damages for libel in the High Court, the money going to the charity Families at Risk, of which Cleese is a trustee, over a piece in the *Daily Mirror* which alleged that he had become increasingly like Basil Fawlty, flying into irrational rages and tweaking the ears of fellow actors during the filming of *A Fish Called Wanda*. His solicitor, Roderick Dadak, told Mr Justice Jowitt that the claim was 'absurd'.

'For some reason,' Cleese sighed to the *Daily Mail* shortly before the second series, 'people assume there's a lot of Basil Fawlty in me. Would they go up to Olivier after he'd played *Othello* and say, "I suppose there's a lot of the Moor in you, Larry?"' Yet some – admittedly a minority – who have met Cleese both before and after his years of psychotherapy still feel there is a great deal of anger lurking beneath his immaculately polite surface. He admits to a vague obsession with Hitler and certainly ranted convincingly as a boy at Clifton College. Since then, he has always played enraged roles with magnificent gusto. The kind of role an actor is good at, however, tends to be a red herring when trying to assess his true-life character. 'I'm going to say something very arrogant,' Cleese told a *Los Angeles Times* interviewer, talking about his 1980 role as Petruchio in *The Taming of the Shrew*. 'I can act. Most people don't think I can act. I don't mind. It's a perfectly reasonable assumption. Most people think I can play Basil Fawlty because I am Basil Fawlty.'

Terry Jones believes Cleese used Basil Fawlty as a way of coming to terms with himself. *Fawlty Towers* 'gave him an outlet. I think John was brilliant in that because Basil Fawlty was such a monster creation. It was as though the more psychiatric help John sought the less he needed to express himself with things like *Fawlty Towers* – if you like, the less he felt he needed to be funny.'

So, if Jones is right, *Fawlty Towers* helped Cleese *act* out the anger that he had learned from his parents to suppress in the classic middle-class English way. But, post-therapy, he takes pride in having learned to release his fury in real life too, when it is appropriate. 'The first time you use anger to complain it's like going through the sound barrier,' he says, but warns, 'If you've never let your anger come out it can seem beforehand like a terrific risk.' A writer for the *Christian Science Monitor*, Christopher Swan, saw genuine Cleese anger for himself in a Boston hotel room, when his interview with Cleese was interrupted by a fire alarm going off. Swan wrote: 'A deafening voice comes over the public address system, airplane-captain style, telling us that it's a mistake. Then the whoops get even louder. And, suddenly, he's off. "Oh, shut up!" he screams. "*Shut* UP! . . . I'd just like to say that we are at 23,000 feet, and if you look out of the window on the left, you'll see my granny's house down there. The temperature in Buenos Aires is 16 degrees."'

However, another American journalist, Bill Bryson, concluded for the *New York Times* that Cleese is the antithesis of his angry characters: 'Even his snidest moments tend to be rather tame. He recalls with some pride a letter he once wrote to the Electricity Board in which he provided a long list of complaints about poor services, but then added the closing remark: "However, I should like to congratulate you on the continuing excellent quality of your electricity." That is about as vicious as the private John Cleese gets.'

Cleese has come gradually round to confessing that he just *might* be the real Basil. He acknowledged at one stage that there was something of his father in Fawlty – the leaden sarcasm and thesaurus-like abuse – and then on Yorkshire Television's *Where*

Madeira Cove, Weston-super-Mare, in the 1930s — a slightly seedy seaside resort with
an overactive tide

Above: 'Christopher's Punctured Romance', a New York comic strip, includes a Westchester housewife, *Angst* and a Barbie doll

Right: Cleese inspects the winner of the Modern Venus bathing beauties contest, Weston-super-Mare, 1970

Left above: St Peter's School, Weston-super-Mare, 1940s. Were these the inspiration for the trophy that felled the Major in *Fawlty Towers*?

Left centre: Master and pupil: with 'Tolly' Tolson, headmaster of St Peter's

Left below: Where it all began: No. 6 Ellesmere Road, Uphill, Somerset

Above: The Secret Policeman's Ball,
1979. *From left to right: back:*
Des Johns, Michael Palin,
Rob Buckman; *centre:* Hatoff,
John Cleese, Peter Cook, Hatonn;
front: John Williams, Eleanor Bron,
Terry Jones, Rowan Atkinson

Right: With John Bird in the Video
Arts film *Cost, Profit and Breakeven,*
for non-financial managers, in 1981

Left above: The Pythons *(from left
to right):* Terry Jones, Graham
Chapman, John Cleese, Eric Idle,
Terry Gilliam and Michael Palin

Left below: On *Sez Les,* 'Television's
popular mirth and melody show',
in 1974. Les Dawson is on the left

Left: Basil Fawlty, a man on the verge of a catastrophic breakdown. Fans include Martin Scorsese ('So tasteless, it's hilarious')

Right above: Haffdan the Black in *Erik the Viking*

Right below: Aka A Guppie Called Jack, The Last Prawn, and Wanda, the Diamond and the Good Guys

Above: The Gleneagles Hotel, Torquay

Right: Now O'Lonnie's Bar, New York, in 1964 this was The Living Room, where Connie Booth met John Cleese

Une histoire de meurtre, de cupidité, de luxure, de revanche
et de poisson.

JOHN
CLEESE

JAMIE LEE
CURTIS

KEVIN
KLINE

MICHAEL
PALIN

UN POISSON NOMME WANDA

(A FISH CALLED WANDA)

SZECHUAN ARMOA
CHINESE REST TEL 758-1550

917
FREE DELIVERY
Tel. 758-1550

The funniest man in the world? John Cleese, Alyce Faye Eichelberger *(left)* and Cynthia Cleese

There's Life programme in 1984 he explained the Cleese/Basil relationship further to presenter Dr Miriam Stoppard. It had always irritated him, he said, when people assumed there must be a lot of Fawlty in him. But then Dr Robin Skynner, his analyst and co-author, suggested that when people said this, they were probably trying to avoid admitting that there was a lot of Basil in *them*. Cleese, Skynner said, had become almost a national scapegoat for every uptight Englishman trying to avoid his own reflection in the mirror. Cleese went on to say that he found that you could often discover what you least liked about yourself by examining the people you liked least. 'I started to think why do I hate John McEnroe the way I do?' Cleese said, 'and then I realized that he was a young American version of Basil Fawlty.' He acknowledged that, for example, at parties when someone was boring him, he often felt the urge to push a sponge cake in their face. He had never done so, but was relieved that at least he could act out such behaviour.

'Ten years ago,' Cleese concluded, 'I thought of myself as a much nicer chap than I think of myself now. Nowadays I know what a shit I am. There it is. People still seem to like me mostly, but I really know how awful I am inside, and it doesn't seem too bad to me.'

Despite this one semi-lapse, Cleese still prefers to talk about Basil Fawlty's anger as a more general English phenomenon. 'One of the reasons why Basil Fawlty was a very successful creation in the long run was that he embodied the kind of thing that the English feel sometimes, which is because they can't say, "I'm sorry, this is foolish, not good enough," or, "I bought this pair of shoes and want you to replace it",' he explained to Melvyn Bragg on *The South Bank Show*. 'Because they can't do these simple acts of self-assertion, they tend to develop on the surface a kind of brittle politeness and underneath a lot of seething rage. And I think that that was one of the reasons why they could identify with Basil, also find him funny and, at the same time, quite like him.'

It was not only Basil's anger that captured the British – or at least the English – imagination. His snobbery was also well observed. Perhaps the most embarrassing moment in *Fawlty Towers* comes in the first episode, when Basil insists on accepting a cheque for cash from a phoney 'Lord Melbury', despite Sybil's suspicion that he is not necessarily all he seems to be. A caricature of English obsequiousness to the nobility? Perhaps, but consider the case, as reported in July 1991, of Mr Paul Bryant, owner of a Fulham electrical appliance shop, who accepted a cheque for £175.75 from a titularly genuine but otherwise notoriously dodgy young peer. The Barclays cheque, signed in insouciant Lord Melbury style with the surname alone, bounced merrily back from His Lordship's Oxfordshire bank. 'Because he is a member of the aristocracy I never bothered to ask for his banker's card,' Mr Bryant explained. 'Well, you don't, do you? You just trust him.'

Cleese was inventing Basil Fawlty at the same time as he started going to his weekly psychotherapy group. What he was quite unaware of, having read little on the subject and being new to 'the world of shrinks' as he has called it, was that Basil was a casebook rendition of a man on the verge of a catastrophic breakdown: 'It's pretty accurate, funnily enough. I wrote it on intuition. It was only later when I had to think about it more that I realized that psychiatrically it was very accurate. I remember reading a book on transactional analysis after the first series. It was called *I'm OK, You're OK*; it was a best-seller. And there was a list of characteristic phrases and gestures that people use when they're "stuck in the parent", which is absolutely Basil. If you want to know how to play him, just read that page, it's extraordinary.' Even his gestures were spot on, he was once assured by the chief psychiatrist at Broadmoor, though he has to confess (guardedly, given the Broadmoor shrink's enthusiasm for Cleese's body language) that Fawlty's walk was nothing more than his own.

'It's something to do with reducing the wind resistance. I'm very peculiar when I move. I wish I was an elegant mover, but I'm not, and I don't have to exaggerate it much, unfortunately, to look like Basil,' he says ruefully. Tony Staveacre, author of the book *Slapstick*, studied Basil Fawlty's walk with loving care to achieve this description: 'Unlike Monsieur Hulot, Fawlty seems to slant *backwards*, usually because his brain has not caught up with the fact that his legs are on the move again, in a desperate dash to head off approaching, inevitable disaster. Occasionally the time-lag between head and heels is so marked that he appears to be in two scenes at the same time – arriving legs make a whirlwind diversionary entrance while departing head is still explaining, ranting, prevaricating, grovelling.'

On 8 May 1977, at Sir Bernard Miles's Mermaid Theatre in London, the *Monty Python* team, plus Peter Cook, Dudley Moore, Jonathan Miller and Peter Ustinov, put on a show called *An Evening Without Sir Bernard Miles*, a record of which, *The Mermaid Frolics*, was released. The show included a noteworthy sketch in which John Cleese and Connie Booth played an upper-class couple called Fiona and Simon, dining in a posh restaurant, who address both themselves and each other as 'one' until they become thoroughly confused.

In 1977, when John Cleese and Connie Booth started on the second series of *Fawlty Towers*, the working atmosphere was very different from that of four years earlier. Exactly a year before the Mermaid show, Connie had told John, in a New York hotel room, that their marriage was over. When they came back to London after the *Monty Python* stage show run in New York, the reality of separation set in. Characteristically, Cleese set about the practical, non-emotional side of being a full-time bachelor again, rather than one who oscillated in and out of the marriage as he had done for two years, by assiduously learning a new skill: he took himself off to Hintlesham Hall, Robert Carrier's culinary academy in Essex, for a cookery course.

Amply lubricated by counselling and psychotherapy (as well as money, the missing link in a lot of would-be ideal marital breakdowns) in many respects it was the perfect divorce. John and Connie have remained friends to this day. They lived at the outset in different sections of the same house, shared care of Cynthia, then six, and took holidays together with her. Moreover, they succeeded in writing the second series of *Fawlty Towers*, commuting between each other's homes to work office-hour days. Cleese regards the second series, which includes 'The Psychiatrists', 'The Dead Body', and, lastly, 'Basil the Rat' episodes, as the best work he has ever produced.

'I know it sounds rather silly to say we have separated while we are still living under the same roof, but we are staying here now because of our child. We will decide in a year's time whether or not to sell the house and go our separate ways. . . . We decided over some months. . . . We are still very friendly,' Connie told the *Daily Mirror*. 'I don't like the idea of just disappearing, it's ridiculous,' commented Cleese. 'Having done the psychotherapy we don't think in terms of whose fault it was. It was very much a fifty-fifty thing.'

Some friends were distraught by the separation. Tim Brooke-Taylor said at the time: 'My wife and I like both of them equally – and it's not many friendships where you can say that. . . . I'm pessimistic about them coming together again, but I would like it. He's potty about his daughter Cynthia.'

Cynthia reciprocated her father's feelings. She would later admit that she was in no doubt that the very public and traumatic divorce not only forced her parents apart, but also emotionally separated her from Connie for several years, even though she lived with her when she was not at boarding school, which she attended from the age of nine. Cynthia says:

> My father was successful and everything seemed to come so easily for him, while at the time, she [Connie] was struggling to establish herself. She was defensive and easily threatened when it came to her career, and in some ways she still is. I think that was one of the main reasons for the divorce. My mother really wanted a daughter but I think I was too boisterous and independent for her in the early years. She would tell me not to talk too much and avoid dominating the conversation if I was at a dinner party with her, but I've always been the kind of person that would just say something if I wanted to . . . .
>
> It is only in the last few years that I have started really talking to my mother properly. It took me a long time to recognize that I could talk to my mother about all sorts of things, just like mothers and daughters do.

As a young adult, Cynthia shed further light on the Cleese/Booth separation: 'My father has always had an attraction for women who want to be fathered, to be looked after. He liked it if they had complications because he could try and help them sort it out, but it never worked like that.'

Splitting the Woodsford Square house into two did not last long. By early 1977, Cleese had moved into a rented flat in a pink house in a pink-and-white blossomed street in Notting Hill Gate only half a mile away. He was intending to buy a house just round the corner from Connie. The flat had wooden floors and was sparsely furnished. The couple's Siamese cats – Cleese loves cats, and had recently given an Abyssinian to his mother – had symbolically separated along with the Cleeses. He kept Vanilla, while Connie kept Nez, Vanilla's mother. Independence was suiting Cleese well. He and Booth had plotted two of the new *Fawlty* episodes, but written no dialogue; she was on tour in Tennessee Williams's *The Glass Menagerie* which came to London at the end of May, he was working on *Life of Brian* and they had both starred in a badly received Holmes and Watson television drama with Arthur Lowe. But Cleese and Booth were not yet planning to divorce. 'I just leave my options open,' he told the journalist Tim Satchell, who visited him during the week of the Mermaid Theatre show for a 10 a.m. breakfast of orange juice and percolated coffee with honey. 'We live separately now and the relationship is very friendly. And we work well together. I think there's much too much togetherness in marriages. And when you discover a sort of independence it's very nice. It sounds cold-blooded but I think that it works much more than the excessively romantic attitude which we do get pushed at us.'

In September, Cleese and Booth went on a fortnight's holiday to Jamaica with Cynthia. 'We remain very good friends,' Cleese reiterated. 'I think it is sad that someone who for ten years has been the closest person in the world to you should suddenly become the most distant. If you can work out all the adolescent business of blaming one another, there is no reason why you can't remain friends.' Connie also went to Barbados three months later with Cleese and the other Pythons who were finalizing the script of *Life of Brian*.

Although the divorce was becoming increasingly inevitable, both Cleese and his wife were adamant that counselling and group therapy had been a success. 'Some people go into therapy to try to save their marriage. But sometimes therapy can make you realize that the marriage has to end,' Cleese explained. Booth did not say much about the break-up at the time, but nearly ten years later, when she and her ex-husband still spoke every week and lunched together, she admitted, 'If it hadn't been for group therapy I don't think we could have worked on the second series. We were able to begin to see each other more objectively, which made a bridge for us while we were facing the fact that we might have to separate.' She did add sadly at the same time, however, that living on her own she did not laugh so much.

Fawlty Towers was a shared dream, almost like a baby to Cleese and Booth. But despite the fact that it marked the end of their marriage, she was still happier writing it than at any other time. She finally had some feeling of her own self-worth, which may explain why she was able to remain so friendly with Cleese; she had come out of the nearly twelve-year-long relationship 'improved' in many ways that she had badly desired. She did not even feel any urge to go back to the USA, as sharing Cynthia was working out well, and continued to do so.

In October 1977, close to his thirty-eighth birthday, eighteen months after the final split with Connie but a year before their divorce, Cleese bought an enormous house in Holland Park from the pop singer Bryan Ferry. Because of his own size, Cleese delights in large things – the house, Rolls-Royce and Bentley cars, and heapy portions in restaurants. (At Lilly's, the restaurant next to his office, the staff automatically serve him bigger help-ings.) Ever mindful of his parents' continual home shifting back in the West Country, John was determined at last to put down roots in the house he had found, and has done so; fourteen years later, with a second marriage come and gone and a new permanent girlfriend *in situ*, he is still there, a hundred-yard walk from his office. Ferry had lived in the house with Jerry Hall; the day Cleese came to see it, he recalls, 'I took one look at him standing in the hall, thought of Basil Fawlty, and just cracked up with laughing. I had to hide in the cloakroom to control myself until I could make a re-entrance.' Cleese ('All I've got to do is say "Hello" perfectly normally for people to go off in howls of laughter. . . . Sometimes I envy people who are taken seriously') reportedly beat Ferry's price down from

£120,000 to £80,000. 'It's a good move to buy a house from a pop star. They've got so much money they don't haggle much,' Cleese commented with satisfaction. On the Barbados trip in January, the Pythons spent time with Jerry Hall and Mick Jagger, with whom she was now living; Hall saw fit to mention one evening that the house John had just bought from Ferry was haunted. A furious spectre of the now late Donald Sinclair, ex-proprietor of the Gleneagles in Torquay, was simultaneously roaming the corridors of the Fawlty Towers prototype, staff there reported.

Cleese sued for a 'quickie' divorce on 31 August 1978, two weeks before going off to Tunisia to shoot *Life of Brian*; the divorce came through while he was away. Six months later, Cleese and his ex-wife were hilariously rehearsing their new *Fawlty Towers* episodes, racing in and out of a three-doored room in his new house. The house was not yet decorated, but boasted a huge pine table which came from HM Prison, Holloway, and had the names of former inmates scratched into it.

The couple had by now resolved not to write together again. 'We feel that now we are separated we ought to live that way,' Cleese said. 'Working on these scripts means you spend more time together than the average happily married couple. It is quite amazing that we have continued to work like this. I suppose it's because we make each other laugh.'

Dictated largely by Cleese and Booth's personal circumstances, one of the keys to *Fawlty Towers*'s success was the fact that only twelve episodes were ever made. For a comedy with one over-riding character, even this was a huge achievement. 'We made eight hours out of Basil Fawlty. Shakespeare only managed four with Hamlet,' Cleese crowed. Since 25 October 1979, when 'Basil the Rat' concluded the second series, the two series have been frequently repeated, with audiences growing rather than diminishing. A repeat showing of the first series in November 1985 had 12.5 million viewers for the opening episode – the largest single audience ever for BBC2. Since then, the home video market has exploded and viewers have discovered that *Fawlty Towers* has the same quality as a well-thumbed book – it bears seeing again and again. In Britain, 690,000 *Fawlty Towers* videos at £10 each have been sold; the BBC has also had big export orders from Japan, Australia, Israel, Germany, the USA and Holland. During the Gulf War in January 1991, President George Bush claimed he relaxed at Camp David by watching *Fawlty Towers* videos – 'We roar and roar at them,' he said.

The second series was again influenced by more of Cleese's personal experience of hotels and restaurants. As far back as 1965 in New York he had been listening carefully to actor friends who waited at table both at the restaurant where he met Connie and at the Ginger Man, a dark Parisian-looking theatrical haunt on West 64th Street, just off the better end of Broadway. Some ideas never made it into the show, but give a hint of what might have been in a third series. 'We thought it would be funny if somebody came in to the hotel who got very small portions. I stayed at a hotel in Weston-super-Mare a while ago and I noticed you got exactly what the menu said. For "Egg, bacon and tomato" you got one egg, one rasher and half a tomato. As Basil has a very literal, legalistic mind – he's a litigious individual – he could get into a row over whether you'd expect to find Margaret Thatcher in a cabinet pudding.' Another idea was to base an episode upon a tax inspector.

The basis of two of the best *Fawltys* came from other people. 'My friend at Langan's, who trained at the Savoy, told me without a moment's thought that the worst problem was the dead bodies, people pegging out inconveniently,' he said. 'The Savoy gets ten or twelve a year. Naturally they don't want to disturb the surviving guests' breakfasts by taking corpses through the dining room. Terrible problems of rigor mortis they have in the service lifts.' 'Basil the Rat' was originally prompted by a viewer's letter about an incident in a real hotel. 'Apparently the owner suddenly burst in carrying a shotgun, which I thought was very Basil. He said he was going out to shoot some rats. Then he was overcome with compassion for the rats, and he stormed back in saying what harm had rats ever done him? He should be shooting some of his guests!' Cleese is also keen to give credit to the BBC Special Effects Department for producing a rat so realistic 'I almost kissed them. We got about sixty seconds out of that rat sitting in the biscuit tin.'

The second series took a harder physical toll on Cleese. During the first, he could rehearse Basil for a whole day without tiring.

Now he got muscular pains in his neck, back and shoulders keeping up the tension the part required. Cleese worked out that this was because he had relaxed in the three years between series and now had to contrive Basil's manic erectness more. He and Booth tentatively discussed doing a *Fawlty Towers* film script. 'Connie's idea was to send Basil on holiday to Spain where he gets an hotel just as bad as his own and has appalling service.' An alternative involved Basil's plane being hijacked. Stoked up by a sixteen-hour wait at Heathrow, he overcomes the hijackers single-handed, becomes a hero, but when it turns out they will have to return to Heathrow, he hijacks the plane himself and demands to be taken to Malaga, where he enjoys a happy fortnight in a Spanish prison. So popular was *Fawlty Towers* by now that members of the public were willing it to continue. Richard Heller, at the time a principal in the Civil Service and shortly to become political adviser to Denis Healey, wrote to Cleese at the BBC with a particularly splendid idea for a new Fawlty series. In it, Manuel wins El Gordo, the multi-million-pound prize in the Spanish National Lottery. With the money, he naturally buys a huge hotel but decides to advertise in Britain for a manager. Since Manuel learned his English entirely from Basil he words the advertisement in Fawlty terms, especially the last line, 'No riff raff need apply'. With Fawlty Towers down in Torquay falling into ruin, the ad catches the eye of Basil and Sybil, who get the job. One scene in Heller's proposal has Manuel climbing on to a chair to hit Basil.

Already replete with awards from the first series, *Fawlty Towers* now attracted still more. What started as a gamble, because it would inevitably be compared with *Monty Python*, turned out to be more popular − even John Cleese's mother liked it. There was a flurry of upset over him, however, when he went to pick up one BAFTA gong from Princess Anne and Morecambe and Wise and didn't say a word. 'My departure wasn't a snub,' complained Cleese when the tired, inevitable 'royal slight' story grew wings. 'I was going to say a few words and crack a joke apologizing for not being present to accept the award. But Eric and Ern had already got a laugh out of that. I thought the best thing to do was to say nothing and simply turn round and walk off with a wave. People may not appreciate it, but I'm really not very funny without a script.'

The truth is that he *was* a funny man without a script, but, by 1979, a combination of the disrupted relationship with Connie, the more mellow attitude bred by psychotherapy and the grinding effect of continual recognition in public places made him less inclined to be funny to order. 'Like all great comedians,' observes Jeffrey Archer, 'he needs to be given the stage, rather than take it. If you offer him the stage, he'll take it. If you don't offer it, he'll remain silent.' (Some while before Jeffrey Archer, Plato noticed the same phenomenon; in the *Symposium*, he describes a drinking party at which Aristophanes, the greatest comedy writer of the day, was present. Although well-liked and convivial, Aristophanes was inclined to take himself a little seriously: 'I don't mind being thought amusing – that's my job – but I don't want to be thought ridiculous.')

'I used to do daffy, funny, spontaneous things years ago with great delight,' Cleese said, 'but if I try and do them now I'm usually recognized. And therefore it's now "the bloke from the box" doing something funny. That's why I enjoy writing more. I cannot go into a restaurant without someone coming up to me saying "You will never believe this, but we have a waiter here called Manuel."' His aim in life was now to be quieter, more contemplative, to 'sit in the garden and read books', as he often stated.

The 'Dead Body' episode of *Fawlty Towers* was entered for the Golden Rose of Montreux television award by the BBC in 1979, a rather risky decision by the corporation, considering how much of the humour was at the expense of Manuel and that there would be Spanish judges at the festival. The episode was shown at 9 a.m. on a Sunday morning; in the end it was the Swiss, with their legendary sense of humour, who sank Cleese's non-existent hope of winning. 'Funny foreigners may be a joke to the English. But not to us. We are your funny foreigners. Manuel is a character in dubious taste,' sniffed a Swiss television man.

In the event, Cleese had a truly Pythonesque ace in a hole – he also had an entry in the competition for Norway. Neither was this a flag of convenience operation: *Norway: Land of Giants!* was a real Norwegian film. 'It's a bit embarrassing. The Norwegians had seen me in *Fawlty Towers* and asked me to help them out. At that time the BBC hadn't decided to enter *Fawlty* so there was nothing I could do about it. On the past record of this place I reckon I've got more chance of winning with the Norwegians' entry than with the Beeb's.' He was right. His Norwegian film won the City of Montreux Prize for the funniest programme and the Press Jury Prize. In *Land of Giants*, Cleese starred as the deadpan commentator, Norman Fearless, complete with Fawlty moustache, to a montage of sketches, which, rather admirably, were a massive send-up of everything Norwegian – everyone wears skis and back-packs, even in bed; the Norwegian abroad behaves like a lout; Norway's most celebrated inventions were the cheese slice and the aerosol; Ibsen was the only famous writer to come from Norway, and even he lived abroad. Self-inflicted racism, it seemed, was perfectly acceptable to the judges.

Despite that Swiss executive's misgivings, *Fawlty Towers* was for eleven years the BBC's best-selling overseas programme, reaching forty-five stations in seventeen countries. It would have sold far better had Cleese not refused to let the Americans lop a disastrous eight minutes off each half-hour episode to make space for commercials. His principles lost him a lot of money, though. As had happened with *Python*, the Public Broadcasting System showed the episodes uncut and secured cult status for Basil in America, albeit in the mid to late 1980s, several years after Britain. The payment system was complicated, but it worked out that each time a PBS station broadcast a *Fawlty* episode, Cleese earned roughly $2.04. In many cities, PBS stations would hold Fawltythons, and show all twelve episodes of the latest 'Britcom' in one exhausting night, bringing the lucky Cleese nearly £12. In Miami, there was a Fawlty Festival, complete with scores of Basil lookalikes. One American fan, instinctively appreciating just the kind of thing that would be to the taste of Cleese, a collector of distinguished nineteenth- and twentieth-century watercolours, sent him a facsimile of his features woven into a carpet. For a long time he kept it as a doormat in his office.

Leading the Fawlty worshippers was the *New York Newsday*

television critic and columnist Marvin Kitman, who regularly reported American Fawlty news, such as when a New York reader's son was asked in class to name a city in England; while the other boys said London, her eight-year-old piped up with Torquay. Kitman, who, to put him in correct perspective, is also a major admirer of Benny Hill, formed a Basil Fawlty Brigade which in 1986 supported the 'Basil Fawlty for Prime Minister' campaign and gave out 1,007 badges bearing that slogan. Kitman relaunched the campaign in 1987 when a by-election came up in Britain. Delightfully, fans wrote to Kitman, most of them demonstrating an exquisite misunderstanding of *Fawlty Towers*, to explain why they wanted Cleese as PM. Joe Barry of Miller Place let on that he was 'dying to see John Cleese in one of Margaret Thatcher's dresses'. Sybil Sahasrabudhe of Selden wrote a campaign song to the tune of 'America the Beautiful' too painful to reproduce here. M. Wilson of Smithtown even started a 'Manuel for the House of Commons' movement. Kitman wrote to Cleese, giving him their support. He gamely wrote back: 'I am happy to confirm that I will not stand for election. If drafted, I will not accept. If elected, I will not serve. If I do serve, I shall pretend I'm not.' The doughty Kitman was not put off by his candidate's stubbornness. In August 1988, he ran a poll asking his readers who they would vote for in the presidential election out of Cleese or the other candidates. The results were: Cleese 63%, Dukakis 4%, Bush 7%, others 26%. The only question begged by the exercise was, who went to the trouble to write in *not* to support Cleese?

Predictably, American attempts to copy the *Fawlty Towers* formula have been catastrophic, showing only how uniquely British the concept is. Cleese sold the format rights to a packager, Herman Rush, who let them lapse, and they then passed around Los Angeles largely unwanted. A pilot called 'Snavely', starring Harvey Korman and Betty White, nearly saw the light of day but clearly did not work. 'The producers feared it was too mean-spirited,' Cleese says. 'In America now,' he explained to the *LA Times*, 'comedians want to be lovable. W. C. Fields was a total bastard, but rather him than thirty-three of the "but seriously, folks, it's just a joke" types. That was the trouble with the Korman version. There was a noticeable attempt to reassure the audience that the people in the show were all right, folks. Korman would give a slightly reassuring smile now and then. He'd allow little moments of warmth to creep in. Disastrous.'

Some while later, he had what he describes as the most extraordinary Hollywood experience of his life. 'I was at a house party in England and two Americans introduced themselves. They said, "Our company owns the *Fawlty Towers* format. And we're just about to make six of them"', Cleese recounted in *Playboy*. 'My heart leaped to the sound of cash registers, and I asked, "How nice, but would a series about a small private hotel be understood in America?" "No problem with that," they said. "Have you made any changes at all?" I asked. "Just one," they replied. "We've written Basil out." And you know, there's just this moment when you stand there smiling politely, thinking everything you've ever heard about Hollywood is true.'

Amazingly, in 1983 Viacom and ABC actually made *Amanda's By the Sea*, with Bea Arthur of *The Golden Girls*, and, as promised, without even an approximation of a Basil Fawlty character. The one remaining unwiped episode of *Amanda's* resides on its own at Viacom's London office in Conduit Street, where none of the other videos, one suspects, will talk to it. It is a breathtaking piece of work.

The hotel building at least is remarkably similar, if a little more ornate than Fawlty Towers. The layout is identical, the bell on the front desk (along with a Manuel-type waiter, the only feature left untouched), the room behind the desk, the staircase, the kitchen and dining-room all somehow eerily in place. Beatrice Arthur plays the widowed Amanda Cartwright, who in rudeness is perhaps the cube root of Basil. Amanda has a witlessly truculent son Marty, and he a glamorous but empty-brained wife Arlene. Manuel (renamed Aldo) is a Mexican, who imitates Andrew Sachs's bow-legged, confused stagger to perfection, a great achievement for the actor when his lines are not even microscopically funny. *Amanda's By the Sea*, on which Cleese refused to allow his name to appear, was a dreadful slur on the bad name and misanthropy of Basil Fawlty.

For one thing, the show contains such outrages as hugging — real fatuous, American hugs. The gruesome fascination doesn't end there. The emotions on display span only the traditional A to B, but there are at least twenty-five different lingering glances as the actors wait for studio laughter to die. The miracle is that the laughter began in the first place. The comic epicentre of the remaining episode is that twenty cases of fresh okra have been delivered, as a result of a misunderstanding. In a faint echo of a Basil line, Amanda proposes rhetorically that she might institute an Amanda's By the Sea All Okra Alternative Menu. When her dead husband's interfering brother comes to the hotel to try to get her to retire, Amanda complains, 'I am happy, this hotel makes me happy.' The slapstick peak of this particular episode comes when Zak, the brother-in-law, accidentally puts chilli powder in Amanda's cocoa. ('What did you put in this? It's chilli powder!' she yells.) The end shows Zak, having left the kitchen, shaking his head and saying, 'That's one hell of a woman'; cut to Amanda, expression frozen and cocoa in hand, looking astonished and saying, 'I'm going to kill that man.' That's it, folks. No jokes. The show was taped at ABC in Hollywood and created by one Elliott Shoenmann.

Long after the last *Fawlty Towers* episode was made, Cleese hired Andrew Sachs for a Video Arts training film. Sachs played a snooty restaurant proprietor, Cleese a rep selling glassware. Sachs mentioned on the shoot that this was the first time he had seen Cleese in six years. Cleese was quite embarrassed when the *Sunday Times* made a note of the meeting: 'Do you know, *Fawlty Towers* didn't enter my head when I asked Andrew to do this film. And quite honestly I had no idea that we hadn't even met since the end of *Fawlty* until Andrew pointed it out. It's odd how you can be so close to someone for so long and then simply not see them for years on end.' Cleese always likes to create families around him, but he has a facility for moving on to the next item on life's agenda without indulging in nostalgia about the last. He readily admits that he treats each group of people he has worked with as a temporary family: 'And yet the fact is I've felt each family has outlived its use. And I usually feel that before anyone else does.' It is almost as if having so many confidants prevents Cleese from seeing any one person for too long, thereby making it difficult to get too close to him. (Tony Hancock also had a vast number of friends, few of whom ever got to know him well; Hancock also had an abiding interest in serious matters and carried a copy of Bertrand Russell's *History of Western Philosophy* around theatre dressing-rooms with him, along with a teddy bear.)

The end of *Fawlty Towers* coincided with the end of Cleese's marriage and the emergence of a new, more mellow, psychoanalysed self. In his professional life, he moved on to writing with his analyst Dr Robin Skynner with scarcely a glance back at *Monty Python*, moved on to developing a film role that took him away from Basil Fawlty (the more vulnerable and sympathetic persona of Archie Leach in *A Fish Called Wanda*). *Fawlty Towers* represented, perhaps, a certain neurosis in Cleese, and when he had conquered that neurosis he no longer needed or wanted to be reminded of it.

His affair with Connie Booth – the meeting in the restaurant, his ignoring her at first, the years of conducting the relationship across the Atlantic – read like most people's idea of a romantic idyll. He came out of the marriage almost bomb-proofed against any future attack of romance. It is arguable that he regards romantic love as no more than the sanctification of the characteristics of depression – clinginess, dependency, missing people, suffering. 'The myth of the perfect Hollywood romance is responsible for a lot of broken marriages. I have a feeling I could marry a wide range of people,' he has said. 'If I finish up being married five times for seven years each time, that for me will probably be more interesting than once for thirty-five years. I know you are not supposed to say it, but why not?'

Even after his second separation he was adamant on the point. 'I don't think you can regard marriage as a failure just because at some point you separate and get divorced. Otherwise, you'd have to assume that every marriage was a failure unless it ended in death. I don't think life is about avoiding mistakes. I think it's about making them and coming to terms with them and actually getting to a more interesting place as a result. Playing safe is the worst thing anyone can do.'

From a painfully embarrassed public schoolboy with no experience or understanding of women at all, through a tall, odd young man who only lost his virginity at twenty-four, to a star with two highly civilized divorces behind him, it is easy to see how John Cleese must have felt proud of his development by his forties. He had learned to give and seek affection, which he used to think contemptible. And he had learned more than most men ever know about women, developing an understanding and respect that would have made him an even greater oddity in the Footlights bar back at Cambridge.

'Women are terribly good at understanding people emotionally, even men,' Cleese said in the *Daily Telegraph* in 1980. 'I told my nine-year-old daughter about breaking up with a girlfriend and she understood perfectly. They're much better at us than we are at them and they really should start writing their own brand of humour because it will open up whole new areas.'

9 *Psycho-Drama*

There is a story about the famous Swiss
clown, Grock, who became so terribly
depressed on a tour of England that, using
his own name, he went to see a psychiatrist.
The psychiatrist finally said: 'Look, what you
need is a good laugh. Why don't you go and
see Grock at Earls Court tonight?'

John Cleese, while making *Clockwise*

The British attitude towards psychiatry and psychoanalysis
was encapsulated by the Scottish columnist Peter McKay,
writing in the London *Evening Standard* in 1990: 'Psychiatry –
certainly the kind where self-absorbed bores pay analysts to
listen to their self-pity – should enjoy roughly the same status
as fortune-telling,' he snarled.

Significantly, it took the American Connie Booth, who had
been in analysis in New York before John Cleese met her, to
persuade him to seek similar treatment when their marriage
began to flounder. He was unable to decide what to do post-
Python, and he often felt ill and unhappy. Over a decade on
from their divorce, Connie sometimes wonders quite what she
unleashed in John; so impressed is he with the benefits of
psychotherapy that he has become one of its leading advocates.
It is possible that he will end up one day better known for his
evangelistic espousal of psychology than for comedy, nor would
that displease him.

Although at the age of sixteen Cleese had expressed an interest in becoming a psychoanalyst, it was not an idea that had consumed him for long. 'I was very rigid, very Weston-super-Mare. I had a very British attitude towards therapy. Couldn't see what it would achieve. I felt very normal. I was successful. I wasn't aware of feeling depressed, just a bit irritable. In fact, you could say I had the normal state of mind of a sixty-year-old colonel.'

For three years, eight to ten months of each year, Cleese had been suffering mild flu symptoms. 'Like a good public school chap, I assumed it was for physical causes and I went and had it checked out a couple of times by all the specialists and they could find nothing wrong. Then, to my astonishment, a very nice Australian doctor had me fully checked out physically and then suggested afterwards it might have a psychological/psychosomatic basis.'

He says he was shocked and alarmed by this suggestion, but on the advice of a friend went to see Dr Robin Skynner, which he thought 'a very good name for a shrink'. The night before he saw Cleese, Skynner, a Cornishman who reassuringly looks and dresses more like a farmer than a psychiatrist, happened to watch the *Monty Python* 'Confuse-A-Cat' sketch on TV and wasn't sure what to expect from his new client. After four sessions with Cleese, Skynner pronounced him a suitable case for group therapy, his speciality. Something in Skynner's approach had appealed to Cleese's scientific belief that every problem has a technical solution. He reconciled the intuitive English reaction against shrinkery with his inclination to treat the components of himself objectively, as if they were parts of a machine.

So at the time he was starting to write *Fawlty Towers* with Connie, Cleese joined a weekly psychotherapy group with seven others, run by Skynner and his wife Prue, who live in Hampstead Garden Suburb. Skynner, late of the Maudsley Hospital, is a co-founder of the Institute of Group Analysis and Institute of Family Therapy. The meetings were held late every Thursday afternoon for an hour and a half at the Institute in New Cavendish Street. All the other group members were highly successful but miserable professionals, a disproportionate number of barristers among them. Within two months of starting in the group, Cleese's flu symptoms disappeared. He did not leave the group until late in 1977 when he bought Bryan Ferry's house in Holland Park and, by his standards, put down roots.

The three years that Cleese spent fighting, in his words, 'wanting to be Tarzan, always looking after smaller Connie', was a relatively short period for analysis: as he said, 'I once asked Woody Allen how his psychoanalysis was going after twenty-five years. He said, "Slowly".' In Skynner's group, however, it only took twenty minutes or so before these terribly correct English people, some there to mend their marriages, others looking for proof that relationships could not continue, were admitting their problems to one another. 'We laughed a lot,' Cleese says; it also turned out to be the most interesting experience of his life. 'It's largely a question of having your ego cut down to size. Most of the things we've got wrong can be explained by having an ego that's too big.'

The therapy did nothing as simplistic as 'cure' the depression. After John and Connie finally split in 1976, he was depressed for a year. Even today, he still suffers from depressions, but understands how to live with them, acknowledging what they are, looking after himself while they are on. 'Now I say "here we go again" and view them as a rather inferior soap opera,' he explains. 'People now find me calmer. One of my faults is that I have taken work too seriously which means I get quite wound up about things. Now I think I have grown up a bit. I do my best to get things right, but at the end of the day I'm not so wound up. So I think people find me more open and less defended than I used to be. There's no question that my public school upbringing plus – let us put it nicely – having a vaguely artistic temperament causes a certain amount of tumult to be held in.'

Cleese has remained friends with many psychiatrists to this day. In the mid-Eighties, he used to stay regularly with a Dr Robert Sharp in Huggler's Hole, near East Knoyle in Wiltshire. He also still occasionally visits a psychiatrist as a patient but they talk about everything. Recently, as he was leaving, one shrink asked, 'Oh, by the way, how are you?'

The fact that Cleese has willingly kept journalists up-to-date with his psychoanalytical journey makes his a very unusual case indeed; although there are huge black areas that only he and his analyst know about, a great deal of the saga has been played out in public. But Cleese's refreshingly candid attitude to the press, an aspect of the American openness he adopted when he first went to the USA, has caused him now to be hoisted by his own petard, albeit sometimes cackhandedly. Cleese had already found that the media's handling of such intellectually uncomplicated issues as the Ministry for Silly Walks sketch was enough to give him the vapours. When he made the brave decision to tell all to journalists about his therapy, it was hardly surprising that the press immediately labelled him as barking mad and on the verge of being shipped off to an asylum.

Journalism does not lend itself easily to portraying shades of grey, as Cleese must have known, but his occasional naivety can never be underestimated; in a culture that merrily jumbles psychiatry, psychotherapy and even mental handicap into one bundle, he remains bitterly angry at being treated as a howling-in-the-corner basket-case. 'I was never not functioning,' he has explained repeatedly, 'but at weekends I tended to sit around and just feel rather melancholic.'

'I love to get things clear, absolutely clear,' he informed another interviewer, William Marshall. 'There has been this distorted image, this figure sitting in a corner paralysed by depression, all that kind of crap. Lot of *crap*. It came at a time when I was doing extremely well professionally, but at the same time my first marriage was breaking up. But people tried to give the impression I was some kind of a very tortured guy.' 'And you weren't?' asked Marshall, courageously. 'Well, no, I don't think above averagely tortured. I suppose I'm your average tortured guy, really. Life can't all be pure happiness or pure misery. . . .'

It was not only the newspapers that saw the story in 'sad clown' cartoon terms. Cleese and Skynner wanted to share the fruits of their discussions with a larger audience, so before they wrote their book, *Families and How to Survive Them*, they sent scripts for a ten-part television series on human relations to London Weekend. Television, with its less enquiring mind paradoxically combined with greater intellectual self-belief than newspapers, is usually adored by showbusiness people, but London Weekend greeted the idea with a yawn. Cleese told the writer Stephen Pile: 'Television is not interested in ideas. It employs people who either cannot think at all or have no insight. "Where are the pictures?" they keep saying. If Jesus Christ came back to this planet for twenty-four hours and agreed to do an interview on *Everyman* they would say, "Well, he's an outstanding talking head, but where are the pictures?" Put all this in if you can. I hate the bastards.'

In the event, *Families and How to Survive Them* (working title 'Kitchen Shrink') was published in the early 1980s to a stony reception. A series of dialogues between Cleese and Skynner based on tapes they made a couple of days each week, its broad theme was how people tend, from childhood, to 'screen off' or block difficult feelings and emotions, just as their parents did before them. Designed to be jargon-free in a subject area that worships self-aggrandizing mumbo-jumbo, *Families* got little publicity and the psychiatric world seemed unimpressed. But it sold 400 copies a week by word of mouth and a healthy 80,000 copies in the first year. Relate (then called the Marriage Guidance Council), to whose Bristol branch Cleese donated £10,000, uses it as a set text for trainee counsellors. The book was not successful in America; 'I think it's hard for Americans to think that something that is serious can be put across in a way that is fundamentally light-hearted,' Cleese said. *Families* was gruelling to write – the chapter on depression revived too many memories and gave Cleese ten days of deep gloom – but he claims that he never made a penny from it. It remains, however, along with *Fawlty Towers*, *Life of Brian* and *A Fish Called Wanda*, Cleese's proudest achievement. Skynner also found writing it a rewarding experience: 'John has an extraordinarily fine mind. I will present something to him from my knowledge of psychiatry and he will go off at a complete tangent, turn it on its head and give me a completely new insight into it.'

By the early 1990s, psychotherapy was starting to enjoy a small boom in Britain, but when the Cleese/Skynner book came out in 1983, the word hardly existed in the popular perception. Oliver James, a young clinical psychologist interested in popularizing the whole psychology field, wrote to Cleese after reading *Families* to comment on one or two points. Cleese replied with a very serious letter, and, like a couple of polite turn-of-the-century Viennese psychoanalysts, the two conducted a correspondence from addresses a few streets apart. James told Cleese he had an idea of making a psychological TV profile of the man who killed John Lennon. Soon, at Cleese's behest, he and James met for lunch at an Italian restaurant in the Fulham Road. James, who later became famous as a TV psychologist, was surprised to have been invited.

> He was exceptionally kind to me. I think he just thought, 'Here's somebody who's batting in the right direction,' even though I don't think he was that interested in what I was doing. I think he is a magnanimous and decent sort of person, albeit quite patriarchal and enjoying doing it, as well he should. He arrived on a cold spring day in 1983, a cashmere jersey round his shoulders. He had this thing about having walked, and spent time looking in shops because he was trying not to work all the time. I remember being quite struck by that.
>
> We sat down and within about two minutes of being seated, having got the menus, and him saying that the calves' liver was particularly good here, he took a deep breath and said, 'Do you feel that there is anything that you know for sure that is true?' That was the exact question, and I was completely staggered. I was really thrown by it. Although that was the sort of question at that stage of my life I really liked, one you could get your teeth into, it was a really heavy number. It wasn't so much the fact that here is an extremely famous person, whom you've only met for a couple of minutes, taking you out for lunch, but that it's a very, very difficult problem. It's a technical philosophical question regarding epistemology, but it's also an existential problem – do you feel inside yourself that anything is true, that you have any truth in you or that anybody else has any truth in them?
>
> Anyway, I said that I felt absolutely sure that certain things were true, although I trembled to say that because I knew that he was going to go for the jugular immediately. I think what I offered was certain things about the effect of childcare on one's personality as one grows up, and that there were

observations that George Orwell had made which I felt proved conclusively that there was such a thing as truth.

John didn't seem to believe that. He was sceptical. He didn't believe for sure that anything was definitely true, which seemed rather a miserable conclusion, a terribly unhappy thing to say both about yourself and your relationship to the world. If you say that you don't believe that anything is definitely true, that means you must always be sceptical of your own persona and your own motivation. That's a feeling of hopelessness.

I think I would describe his demeanour as really extremely earnest. There is this astonishing discrepancy between the man who's made you laugh more than anyone else and this man who is probably more humourless than anyone else you've met. There was no point in making any jokes, and he didn't make any. It's very odd to have a meal in which there is absolutely no humour. What I do remember was a great deal of spin on almost everything he said; you couldn't be quite sure of everything he said, though I don't think at any point I doubted for one moment that he seriously wanted to know if I believed that there was anything that was true.

As a result of the testing lunch, James put his ideas to Video Arts, and the film was made. He also found himself contrasting that strange meeting with a dinner party on a later occasion with Eric Idle; Idle had the entire table helpless with laughter for long stretches. 'It was terribly sad,' says James, 'that there was no television camera to record it. It was quite extraordinary.'

One of the most commonly held views about John Cleese is that he has forfeited his comic muse as a result of psychotherapy, that 'a calmer Cleese is a duller Cleese' – this despite the fact that he wrote the second series of *Fawlty Towers* towards the end of his group therapy period. The evidence usually marshalled to support this argument, which is no more easy to prove than the effects of psychoanalysis itself, is familiar: that Cleese takes himself too seriously, that he takes his distaste for nearly all the *Monty Python* output too far, and that *A Fish Called Wanda* – the most successful British comedy film ever – was actually not very funny at all, an assertion which if widespread would make

Cleese the most accomplished failed comic of all time. The 1988 break-up of Cleese's second marriage, coming under the media category of good old-fashioned misery (which as everybody knows makes clowns funnier), even gave some showbusiness writers the hope that Cleese's subsequent *Angst* would give birth to him inventing new, funny comic roles, a notion he squashed by telling the *Independent* that his life had 'got better and better every year – let me be accurate, for the last twelve years'.

Robin Skynner has no time for the accusation that taking the treatment has dampened his friend and former patient's comedy: 'John is naturally a very good-humoured, high-spirited person to be with. I don't think he needs to be funny to counteract some other tendency; that's not the impression I get of him these days,' he told the *Sunday Times* in 1988. Antony Jay said: 'I don't think he's changed that much. He may feel better inside, but he's still the same character.' Another friend says: 'John relaxed is staring at the ceiling drumming his fingernails.' Loss of creativity was an issue Cleese and Skynner looked at in their book, Cleese saying in the dialogue that he had friends who were avoiding therapy in order to preserve their creativity. Skynner argues that his experience, and that of other therapists, is that creative people become more creative after therapy; Cleese replies that his creativity did not necessarily increase, 'but I feel I've been freed to use it more widely; with less constraints, as it were.

'I think if you get a bit better adjusted you may lose a little compulsion to work. But my experience is that the more relaxed you get, the more creative you become. I mean *Wanda* is a much wider sweep of creativity than anything I did ten years ago.' This was in 1988. Interestingly, when asked in 1990 if he had been scared that therapy might make him less creative, Cleese took a different tack: 'No, I didn't give a damn. It's always struck me that life is a great deal more important than art. If I were given a choice between being Vincent van Gogh – one-eared, dead at thirty-seven, one review and one painting sold in his life – or being one of those unknown portrait painters who lived with six kids in a lovely big house, I'd be a portrait painter every time.'

Creativity, of course, did not have to mean being funny. Terry

Jones said at the time of the release of *Wanda*, 'John is capable of gloriously silly moments and when it happens it is wonderful. I just wish he would be silly a bit more often. He can also be a very serious man. He is very interested in what makes people tick and can be a bit introverted about it all. He has had an awful lot of psychiatry and I think that has helped him. All comedians go around with this fear of people wanting us to be funny and I think John carries that more than most. I don't worry about John too much because John worries about himself so much he doesn't need anyone else to do it for him. All his work with Robin Skynner has helped him sort himself out. He is much more comfortable than he used to be.'

Which was exactly what disturbed the writer John Morrish. He asked, in 1988: 'If a man's career is apparently based on the public exorcism of his own devils, what happens when the devils are tamed?' Morrish also noted similarities between Cleese's characters: Fawlty, Major Flack, Sheriff Langston and Stimpson were 'cold, pompous, bad-tempered, snobbish, a man at break-ing pitch. . . . One thing Cleese doesn't do is act. He hasn't really needed to – until now.' Morrish had a point; the man who at eighteen humiliated his own Classics master in front of his schoolmates and once snarled that he wished the Fleet Street gossip columnists would have a bash at Mother Teresa was by 1990 averring that he regarded the Nutrasweet Huxtables from TV's *The Cosby Show* as the embodiment of the ideal family.

Terry Gilliam was also keen to analyse Cleese at the time of *Wanda*: 'Frustration is the key to understanding John. He would love to bring reason into his life. He loves the idea of trying to control the world when it is clearly out of his control. I don't know why he wastes his time on analysis when he cleans his system out so well on film. John would say it's not important for him to make people laugh, but he'd be fooling himself. With *Wanda* a hit, he's on top form – bouncier than I've seen him for years.'

Brian Appleyard, one of Britain's most perceptive journalists, remained unconvinced by the psychoanalysed Cleese: 'Once psychoanalysis persuades you that you know what you're like, you become impossible. You discuss yourself with happy, irre-sponsible enthusiasm. You develop the concerned stare of the social worker, designed to establish that whoever you are talking to is either completely mad or terminally repressed. And you embrace your own flaws, such as inconsistency, happily imagining them to be lovable. Cleese is not quite there yet, but a perilous glibness has begun to intrude.

'He still aspires to a sort of limbo of languid incompetence,' Appleyard went on. Cleese told him that he was 'thinking of forming a lunch club called BLOCH – the British League of the Completely Hopeless. To join you have to take an oath saying: "I now realize I am completely hopeless." My main problem is I have to spend time with people who have not realized it.' In Appleyard's view, 'All those contradictions, the faintly smug air, and the implicit disclaimer that comes with every quote, leave one with the sensation that conversation is telling you less rather than more about the man.' It is an indicator of Cleese's admiration for informed argument, or perhaps of his ability after three years of group therapy to take criticism on the chin, that he remains highly respectful of Appleyard while scornfully dismissive of those who write reverential stories which invariably open with: 'And now for something completely different. . . .'

Cleese and Skynner's latest collaboration is another book, *Life and How to Survive It*. The book 'is very much about the healthy function of groups. It's stuff that's going to give us a lot of new films for Video Arts. It starts not with groups but with families.' Part of the book is about research done by a Jerry Lewis, who studied middle-class white families in Dallas and working-class black families in New York and found them all unhappy to varying degrees. The first chapter, Cleese says, will amplify his intellectual distrust of the concept of romantic love.

Life, as a sequel to *Families*, thus introduces Jerry Lewis as another fixture in the pantheon of intellectual gurus to whom John Cleese adheres. There was a strong whiff of self-parody in the lines Cleese wrote for Chapman and himself in *Life of Brian*:

Brian [Chapman]: 'I'm not the Messiah.'
Arthur [Cleese]: 'I should say you are, and I should know. I've followed a few.'

Cleese has always revered experts. As early as 1977, Tim Brooke-Taylor had indicated that Cleese was a 'sucker' for 'intellectual names'. More recently, Terry Gilliam has pointed out that Cleese 'surrounds himself with professional help – psychotherapists, trichologists, dentists, who, he feels, can give him greater insight into the world'. (A newer addition to the list is fitness instructors.) There is something curiously childlike about Cleese's eagerness not just to consider but to embrace new philosophies. It is as if he wishes continually to reinvent himself – the anti-establishment comic, the journalist, the businessman, the academic, the politician, the earnest advocate of therapy, the laid-back, tanned Hollywood star, the fitness-conscious sex symbol, the philosopher. And always, in each new reverie, there is a strong parental figure for him to respect, a father to supply the authority that poor, kind old Reg Cleese could never quite muster. Like a rarefied version of the great British hobbyist collecting stamps or beermats, it is unlikely that John Cleese's guru collection will ever be complete.

Nor does it contain exclusively the quirky and esoteric gurus he favours, the lesser and rarely spotted pundits such as G. I. Gurdjieff, Robert McKee, P. D. Ouspensky, Erich Fromm, Maurice Nicoll, Jacob Needleman and Norman Cousins. Henri Bergson is an old favourite, the Dalai Lama and even Jesus Christ have occupied a favoured spot in the collection, as have some less likely mentors. 'Video Arts films have very much caused me to keep my eye open for "Am I getting good service? Am I not getting good service?"' he expounded in a Radio 4 interview. 'Not quite so much in the judgemental sense, but because it becomes such a pleasure when you get somebody like the girl who sold me a pair of shoes two weeks ago who really knew what she was doing. You get such pleasure out of it because you're in the hands of experts.' When asked how and where he would most like to sightsee, he said sitting on a boat on the Nile: 'I would like two or three experts at my command to tell me all about the history, geology, flora and fauna of the Nile Valley.' And on the *Wogan* television show he discoursed, 'If I thought my comedy was going off I'd go and talk to someone who knew about comedy. . . . Same if I wanted to learn to be a better golfer, you know. You go to somebody who's an expert.'

He does not even find reading the works of his gurus particularly easy: 'I have the most appallingly slow reading speed, so sometimes it would take me about four weeks to get through a Jeffrey Archer. So, as my life consists of another thirty years or something like that, I can't afford to cruise through pop novels as people do on holiday. I tend to read fairly factual stuff and that drops into various areas. I'm very interested in psychology and psychiatry – I find very frequently the books are fascinating theoretically, but don't have any impact on me as I read them.'

Some believe, however, that as part of his consistent change-for-change's-sake policy, Cleese is moving on even from guru worship. One Oxford don invited to a dinner party with Cleese and his present girlfriend, an American psychoanalyst, Alyce Faye Eichelberger, was warned to expect an Oliver James-type meal of scholarly debate with every course. To his bemusement, the don was seated at the opposite end of the table from Cleese, next to and downwind of a busy evening in the cat litter tray, and barely exchanged a word with his host. 'The dinner parties have become terribly domestic. There's nobody who's going to be illuminating or drive the conversation in any other direction,' one friend says. At another recent dinner, the editor of the *Daily Telegraph*, Max Hastings, was steered into the kitchen by a reportedly chortling Cleese to be shown that the meal had been cooked by none other than the *Telegraph*'s head chef. Sophisticated joke? Obscure intellectual point? Hastings was baffled.

Leaving aside the possibility of guru fatigue, there is little sign of Cleese's seriousness waning. He is becoming increasingly interested in religion. 'I've had one or two experiences, which I don't want to talk about, which suggest to me that there is some spiritual dimension to the universe,' he told the author John Hind. 'And I simply say that it was a surprise when I came to believe it, because at seventeen I'd given up the C of E as being too unintelligent to be of interest.' Cleese has recently expressed an interest in meditation and Buddhism, and in 1991 he and Robin Skynner went on a semi-spiritual pilgrimage to Tibet where he made a video with the Dalai Lama.

Apart perhaps from psychotherapy, the most important philosophical influence on him in recent years has been the quasi-religious teachings of George Ivanovitch Gurdjieff and his disciples, Peter Ouspensky and Maurice Nicoll (Nicoll was a British pioneer in psychological medicine who taught on the inner meaning of Christian ideas and wrote one of Cleese's favourite books, the tinder-dry *Psychological Commentaries on the Teaching of Gurdjieff & Ouspensky*). Cleese was introduced to Gurdjieff's work in America by the man he regards as the only truly grown-up person he has ever met, the late Lord Pentland. Pentland, who died aged seventy-seven in 1984, was a tall and lanky eccentric, son of the Scottish Secretary in Asquith's government and great-nephew of the first man to cross the English Channel in a canoe. A studious-looking 21-year-old in 1928, he was president of the Cambridge Union, a leading young Liberal, joint editor of *Granta* and already famous for taking a rare step for an aristocrat – going into the business world. Pentland was entranced by Gordon Selfridge when he spoke at a Cambridge students' meeting about the more refreshing attitude to business in America compared to Britain and made his decision to get an engineering apprenticeship, then go into trade, on the spot. Instead of shooting grouse in the summer of 1928, as a young nobleman would have done, he got a job in the engine room of the liner *Mauretania*. Little was written of it in his lifetime, but Pentland also set up an institute in America for the study of Gurdjieff, who died in 1949.

The thinkers Lord Pentland familiarized Cleese with, the last of whom died in 1953, come under the category now known as 'esoteric Christianity'. Some of Cleese's schoolfriends remember that as a boy he seemed to get pleasure out of understanding things they could not penetrate; back in Weston-super-Mare it was *The Goons* and complex private jokes at the expense of teachers. It would be ridiculous to say that Cleese in his fifties reads obscure philosophy *because* it is obscure – although for a slow reader to get through dense volumes of Gurdjieff is a major achievement – but if a guru's curriculum vitae could be custom-made to suit John Cleese's sense of humour, it would be that of Gurdjieff, who makes Cleese's attempts at being a polymath seem half-hearted.

A Russian-Armenian of Greek parentage, Gurdjieff was a one-time Tibetan lama and a Russian double-agent working both as a revolutionary and as a government spy and friend to the court of the Tsar. He was shot on four different occasions. He helped to build railways and roads and traded in carpets and antiques, becoming extremely rich in the process. Adept in psychic powers, until 1910 he operated as a hypnotist and wonder-worker, and his main reputation is as an occultist. Gurdjieff referred to his 'repertoire of ideas, techniques and powers' as 'The System' which was to lead mankind away from imminent crisis by making us capable of showing the love needed to follow Christ's teachings.

Gurdjieff was famous for being enigmatic. One devoted pupil, Sophie Ouspensky, wrote: 'Many people got the impression that he was a gourmand, a man fond of good living in general, and it seemed to us that he often *wanted* to create this impression, although all of us saw that this was "acting".' Gurdjieff also had a lifelong predilection for pretty young women, this interest obviously also part of the act. At the Institute For Man's Harmonious Development, which he founded at Fontainebleau outside Paris, Gurdjieff sometimes revolted from the stupidity and narrowness of his own followers and shut himself away to find some better way of fulfilling his mission. At other times, he went so far as to hold gruelling experiments for days on end with unsuspecting groupies to test his techniques, sometimes misleading them to demonstrate the powers of suggestion. In the attempt to 'awaken' people – he believed most of mankind to be asleep – he also started using gymnastics, rhythms and dances of Dervish origins. (Could the silly walk possibly be Dervish-inspired, more of a silly whirl?) To help fund his Institute, Gurdjieff started many businesses, including oilfield ventures and setting up restaurants in Montmartre.

Gurdjieff's training methods were rather different from Video Arts'. He would make followers fast, sometimes for up to a fortnight. He had thirty pithy sayings painted (in Armenian) on the ceiling of his 'Study House', which was decked, among other things, with a stage, cushions, goat skins, Eastern musical instruments, painted windows and indoor fountains. ('Man is born with the capacity for a definite number of experiences. Economizing them, he prolongs his life,' was one aphorism. Another, extremely Cleesian: 'A mark of the perfected man is his ability to play to perfection any desired role in his external life while inwardly remaining free and not allowing himself to "blend" with anything proceeding outside of him.') 'Work' at the Institute wound down after Gurdjieff, a notoriously bad driver, crashed his car into a tree at 90 m.p.h. He turned to writing and people would flock to see him like acolytes on a pilgrimage.

Gurdjieff, John Cleese says, 'has made me realize how much emotions and attitudes that are fundamentally negative are valued in our culture. I'm beginning to prize things like a generosity of spirit. I got into it because two or three friends who seemed to me to possess wisdom, which is pretty rare, were all admirers of this body of thought. . . . This stuff contains for me what I think religion – real religion – must be. I don't think that in our ordinary frames of mind we're anywhere near a religious frame of mind. I think we've almost lost that in the Western world. But if I read a bit of Maurice Nicoll, it moves me to a different place in myself, and it's actually a place I like a lot better than the place that I usually inhabit.'

The basis of Nicoll's interpretation of Gurdjieff is that wars and other bad occurrences are not 'exceptional' but an inevitable consequence of mankind's penchant for negative emotions; we must therefore use negative feelings at a much higher level. 'For example, a man finding himself in the depths of despair, if he observes the situation and tries to remember himself, or tries to give himself any other kind of conscious shock at that particular moment, such as remembering his aim – that is, in other words, if he tries to "transform himself", to transform his mechanical reaction to the circumstances that surround him at that moment – may find to his astonishment that quite suddenly everything is changed, his mood of depression vanishes, and he finds himself in a new atmosphere from which he wonders how he could have been in his former state.' This elevated method of looking at life goes further. Nicoll argued that people consist of an inner essence and an outer personality. However successful one may be in external life, the inner life can be empty: 'The internal life needs developing and this is done by further developing the essence, which can only grow at the expense of the personality, thereby giving meaning to life and the teaching of the Gospels.'

A little less weighty, though it does not sound it, is a new science Cleese recently got into, Psychoneuroimmunology. In March 1988, he got the chance to play guru himself when he appeared at the UK/LA Festival with Norman Cousins, then seventy-two, a former editor of the *Saturday Review* and adjunct professor of the Medical Humanities at UCLA. They were promoting the new science, which proposes nothing more intimidating than the hoary old saying, 'Laughter is the best medicine'. Hearty laughter, the theory goes, releases morphine-like molecules which help to repair sick bodies. Cousins had apparently once cured himself of some condition with nothing more than vitamin C and Laurel and Hardy. Cleese, who said he accepted the invitation 'mainly because I wanted to meet Norman Cousins', and the guru held a ninety-minute dialogue at UCLA called 'New Dimensions in Healing'. Cleese kicked off by asking, 'What's the difference between Los Angeles and a pot of yoghurt? A pot of yoghurt has a living culture. . . . [to Cousins] I was just trying to heal them, Norman.' On the 'mind over matter' theme, Cleese also told a story about a visit he made to the dentist: 'during a heavy drilling session' the dentist gave him distilled water instead of an anaesthetic: 'He said it was a little experiment of his. But my face went completely numb.'

Then there is Jacob Needleman, Professor of Philosophy at San Francisco State University and author of a novel called *Sorcerers*, a metaphysical thriller about the adolescence of a boy called Eliot. Cleese, a friend, is one of Needleman's main promoters and his 'disciple'. While conventional religions present human change and development as an exceptional part of being (an unwelcome destabilizer), Needleman (with shades of Gurdjieff) proposes that 'to be alive, one is always in transition'. And after having been through adolescence, 'you must find different areas of unknowingness to explore'. 'People seem unaware of how extraordinarily difficult real change is,' Cleese, wearing his Needleman hat, told the *Guardian*. 'They can see that something is up, but all they do to change themselves is change the externals of their life; and it doesn't matter whether they go to Buenos Aires or marry somebody different because six months later they're in exactly the same position.'

Cleese's devotion to psychotherapy also helped him to develop his thinking on politics, which was always a minor preoccupation. His family voted Conservative, but he became a moderate Labour voter after Cambridge, supported the Labour Party at the beginning of his showbusiness career and later, after deciding they had 'some idea how to run business, which the Labour Party doesn't', became a fixture in the Social Democrats. He has declared for the Green Party, spoken at the Liberal Democrats' Conference, and expressed his admiration for some Conservative politicians, though in the main the kind of dissident Tories that Margaret Thatcher sacked. He is often asked if he will ever go into politics, having said back in the *Frost Report* days, when supporting Labour was as chic as being an armchair Sandinista in the 1980s, that he thought he would end up a politician. More recently, he has said he might give being an MP a try in his sixties, but he has been unusually consistent in maintaining that he thinks politics is basically not for him. Psychiatry has at once bred his libertarian side and made him see politics as an absurdly paranoid profession.

He says that he realized on entering therapy that 'I've always had a thing which I can't entirely explain about the necessity to be as free as possible. Why that should happen, unless it's a simple reaction to the slightly repressed atmosphere I grew up in, I don't know. But I've always felt very strongly that people should be as free as possible from other people's ways of controlling them.' He is both amused and disgusted by the tendency of politicians (in psychoanalytical terms) to 'project' on to other people the blame for a problem they themselves have caused. In October 1988, indeed, Cleese made a donation of nearly £100,000 to Sussex University to finance a three-year study into the 'psychological phenomenon of projection and denial'. 'That seems to me frightfully important as a bit of understanding of human nature, particularly for politicians, who seem to me a lot of the time to be behaving in a slightly, or even totally, paranoid way.' Cleese will own the copyright on the research and hopes to write a book about it with Skynner.

They were already wading into the subject in *Families and How to Survive Them*, which had a long section on 'Paranoia and Politics'. Their contention was that politicians regard all the unpleasant aspects of themselves as being the sole property of their opponents. So, for Labour, poor economic performance is caused entirely by deficient management and cannot possibly have anything to do with inefficient workers. The greater the paranoia of the politician, the more he will feel he must distance himself from ideologically unsound elements. In *Life of Brian*, Cleese enjoyed expanding on this theory, creating an extreme People's Front of Judaea, whose members hated rival Judaean nationalists more than the enemy, the Romans.

Although many people felt that Cleese had in this wonderful parody already got as many jokes as could ever be squeezed out of left-wing sectarian groups, he went on to toy with the idea of making a comedy series on politics. 'Do you know anyone that you like and respect who wants to go into politics?' he asked an interviewer in 1980. 'It's a really dreary, rotten job. I try to view the world from a psychological rather than sociological standpoint, and when you do that you find the politicians are just working out their childhood problems.'

The basis of the show was to be the satire of the political centre, 'a really immoderate attack on immoderates by outstandingly moderate people,' he said. 'There's plenty of ammunition for someone who stands roughly in the middle politically. Look at mixed-ability schools, for instance. They are supposed to be a good idea, but nobody complains that Nottingham Forest is an elitist football club and nobody would want to listen to a mixed-ability orchestra.' The SDP, which started with high hopes in 1981, claimed Cleese as an early supporter. The former Labour foreign secretary Dr David Owen – another Cleese polymath – was one of the original 'gang of four' and a friend. Cleese by now regarded himself as a 'good old eighteenth-century liberal'. 'The only thing Labour and Conservative can agree on,' he said, 'is that they don't want the Alliance to have any publicity because it's breaking up their paranoid confrontation. Here the two of them are feeling very important and then somebody else comes along and says, "Can we join in?" and they say "Go away, this is private".' Ironically, Cleese later felt that the SDP had let him down by turning out to be as entrenched in paranoid confrontation as the two main parties.

In December 1985, Cleese fronted a ten-minute party political broadcast, made by Video Arts for the SDP. He wrote the script and smiled grimly through the Minister of Silly Walks/Silly Talks headlines which guaranteed that the SDP would get the highest ever television ratings for a party political. The broadcast began with Cleese, yawning, sitting in the traditional sombre office and saying: 'I am sorry, but this is a party political broadcast, and you know how boring they are. This one, I'm afraid, promises to be quite outstandingly tedious, because it's all about proportional representation. [yawn] And don't complain to me it's boring because I know in advance what I'm going to say. So the level of boredom I shall experience during the next ten minutes will be really appalling, compared even with yours.' He then made some jokes and reminded the audience that 'there's probably snooker on the other channel, all three, probably'. It concluded with Cleese addressing someone off-camera, asking 'Was that all right?' The camera pulled back to show David Owen: 'Yes, it's OK.'

The broadcast had a marvellously chaotic aftermath. As Cleese had barely mentioned the SDP, believing he was doing an Alliance commercial, his office when asked played safe and said he was a member of both the Liberals and the SDP – which turned out to be an expellable offence in the SDP. 'Much to my surprise,' Cleese explained – 'I'm officially down only as a supporter of both parties – and a member of neither. Entirely thanks to my own incompetence, I have no party to be expelled from.' This hiccup aside, the broadcast was a success. The party got several thousand complimentary phone calls the next morning and 5,000 membership enquiries. The press loved it, and even Dennis Skinner, the voluble Labour left-winger, was able to add it to his magnificent record of Parliamentary one-liners. He immediately started to call out 'Come on, Basil' every time David Owen got up to make a speech; then once, when David Steel entered, Skinner shouted 'Ay oop, Manuel'.

In May 1989, Cleese managed the political feat of appearing in another SDP broadcast while no longer supporting the party. He had filmed his comic political promotion four years earlier, but he didn't have the heart to refuse when Dr David Owen rang him to ask if the SDP could use a clip to pad out the new broadcast. 'I think it is very sad what has happened to the SDP, but I still believe there is a need for a centre party in British politics,' he said, urging the SDP and Paddy Ashdown's Liberal Democrats to merge. He was now giving support and money to the Ecology Party, 'because it's the one thing I know I believe in. My politics are those of bewilderment.'

A year later, Cleese was spectacularly back in the fold when he addressed the Liberal Democrats' Conference in Blackpool. 'Tonight I am not appearing as the worst hotelier in the Western world,' he told the be-sandalled masses. 'My fifty years have shown me that . . . few people know what they are talking about. I don't mean idiots who don't know. It's everyone.' Cleese called for constitutional reforms, including proportional representation, a bill of rights and a Freedom of Information Act. In several lengthy interviews, he set out something of a political manifesto for his rounded, post-analysis, post-business, post-Gurdjieff self: he believed in delegation, the two-way flow of information and feedback, respect for individuals, particularly eccentrics, and the revealing, rather than the concealment, of mistakes. Cleese was by now convinced that the Democrats' day was within sight: 'I think the door will suddenly open, something will go wrong with the other two parties and that will be our chance. I read enough history to know that these things always take a bit of time – it will probably take us five to ten years.'

A few days later, at the Conservative Party Conference in Bournemouth, Mrs Thatcher, just before being deposed as Prime Minister, borrowed cheekily from Cleese for her closing address. She referred to the Democrats' new symbol, a bird: 'Politics is a serious business, and one should not lower the tone unduly. So I will say only this of the Liberal Democrat symbol and the party it symbolizes. This is an ex-parrot. It is not merely stunned. It has ceased to be, expired and gone to meet its maker.' Satisfyingly for Cleese, the dead parrot then immediately went on to win a landslide victory in the Eastbourne by-election. Margaret Thatcher, on the other hand, fell off her perch within weeks to join the Cabinet invisible.

10 *The Funniest Man in the World*

Never forget that only dead fish swim with the stream.

Said to Malcolm Muggeridge, 1964

W hen John Cleese went to live on his own in his new Holland Park house in October 1977, the first series of *Fawlty Towers* was behind him, the second a long way ahead; his first marriage was in the past, but he had yet to meet his second wife. This was not, however, some empty, wandering period in his life. That same autumn, he brought to an end his attendance at group therapy sessions with Dr Skynner ('coming out' of therapy, for the uninitiated, is a very big decision, taken in consultation with the therapist and the group) and sank his teeth voraciously into what for him and the rest of the Pythons was the meatiest project they had ever considered.

There was a rare accord, almost a sense of mission, among the six that *Monty Python's Life of Brian*, an attack on the idiocy and gullibility of mindless 'followers' of all kinds – but especially of religion and politics – was as important as a comedy film could be. 'I remember *Life of Brian* as being an enormously happy experience because, by coincidence, we all had the same kind of views and feelings about the subject and I think that's our masterpiece. That's what I'd like to be judged by in the future,'

211

Cleese says. Yet none of the Pythons could have known either how good the film would be or how much controversy it would unleash.

The idea for a Bible story was in progress even before the *Holy Grail* film had been completed. At the New York party to launch *Holy Grail* in spring 1975, Eric Idle suggested 'Jesus Christ: Lust for Glory' as a title. Nearly a year later, in a Chinese restaurant in Soho's Gerrard Street, the Pythons were still mulling it over. They started writing the film in December 1976, a month after Mrs Mary Whitehouse had brought a private prosecution for blasphemy against the editor of *Gay News* for publishing a poem suggesting that Christ was a homosexual. The Pythons had donated money to the fighting fund, but the editor, Denis Lemon, lost the case in July 1977 (the month in which the first lengthy draft of *Brian* was completed) and was given an eighteen-month suspended sentence and fined £500, while *Gay News* was fined £1,000.

At the beginning of the collaboration, the Pythons were unsure where the idea was going. Almost the only certainty was that the hero would be called Brian. In one plan St Brian was to be the thirteenth disciple, a businessman who can't make the Last Supper because he is giving a dinner party that night, arranges to meet his co-disciples in the garden afterwards, but goes to a club called The Garden by mistake. 'We tried this,' says Cleese, 'and we found that it just didn't work. Because the moment you got really near the figure of Christ, it just really wasn't funny because Christ was wise and flexible and intelligent and he didn't have any of the things that comedy is about – envy, greed, malice, avarice, lust, stupidity.'

With the filming date looming nearer – a final scripting, casting and water-skiing fortnight in Barbados was fixed for after Christmas 1977 – Cleese was still doing a few comic odd jobs. He appeared on *The Muppet Show* and was suitably impressed, as was six-and-a-half-year-old Cynthia. 'Those little creatures are so realistic that it doesn't seem to require any jump of imagination,' he enthused afterwards. 'Doing the TV show, I had a little scene with Kermit. We did it two or three times and it wasn't quite right – we were rehearsing our way towards a good take. We did the shot and the director shouted, ''Cut!'' I knew it was a good one, and without thinking, I patted Kermit on the head!' (Cleese's enthusiasm for Frank Oz and the late Jim Henson led him to make a cameo appearance as a British aristocrat in the feature film *The Great Muppet Caper* in 1981.)

In Barbados, Cleese got up to swim at 7.15 each morning and relaxed by re-reading his major showbusiness flop from prep school days, *Twelfth Night*. 'He claims that Shakespeare's jokes wouldn't even get on a BBC radio show these days,' Michael Palin noted in his diary. 'John will not be moved from his growing conviction that much of Shakespeare is second rate and panto, and he wanders off in his Muppet T-shirt shouting "Zounds!" and "Forsooth!" much to the amazement of the local labour force who appear in the morning to rake the grass.' A steady stream of showbusiness visitors popped by while the Pythons were in Barbados, including Mick Jagger and Jerry Hall, Keith Moon, Des O'Connor and Alan Price. The final form of the film was now established; Brian Cohen was to be a reluctant Messiah born in a stable next door to Jesus. The others talked Cleese out of playing Brian, 'And they were absolutely right. I was much better doing what I did – it was just that I had never played one character all the way through a film. In fact, I didn't until I played Giles Flack in *Privates on Parade*.' In *Brian* it was agreed that Cleese would play, among other roles, A Wise Man; Reg (of course) – the Leader of the People's Front of Judaea; a Jewish Official at a Stoning; and a Roman Centurion.

The film was to be shot in Tunisia, using Zeffirelli's old sets for *Jesus of Nazareth*. The start, however, was then delayed for six months after EMI's Lord Delfont, under pressure from the Whitehouse brigade (and, as a leading Jewish businessman, doubly sensitive about offending Christianity), withdrew a £2 million deal. George Harrison and his American business partner eventually rescued *Brian* with money from the USA. Shooting, based first at Monastir, then at Gabes, began at almost the moment Cleese became legally divorced from Connie Booth.

For Cleese, connoisseur of bad service, there was a delightful irony in the choice of hotel, the Oasis, a low-slung eighty-roomed white affair on a scruffy stretch of beach. The faded hotel brochure, unchanged today, promises 'For your relax, library, band or stereo records'. 'It was the worst hotel in the world,' Cleese guffawed on *The Dick Cavett Show* more than a year later. 'I went to the front desk just after I got there, and I said to the man in my appalling French, "Excuse me, there's no glass in my room," and he said, proudly, "There are no glasses in any of the rooms." So I said, "Well, could I have one?" And he said, "Why?" And I said, "Well I have a sore throat and want to take a pill," and he said, "Get one from the bar." And that was the first two minutes there. And it went on like that with the two most malevolent breakfast waiters I've ever come across.'

The finished film, shortened by half an hour from the rough cut, took more than $10 million in the USA before it even opened in Britain. It eventually grossed $75 million. Religious objectors there were enormously angry; leading orthodox Jews found themselves in an unlikely alliance with redneck fundamentalist Christians, most of whom naturally had never seen the film but knew someone who had. A Catholic leader declared it a sin to see *Life of Brian*, while more thoughtful Christian and Jewish leaders defended its right to be shown. Two days after the general release in America, Dick Cavett asked Cleese to what extent protesters had increased box office takings. 'Phenomenal,' he breezed. 'They have actually made me rich. I feel we should send them something like a crate of champagne. There's no question. I think originally the movie might have gone into 200 movie houses. And once the protest started it was soon decided to put it into 600. It is wonderful that when people embark upon a course of action, they can really achieve something so totally counter-productive. One can only think that either they're profoundly stupid – and these people are obviously not – or they become so enraged that they are incapable of thinking.'

Throughout the *Life of Brian* debate, Cleese, desperately proud of the film, was at his most rounded and self-possessed: humorous, liberal, polite and logical in his response to accusations of blasphemy. Having an issue of real importance to deal with, rather than tedious discussions about Silly Walks, sparked his intellect as nothing in the entertainment world had previously done. He told Dick Cavett: 'It may sound surprising, but I think *Brian* is a religious film. I think all the messages in it, in fact, are profoundly religious . . . it simply depends on what you mean by religion.' If religion meant accepting everything you were told, then *Brian* was an anti-religious film. Cleese pointed out his favourite exchange in the film, which, he claims, never gets a laugh:

Brian: 'You've all got to work it out for yourselves.'
Crowd: 'Yes, yes! We've got to work it out for ourselves.'
Brian: 'Exactly.'
Crowd: 'Tell us more.'

'I see an awful lot on television the whole time that I find offensive,' Cleese cleverly added, though he hardly needed to use his full battery of debating guns for his converted PBS audience. 'We had a programme called *Stars on Sunday* where all the most lovable of the most lovable singers came on and sang hymns. I just thought it was punishable. But a lot of people thought this was religion, and it sent them off to dinner with a good, warm glow. To me, it was offensive, but I wouldn't try and stop it.'

The Pythons were not quite sure what to expect when they brought the film to Mrs Thatcher's new England in November 1979. Cleese had his mother Muriel on his side, promoting the film on radio advertisements in which she pleads with listeners to see *Brian* and make it a success so that she won't have to go into an old people's home. The commercial won her two awards.

On other fronts, the battle became more serious. The Festival of Light issued a bulletin which stated its case more coolly than the excitable American fundamentalists: 'It's a parody of the life of Our Lord Jesus Christ, showing him as an ignorant zealot in the confused political scene of first-century Palestine. Obscene language is put into the mouth of Brian—Jesus, and his Mother is made into a comic character.' They warned against over-reacting to the film, agreeing that Brian was not Jesus, but still wanted a ban.

On the day of *Brian's* release in Britain, Cleese and Michael Palin were confronted with Dr Mervyn Stockwood, Bishop of Southwark, and Malcolm Muggeridge on *Friday Night Saturday Morning*, a late-night BBC2 discussion show hosted by Tim Rice. The Pythons were surprised to be vehemently criticized by the two deeply respected elders, who said the film was not only blasphemous but also tenth-rate. Cleese and Palin were polite to begin with and tried to quell the feelings of a studio audience evidently on their side. Muggeridge said that if the film had been about Islam instead of Christianity, the people who were currently praising it would be its loudest critics. Cleese, whose debating skills had hardly been stretched by the discussion in America, was on magnificent form. Moustache atwitch with anger, he replied: 'You're right. Four hundred years ago we would have been burnt for making this film. Now I'm suggesting that we've made an advance.' Undeterred by the laughter of the audience, Muggeridge ploughed on to describe it as a 'miserable little film'. Rhetorically, he asked whether *Life of Brian* would be remembered years hence like, say, Chartres Cathedral. It was an impressively sardonic line but Cleese swatted it down with equal scorn; 'Not a funny building,' he shot back, his eyes widening and flashing with a kind of glint that appears in the eyes of a batsman who has just hit six off a wickedly spinning ball. Cleese consistently maintained that the film was an attack not on Christianity but on the followers of false prophets. Stockwood parted by telling the Pythons that they would certainly get their thirty pieces of silver.

In some of Britain's shire counties, thanks to the local councils, they did not. *Brian* was banned in Hereford and Worcester, most of Berkshire, Cornwall and in Harrogate, North Yorkshire (where, to be fair, breathing is also frowned upon). Other councils, such as Surrey, gave it an X certificate. In the West Country, where the Pythons' aged accessory to blasphemy Muriel lived, *Brian* did badly, partly because of a joint letter from the Bishop of Bath & Wells, the Roman Catholic Bishop of Clifton, the Chairman of the Bristol Methodists and the local branch of the United Reformed Church that was sent to all Avon and Somerset district councils. Many demanded an X certificate, although Weston-super-Mare and Bristol made no ruling against the film's AA certificate.

A thirteen-minute short film, shown before *Life of Brian, Away From It All*, attracted a different sort of attention. Written by Clare Taylor, directed and produced by her and Cleese and starring Cleese (uncredited for a joke) as Nigel Farquhar-Bennett, the short was a spoof travelogue in which the narrator parodies the terrible quality of the film and script he is narrating. 'Surely no artist before John Cleese has been given such liberty to bite the hand that feeds him,' commented the British Film Institute's *Monthly Film Bulletin*, a publication for film critics and insiders, which continued: 'His anti-travelogue is being shown in the very cinema Cleese attacks for booking such "cheapo, rip-off fillers". The esteem in which he is held might be measured by his licence to instruct the audience, with obvious passion, to go out and complain to the manager.'

Well as Cleese handled the row over *Life of Brian* and good as the film was, he understandably tired of the issue after a few years. After Graham Chapman's death in 1989, a day before *Monty Python*'s twentieth anniversary, a group of Chapman's friends asked Julian Doyle, who edited *Brian*, to release as a commemorative piece a version he has of the film called *Life After Brian*, which contains all the scenes that ended up cut. The deleted scenes included Eric Idle as Otto, a Jewish Nazi-style leader of a suicide squad who appears without explanation only in the final scenes of the released version of *Brian*. Doyle was not surprised that Cleese used the veto power all the Pythons have to block the uncut version (a full two and a quarter hours) going out even on limited release. 'John said he couldn't be bothered, which is what he always says to mean "no", but then he went into it and said he didn't want the whole issue opened up all over again.'

In the happy afterglow of *Life of Brian*, the Pythons decided quickly to make another film. They had been told by a financial adviser that they 'would never need to work again' if they cashed in on *Brian*'s success. (The adviser was wrong; they did.) Cleese for once did not need persuading to take part in another Python project. The wise Terry Gilliam by now had the measure of his old friend: 'John hasn't changed at all. For the past thirteen years, ever since we started out, he's wanted to get out of the group and wanted to do something else. But as long as we have somewhere for him to lie down and rest his back, he'll probably stick around.' Several fragmented scenes of what was to become *The Meaning of Life* were shot in 1980. Cleese was full of enthusiasm about a script that would, he said, 'evolve' with team members writing in pairs. After nine weeks' work, he admitted they had got no further than a unifying idea. 'We've been agreeing on the humour but not on the theory of the plot [which involves] the Army, public school life and British expeditions – a sort of Empire feel. But it could all change by next week.' It fell to Cleese to suggest they put the project on ice until they found a plot.

He had a pile of television advertisements (in Britain, Australian, Holland and Scandinavia) to make, and a new renaissance to be getting on with – as a Shakespearean actor. Dr Jonathan Miller cast him as Petruchio in his BBC TV production of *The Taming of the Shrew*, part of a season of BBC Shakespeares. It was Cleese's first 'serious' acting role since his schooldays. Miller says he chose Cleese 'because I had seen him in various guises in *Monty Python* and spotted a vigorous stock there, without any leaves or flowers but highly suggestive of what might develop when planted and nourished with a classic text'. He was interested in combining the irritability of Basil Fawlty with what he saw as 'strange sympathetic depths in the man'.

Cleese had hitherto not been a great fan of Shakespeare – on *Desert Island Discs*, he had even declined his copy of Shakespeare's collected works. 'When Jonathan Miller approached me to do Shakespeare, I told him: "I like you, Jonathan, but I hate Shakespeare. Correction – I hate the way Shakespeare is always done. There is a style to Shakespearean acting that I call the Ian McKellen school of acting, which is the declaratory school of acting. I know it's traditional and a lot of people like it and Ian gets a drama award for doing it every year in London, but for me it is silly posturing and extremely affected and absolutely pointless because it does not correspond to any human behaviour I have ever seen except that of actors playing Shakespeare." When I said all of that Jonathan said, "That's the reason I want you to do it."'

Cleese grew a beard for the part and received mixed reviews when the play was screened in October, a few weeks after the Pythons performed at the Hollywood Bowl. Predictably, some critics found Basil in Petruchio, while others were disappointed that they could not. One remarked on Cleese having chosen to play the rather sexy, manly role tenderly and diffidently rather than maniacally. He didn't play it for laughs which led another critic to declare the production disappointingly straight. Cleese himself thought he was being comic: 'This is a comedy, and I just hope people accept it the way I play it,' he told the *Observer*. He added, somewhat plaintively, 'I couldn't play anything serious. People would have all the wrong expectations.'

Before the production, he told Miller he thought of the *Shrew* as 'a lot of thigh-slapping and knocking wine glasses over, a lot of what Jonathan calls "twinkly" and a great deal of loud, unmotivated laughter'. He says Miller gave him another point of view, that Petruchio was really putting on a front in order to win Kate's affection, a deliberately assumed style of behaviour much as a psychiatrist might adopt with a patient. Cleese recounts how he showed the play to a psychiatrist who said: 'This is amazing. I've been absolutely falling over with this first scene between Petruchio and Kate. This is exactly what I do with shrews down to the last inflection, the last semi-colon.' 'Think of it,' exclaimed a revitalized Cleese, 'Shakespeare instinctively knew what psychiatry has taken 400 years to learn.'

The Petruchio beard met its end at seven o'clock one morning shortly after the making of the *Shrew*, in Epping Forest, Essex, when Cleese grudgingly shaved it off to play the part of Robin Hood in Terry Gilliam's film *Time Bandits*. Cleese later learned that Gilliam really wanted Michael Palin for the role, but was advised by Denis O'Brien, George Harrison's partner in Hand-Made Films, that Cleese would help the film sell in America. Cleese performed his role to the brief, which stated that Robin Hood should 'be played like the Duke of Kent'. He duly shook hands with dwarf bandits saying, 'So you're a robber, jolly good', and 'Have you met the poor?'

Meanwhile, the search for a plot for *The Meaning of Life* continued. Inspiration was certainly not forthcoming in July, when ABBA, the Swedish supergroup, were in London to promote *Winner Takes It All* and expressed a desire to link with Cleese in a musical venture. 'It's just that we must work with John . . . he's the funniest man in the world.' Forsaking the attractions of Stockholm, the Pythons at Cleese's suggestion went instead to Los Angeles in September to perform a set of 'golden oldies' (Palin's phrase) and some new material from the group's latest record album. The venue was the Hollywood Bowl, the crowds for four nights as big as 8,000. Cleese was quite candid to a reporter from *Rolling Stone*: 'I don't know if the others have told you the truth. The real reason we're playing the Hollywood Bowl is that we're absolutely stuck on our next movie . . . it made sense to do these shows: we're able to come to Los Angeles, have a holiday in the sun and make enough money to tide us over.'

The *Rolling Stone* piece went on: 'On the fourth and final night in LA the audience is rabid and fanatical, some members dressed in Pythonesque drag. When Cleese walks through the crowd hawking a frozen albatross, half-a-dozen fans answer his cries of "Albatross!" with "What flavour is it?" If he had any trouble finding Jones in the crowd, those fans would clearly be willing and able to finish the sketch themselves.' There were huge ovations for the parrot and lumberjack sketches: 'It's hysterically funny at times, but it's also unsettling. The crowd laughs because it's Python doing their hits, not because they're adding anything to stock routines.'

Somewhere in the audience on one of those four warm nights in Los Angeles, regarding Cleese with what she describes as 'mild curiosity at first sight', was a television producer called Barbara Trentham, then aged thirty-six. Within four months, she would become John Cleese's second wife. Every inch the outgoing Californian blonde beauty, if her 'mild curiosity' joke had an understated English ring to it, it was because English culture was not new to her; she had previously been married to an Oxford hockey blue, Giles Trentham. Even after the marriage to Cleese ended, she opted to stay in England.

John and 'Babs' met at a pre-performance party. 'There I was,' recounts Cleese, 'parading around in drag with this terrible blond wig, false boobs and carpet slippers. And she thought, "This man has to be interesting."' As they discovered rapidly at lunch together, Babs held a lot of attractions for Cleese. She was direct and assertive, and, above all, had a wealth of different interests. An art major, she had been an actress (up to a point – a small part in the film *Rollerball*) and a model with the London agency Models One, had worked in London for Sotheby's and been an on-screen reporter back in America for

CBS News. When she met Cleese, she even possessed that vital, against-the-grain, comic incongruity he seeks out: she was producing and directing film segments for the ABC TV prime-time show *Those Amazing Animals*. This involved a lot of serious contemplation of water-skiing rabbits, dancing oryxes and basketball-playing raccoons, jokey preoccupations that filled the first few weeks of their romance. He found Babs's ability to 'boss twenty men around' on film shoots compelling stuff after nearly forty years in which the two most important women in his life, his mother and Connie Booth, had been shy and retiring. 'I remember two-thirds through lunch saying "I think you should marry me, then I can sit upstairs reading and you can sit downstairs painting." She thought it was some kind of cheap line. Babs has great spark, she's very brave. I'd like a little more courage, I'm still a touch too meek,' Cleese commented after they married.

Babs had just come out of a relationship with Van Gordon Sauter, then vice-president and general manager of KNXT-TV in Los Angeles. Burly and bearded, Sauter lived on a 45-foot Hunter houseboat at Marina del Rey and commuted by Jeep to KNXT's Hollywood studios, where he was known for dressing in khakis and not wearing socks. Just before Babs's meeting with Cleese, Sauter left LA for New York where he became CBS Sports president and got married.

On 15 February 1981, Cleese and Trentham married in Los Angeles, much to the surprise of the British press. She'd refused to marry on St Valentine's Day because it would have been too soppy. Cleese announced the nuptial news to the US press as 'a pathetic bit of tattle'. In London the day before the wedding, the *Mirror* ran an interview with Cleese by Colin Dangaard, who had seen Cleese in the Beverly Hills Tennis Club. Cleese spoke at length about his pet theme of American women, their rare blend of brains and attractiveness, and went on, 'Marriage is one of the few things in the world that is actually worthwhile. Mind you, my taste in women has changed. They no longer have to be beautiful. I have begun to appreciate character over beauty – and a few lines *do* add character. . . . Something happens when you live on your own. You discover it's not so bad. You therefore feel you're going to sell your life very dearly the next time around.' A rather good joke at the *Mirror*'s expense, he married the day after the interview appeared, the ceremony at Barbara's apartment conducted by a hired judge. It had not been part of any plan to marry another American, he later said – but he agreed that the growing tendency did neatly skate round his problem of not knowing where he fitted into the British class system, 'the one thing I'd rather get rid of in this country than anything else'.

The couple flew into Heathrow from Los Angeles a fortnight after their marriage, Barbara clutching a three-foot toy flamingo called Ingrams, which they'd spotted for half price in a shop window and bought out of pity. They announced that they intended to keep up Babs's flat in Los Angeles. Cleese: 'We want to live in Britain because although the people in LA are very nice the city itself is an awful place.' They moved into the Holland Park house, which Cleese was gradually getting round to decorating, and converted an outhouse into a painter's studio for Babs. *En route* to a holiday in Florence, they were hijacked by some reporters at Heathrow. 'With a face straight as a clothes peg,' recorded the *Daily Express*, 'he insisted he was going to Nepal to perform a ballet based on the life of Eric Heffer, MP. His co-star was to be a Yeti.'

Quiet as his first year married to Barbara was – directing Amnesty International's *The Secret Policeman's Other Ball* was the major task of 1981 – the next year was busy. In 1982, he wrote *The Meaning of Life* with the Pythons which went into production in the summer, and starred in *Privates on Parade*, a HandMade film about a British Army song and dance troupe (the SADUSEA, the Song and Dance Unit South-East Asia) performing in Malaya at the time of the 1947 Communist rebellion. *Privates* went into production in May 1982, just as Argentinian troops were invading the Falklands. The first weeks of filming were at Aldershot army base with the Task Force round-up well in hand. Cleese played Major Giles Flack, whom he called 'the second stupidest man on the screen. Well, there is one other character who's stupider . . . probably. Flack is the kindest, most well-meaning complete upper-class twit. He tries to talk to the soldiers in what he thinks is their own language, saying things like "Lor Luv a Duck!" and "Stone the Crows!" And he never realizes that the whole disaster that befalls the troupe – one is killed, another has his balls shot off – is his own fault.'

Cleese refused to take star billing because he regarded the film as a team effort and was incensed that the television trailer for *Privates* centred on a silly walk he had done for the end titles, which gave the misleading impression that the film was some kind of *Monty Python* compilation. Cleese worried that the Americans might not understand the film (they didn't) but thought that after seeing Dustin Hoffman in *Tootsie*, they would appreciate the cultural background to Denis Quilley's drag role. (Unlikely: 'I took Barbara to see our great friend Tim Brooke-Taylor in a pantomime,' Cleese later said, 'and she was distinctly fazed by all this transexualism with principal boys, two girls supposed to be in love with each other and the mother played by a man.')

The Meaning of Life, which was released in Britain in June 1983, four months after *Privates on Parade*, turned out to be the poorest Monty Python effort, as Cleese acknowledges – though he maintains that at least two of the Pythons regard it as better than *Life of Brian*. American-backed, it seemed to be aimed at exploiting the Americans' new-found thirst for outrageousness, which was beginning to pall for the more discriminating among British filmgoers. The group had gone to Jamaica to write *The Meaning of Life*, but the creative block first encountered in 1980 had continued. Cleese suggested they just have a holiday instead. Then Terry Jones, the endlessly enthusiastic director, made them start work at breakfast one morning and by the weekend they had the outline.

Cleese had a thoroughly unfulfilling time making the film. Mike Bygrave, reporting for *You* magazine from the Elstree set, noted how irritable he became on one occasion when they had to wait for the right light. 'What are we waiting for? Is there film in the camera? Is the camera pointing roughly in our direction?' he reported Cleese as snapping. Michael Palin observed that you called him Mr Cleese or Sir if you knew him well. The 'John Cleese in a bad mood' angle eventually got out of hand. A story reached the *Sun* that 120 'black' extras (Glasgow students) had refused to take part in a re-enactment of the battle of Rorke's Drift in Zulu costume on a *Meaning of Life* location in

Scotland. They were supposedly complaining about typecasting. The paper reported: 'As the black warriors downed their spears, the heavens opened and long-legged Cleese leaped about among the extras demanding "Which of you bastards did a rain dance?"' Cleese offered to pay £10,000 to charity if the *Sun* could prove he made the remark. They didn't apologize and stood by their report, so he took them to the Press Council, which upheld his complaint. According to one member of the film crew, the extras were merely griping about being cold; the alleged remark simply never happened.

Cleese called the finished *Meaning of Life* 'a dog's breakfast, with about six great things in it and a lot of stuff that's not up to scratch'. His favourite scene, surprisingly perhaps, was Palin and Jones's obese Mr Creosote vomiting and finally exploding in a restaurant as a result of eating 'just one wafer-thin mint' proffered by Cleese as an obsequious and unflappable French waiter, his funniest part, he says, in the film. Barbara found the sketch 'hard to take' and, for a time, the Pythons didn't think it was funny enough to use. Cleese loved it 'because it has to do with greed which is a fascinating thing'. On the other hand, he took great exception to a speech by Eric Idle at the end of a Boer War sketch. 'He said something like, "You know I killed fifteen people today. If I'd been back in England, they'd have locked me up. Here, they give me a medal." Well, I don't know what that's supposed to say that most people haven't already under-stood by the age of sixteen. It seemed to me not to contribute anything. But the others felt it was an important and valid point.'

As he got older, a lot of Python material seemed puerile to Cleese, even if his colleagues were still in stitches over it. Like a lot of actors, he has never seen the final edit of some of his work, only the cutting-room versions. In 1986, Cleese was editing the first three *Python* series for video and says he was shocked at the standard of the comedy: 'I thought a lot of the material was really kind of weak. The first series intrinsically has the funniest material by quite a long way. The second series is very skilfully done, playing around with the format, making shows intertwine rather nicely, playing tricks on the audience. We got very good at that. But the essentially funny material was from the first series.'

The Meaning of Life was the last true Python film collaboration. Yet also in 1983, more for old times' sake than faith in the script, Cleese agreed to appear in a film written by Graham Chapman, Peter Cook and Bernard McKenna. *Yellowbeard* proved to be a completely disastrous swashbuckling spoof, despite its long list of ill-used stars. Cleese played a Blind ('I have acute hearing') Pew 'whose Mummerset accent,' commented one critic, 'comes off as a misconceived tribute to Tony Hancock's impersonation of Robert Newton'.

The early-to-mid 1980s were a curious time for Cleese, who was now like some vast oil tanker trying to change direction but finding that with the momentum of *Fawlty* and *Python* and the *Python* films behind him, a change of course was a slow process. In June 1983, just before *Families and How to Survive Them* came out, he turned down an offer of $500,000 to play a comedy secret agent, as well as a part in Tony Palmer's *Wagner* which really wanted Basil Fawlty. 'They sent me two pages of script. All the character did was rant and rave and pull a woman's hair. Then they added insult to injury by saying they thought they might ask Prunella Scales to play my wife.' Barbara became pregnant in the spring of 1983, at the time of the release of *The Meaning of Life*, and towards the end of the difficult pregnancy – she had to stay quietly at home for five months – he started planning the one project he had always hankered after, *A Fish Called Wanda*, a film that would be 'state of the art' Cleese, in which he could throw over every cliché that had dogged his career, apply every management technique to the production, and build his best temporary family of actors and technicians around him and the superpaternal figure of his director, Charles Crichton. In the meanwhile, he almost trod water, drumming up interest in psychotherapy, doing Amnesty concerts, commercials and party politicals – as well as two more films, both oddities, and both done primarily to keep income flowing in during the run-up to *Wanda*.

Silverado was a straight (almost) Western, in which Cleese played Sheriff Langston of Turley, an Englishman. It was an entirely American film, made in New Mexico. Cleese was uncharacteristically effusive, according to the studio. Working on *Silverado* had been 'the most enjoyable experience in twenty years' filming. I mean, to come to New Mexico and have free riding lessons . . . just great! . . . Larry Kasdan [the director] has a very good and totally admirable set of values and this is reflected in the team he put together. If the guy in the centre is that good, the whole thing works. I've never grown so fond of a team before; in fact, after a few weeks, I was teaching several of them to speak English. Kevin Kline was doing especially well.' So well, in fact, that Cleese would shortly cast him in a starring role in *A Fish Called Wanda*.

'It was very interesting to be on a film as big as that – three times as big as the biggest *Python* film,' Cleese continued, sustaining the enthusiasm for another American interview in the science fiction magazine *Starlog*. 'Every time I got really comfortable on a horse they gave me a bigger one. I was too tall! They didn't want me to look silly, so the one I finished up on was pretty big, but I adored the riding. Altogether, I went through four or five horses – I don't think they all had to be destroyed after I had ridden them, but every time I got one that I really liked, there was another, bigger one waiting for me the next day. . . . I've no doubt that I shall crop up in other people's films from time to time to earn a bit of money. But otherwise I'd rather sit at home and read a book or two. After all, after twenty years of being a well-known face on the screen I've probably got all the juice out of it. I have a family, a nice house, a nice car and a reasonable income. Now what I want is time to do things which interest me – and money doesn't.'

Two of the 'things' that interested Cleese the most were his adored daughters. Barbara had given birth to Camilla in February 1984, and Cynthia was now in her early teens. Shortly after his second marriage, Cleese told George Perry that Cynthia was 'a markedly healthy, vigorous little girl. She often says that now I've married Barbara it's a bit like having two mothers.' Cynthia later told a rather different story: 'I was always used to being dad's little girl. After he and my mother divorced, I was often the one who went to parties with him, I was the one who acted as the lady when he needed someone to accompany him. My father and I have always been close. I worshipped him and there was nothing I couldn't discuss with him. Neither of us had any hang-ups.

'Suddenly he didn't need me to be the lady any more. I seemed to see the closeness I had always had disappearing, suddenly it didn't seem to exist any more. . . . I remember my father missing three consecutive birthdays because he was on holiday in America with my stepmother. One of them was my sixteenth birthday which was really important to me at the time, and I resented her for taking him away from me and I was just so disappointed that he missed it.'

Cynthia spent a lot of time with her father when at home, but had attended boarding school from the age of nine. She was unsettled and would cry and scream when she had to go to school. She phoned her father every night, desperate to come home. 'My house parents Tom and Jean Wilkinson were wonderful. She was a mother figure in the most maternal way, and that was really important to me.

'I realized that the things that make you develop most as a person are the things that are most dramatic in your life. I now believe that the fact that my parents were divorced might actually have been a good thing, because . . . it brought me close to both of them, rather than just my dad. I don't know if that would have happened had they stayed together.'

Cleese prided himself on being a good father, determined not to repeat the mistakes his parents had made. He was not averse to disciplining Cynthia, yet just before Camilla's arrival he advised: 'One of the great dangers in life is to believe that any adult knows what they are talking about. I'm just trying to tell this to my twelve-year-old daughter and I think she's getting it.' His daughters would reap the full benefit of their father's psychotherapy. While Cynthia showed a healthy indifference to *Families and How to Survive Them*, her father joked: 'She'll probably need some of it later, because I assume we probably screwed her up like everyone else screws up their kids.' Cleese believed in asking Cynthia for a cuddle when he felt depressed and today says: 'I think you should have only a very few rules, but stick rigidly to those you have. I think, also, it is fine to quarrel in front of your children. Life is not dramatically changed by the odd outburst.'

Clockwise was Cleese's last essentially British film, so British that it failed to open in even one American city and was found to be a good deal too parochial for large sections of even the British audience. It was Michael Frayn's first screen comedy and producer Michael (*Jewel in the Crown*) Codron's first film. Codron had asked Cleese to perform in plays, but he had turned them down because 'I have better things to do in the evening than get up and say the same words every night.' For Cleese, Frayn's script was the best he had read, 'with the possible exception of *Life of Brian*. . . . The same day it landed on my front doormat, I rang my agent and said, "I have to do this."'

Clockwise was filmed in Birmingham, Shropshire and Hull. Cleese, according to Frayn, had a clause written into his contract specifying his right to choose the location caterer. For some odd reason, his physical integrity became a major theme of the shooting of *Clockwise*. 'I wanted to see if I could get through eight weeks' filming and finish in reasonably good form, feeling physically OK and mentally together and not exhausted. And I managed it fine by the simple expedient of getting to bed very early and having my masseur work on me for forty-five minutes every night.' But within eight days Cleese smashed his left knee on a staircase and pulled a hamstring chasing a train on Hull station. 'It felt a bit like going out to war and I thought: I hope I come out of this alive.'

He continued the medical theme in a post-release interview with the *San Francisco Chronicle*: 'At my age – I'll be forty-seven next month – it's not quite so easy to do all that running around. On the first day I banged my right knee running around in a confined space. For the rest of the week I was getting out of a small car and putting all the weight on the other knee. On the first day off, I had fluid on the right knee. So I sat in my room putting packets of frozen peas on it to reduce the swelling. I bound it up and the next morning I was supposed to be running around in the train station. At half-past three I tore my left hamstring. With seven weeks of shooting to go, I had the body of a seventy-nine-year-old man, with still a lot of capering around to do. . . . If I liked acting at all, which I don't, I would like to do something that doesn't involve a lot of running around.'

Given such an attrition rate, and Cleese's dislike of filming, he might have been expected to be a bit testy on the set of

Clockwise, but in fact was at his most charming. At a party at the Station Hotel in Hull, Michael Codron thought it prudent after all this to introduce Cleese to the location nurse, Barbara Carson, who was then twenty-six. As Carson remembers the occasion:

> Cleese was absolutely charming when I was introduced to him. My last name was Metcalfe then, and when he heard this he went on about some football player he used to know who played for a Northern club, and that was it for the rest of the film shoot – whenever he needed me he used to yell: 'Metcalfe', because he thought it was a marvellous name.
>
> He was charming rather than funny. I think everybody always seemed to expect him to be funny, so he often put on a show for them, messing about, pulling faces, using the mannerisms that he had, sometimes doing silly walks for the film crew when people were tired or fed up. On the last night he had a dinner for everybody, and he sent a funny note to us all inviting us along. He was very popular with the film crew. Nobody had a bad word to say about him. He never acted self-important, never came on the star.
>
> I didn't actually do much nursing. Cleese used to joke about his hypochondria because he thought everybody was expecting him to be ill. But when he was running down the platform one day he pulled a muscle or something, so we had to get the local doctor to come in and see him. Cleese was very charming with him.
>
> My father had died earlier in the year, and one day Cleese had nothing to do, so he asked me if I'd like to go over his lines with him – it was the speech he makes at the end of the film. So we worked on it in his huge long trailer. Every time I said 'No', when he hadn't got it right, he'd look incredulously at me. And he just kept talking to me, and seemed genuinely interested in me. He was asking all about my dad and he was wonderful because I was still very upset about my dad at this stage. He gave me a copy of *Families*. He really made me feel a lot happier inside because I was really depressed at the time.

Ultimately, *Clockwise* interested Cleese from a psychological standpoint more than it did the film's audience, even though it still led to him, now forty-eight, being voted Funniest Man in Britain by young Radio One listeners, and winning an *Evening Standard* film award. (In the radio poll, conducted by Steve Wright, Lenny Henry came second, then, in order, Michael Barrymore, Ben Elton and Rik Mayall.) Cleese was at pains not to make Stimpson, the hero, too much like Fawlty, and the director Christopher Morahan asked him to redo a couple of takes when he felt he'd gone over the top. Cleese says *Clockwise* used to drive time-neurotics potty: 'The only problem with the film is that it does make some people too nervous. . . . *Clockwise* is a very held-in film about a very held-in personality, and it does amuse me that the only other country that liked it at all was Sweden. Presumably they found Stimpson quite extrovert.' The only other place that took to *Clockwise* was Israel, a country whose people are rarely accused of being introverted.

Cleese was in America for the *Evening Standard* award ceremony and so recorded an acceptance speech. 'I made one of those speeches,' he recounted in *Life* magazine, 'in which I thanked *everybody*, from Søren Kierkegaard to Mamie Eisenhower to the London Symphony Orchestra to my mother to Donald Duck. I mean, my list was at least three minutes long. At the end, I said, "This award is not really for me, it's for all of you. Sorry you can't share it." And then I dropped the vase and it smashed. . . . They really loved it.'

11 *The Wanda Years*

I've been living off *Fawlty Towers* in terms of
reputation for ten years. It's just that when I
do things I put an awful lot of time into
them, and I felt that before I died I would
like to do one film that was my own.

John Cleese, on *A Fish Called Wanda*

'I didn't want to come to America and be a big star – it just
isn't what my life is about. It just never occurred to me. It
has suited Dudley Moore fine, for example. He has done marvellously well, but it never occurred to me as being a possibility,
and it would never happen. It's just not what I want to do
with my life. I've been enormously happy working in England
because of the freedom I have.' Just before the American release
of *Silverado* in 1985, Cleese had adamantly explained to *Starlog*
magazine exactly how he did not want his showbusiness career
to go.

Unsuitable film offers still came in sackfuls, and some producers wrongly thought Cleese had bitten when his response
was positive. He liked attending script meetings and, having
shown enthusiasm for an idea, would then have to explain: 'No,
you don't understand. I don't want to be in your movie. I simply
got excited by the ideas in it.'

Yet within three years of *Silverado* – a sequel to which was
being planned in 1991 – Cleese had succeeded in becoming an

unlikely Hollywood hero by making *A Fish Called Wanda*, the most British of films, within a triangle of Oxford, Heathrow Airport and South London. A survey of American women, conducted by a magazine group based in Alaska shortly after *Wanda*'s release, voted English men the most 'sophisticated, noble, cultured and intellectual' and found Cleese to be the hottest hunk of the year, part of a wave of Cleese-as-sex-symbol publicity which, even with his considerable and self-acknowledged vanity, he found hard to stomach.

Although he first discussed the *Wanda* project in the early 1970s with Charles Crichton, the Ealing comedy director, it only became a serious proposition in 1984, a few months after the publication of *Families* and the birth of Camilla. Cleese regards the Archimedes moment as being in 1983, when he and Crichton spent several days sitting by a pool in the south of France. On the last day, Cleese suddenly had an idea. He scribbled 'Maybe the Gang Boss has a Girlfriend' on a piece of paper. In 1988, it was still pinned to his study wall. The few years between the arduous poolside sessions and the film's triumphant release were another rocky passage in the emotional journey of his life; by the time the film came out in the USA, he and Barbara were separated and he was no longer living (a temporary break as it turned out) in the Holland Park house he loved so much.

There was no clue that things were going wrong again when Penelope Gilliatt visited the vast Victorian house for a *New Yorker* interview weeks before the separation. Cleese, hunting for the coffee grinder in the fridge, even used the same affectionate joke about Barbara as he did about Connie Booth at a similar time in their marriage: 'My wife, Barbara, is American,' he muttered, 'so she puts everything in the fridge: Hoover bags, sticking plaster.'

From the start of the trial separation, Cleese and Trentham spoke to each other every day and he made sure he went home every evening to read a story to Camilla, who was coming up for four years. The mood of the separation was very nonchalant – he made a vague reference to pressure of work, reflecting that maybe the marriage had been a risk, and that he and Barbara did not have enough in common, but adding, 'When you get to my age it doesn't matter that much. I'm going to be dead in twenty years anyway.' There was no third party, both Cleese and his wife agreed, and they said there was a chance of a reconciliation. The fact that Cleese had just written a book called *Families and How to Survive Them* might have been an embarrassing sticking point, but he sidestepped it judiciously, pointing out that as far as he was concerned, he had survived. The split and eventual divorce, which cost him £2.5 million, confirmed for him what has become another Cleese theme – that life is not supposed to be purely about avoiding mistakes; he argues that a marriage is not necessarily a failure just because it ends. The break-up with Barbara received none of the public analysis by Cleese that he had given his separation and divorce from Connie. Both Cleese and Barbara pride themselves on remaining good friends; she lives a few streets away from Cleese, where she is still trying to establish herself as an artist, and the couple share Camilla, whom Cleese, the father of two daughters, jokingly introduces from time to time as his son.

What really went wrong between Cleese and his second wife? His friends see the marriage as having been more of a transitional relationship, a bridge for him from the blackness and loneliness of the post-Connie world to the relaxed maturity he has now settled into. 'It's not a question of what was wrong, there was never anything particularly right,' confides one friend about the Cleese/Trentham marriage. 'He was just John, and there was this incredibly outgoing Californian blonde with an electric smile breezing into the room on his arm and saying "Hi!" It always seemed a bit odd.' It is possible that the marriage started out on an inadvisable footing, that the initial chemistry was confused by a catalyst. Much has been made of Connie, Babs and Cleese's current girlfriend Alyce Faye Eichelberger being blonde and American, but the first two have something else in common. When Cleese initially met them in America, he was performing on both occasions (in 1964 *Cambridge Circus* and in 1980 *Monty Python Live at the Hollywood Bowl*). He met both his wives when he was riding high, the centre of attention. In both cases, their initial role was almost as fans, and his as the star. Psychologically feeling on top of the world and therefore possibly more reckless, he proposed to both Connie and Barbara very rapidly.

At the start of *A Fish Called Wanda*, there was nothing rapid or incautious about Archie Leach, Cleese's character. Leach helped Cleese say everything he ever wanted to say about being English, but only as the role got rewritten and rewritten did it begin strongly to resemble Cleese. As Cleese has said, the straitlaced barrister was not only an awful wimp but 'very proper, stuffy and uptight', and therefore an unsympathetic character, in the original draft. At a read-through eight months before they started to rehearse, 'we [Crichton, Curtis, Kline and Palin] all went to the kitchen after to make coffee and came back and sat down; they all said, "Make him more real". So I simply rewrote the character to be a bit more like me. Softer, more vulnerable and affected by Wanda, more romantic about her as opposed to just wanting to get into bed with her.'

The final Archie was to Cleese the sort of Englishman 'who is actually alive and adventurous and open-minded, but has an emotional conditioning so deep it's a lifetime's work to escape from it'. It was the producer, Michael Shamberg, who insisted that the love affair was crucial and, in retrospect, Cleese admits he was right. 'I just thought he was being soppy. Charlie [Crichton] and I are both pretty black so far as our sense of humour goes, and anything bordering on sentiment has us curling up. Charlie more than me because he's Scottish.'

The plot and even the name of *A Fish Called Wanda* remained largely a secret – a marvellous long-term sales technique which Cleese was employing again in 1991 with the always tentative announcement of a new film – not a sequel, but starring the same actors. In 1986, two years before the film was completed, Cleese told interviewers: 'I think it will be called something like A Goldfish Called Wanda, although Jamie [Lee Curtis], who will play Wanda, wants to be called Jack, so it may come out to be more like A Guppie Called Jack. I think I would rather have it be called The Last Prawn. It's a wonderful title, and all you need after that is a movie to go with it.' Earlier in the year he said it would be called either Corruption or A Goldfish Called Wanda, which *The Times* reported as A Goldfish Called Wonder. He also announced variously that the film would be called Wanda, Wanda the Parrot or Wanda the Policeman.

Cleese and Crichton (who had made *Hue and Cry*, *The Titfield Thunderbolt*, and *The Lavender Hill Mob*) went to thirteen drafts of the script. 'At one point Charlie's back went and I thought, "Well, he's not going to be able to direct this, so I shan't bother making it" and I was perfectly happy with that. Then his back got better, so we upped and off again. . . . He's 168 years old and he mumbles so you have to listen very carefully to know what's going on at all. . . . We nearly did a film together back in 1969, but it all went wrong and we walked away from it. I always thought he'd be wonderful to work with, though, apart from his mumbling.' Born in 1910, Crichton had a genuine claim to being an Edwardian gentleman. He was seventy-eight when *Wanda* came out, and had started making films before Hitler came to power. 'He's the only director I've ever worked with who's still suffering from the arrival of the Talkies,' Cleese has said. 'Charlie hasn't made a feature for over twenty years because they're all looking for exciting young directors, whereas *I'm* looking for unexciting old directors – who know what they're doing.'

On the first day of shooting, Cleese gave Crichton a T-shirt reading 'Age and Treachery Will Always Overcome Youth and Skill'. The old man was, needless to say, another guru/father figure for Cleese to sit at the feet of. Cleese recalls, 'Once during the script stage of *Wanda*, we were talking about the way the threads of the plot could be edited together as A, B and C. And he said, "You must never cut ABC, ABC, ABC." And I said, "All right, Charlie, you know about these things. But why not?" And he said, "Well, *I* don't know, but I was told that by the man who used to edit the *Keystone Kops*."'

Although Cleese assisted ('interfered', he says) in the direction of the film, a pursuit he regards as having 'all the appeal of waiting twelve weeks for a plane at London Airport', he insisted that Crichton got a sole credit. Cleese's name was listed on the credits as co-director until the last day's shooting, when he had it removed. He loyally maintains that he only had his name down as a co-director in the first place to encourage MGM who might have worried that Crichton would die of old age half-way through the filming.

The process of wooing the actors he wanted for *Wanda* was as painstaking as its creative gestation. Kevin Kline, better known as a Shakespearean actor, who had impressed Cleese when they did *Silverado* together – the pair immediately took to one another – spent an age deciding whether or not he wanted the part. Cleese went on holiday to Jamaica with Kline to persuade him. 'I often tell him that the reason he did *Hamlet* on Broadway was because it gave him the chance to play somebody who could make a decision more quickly than he could.' The persuasion process sometimes worked the other way round. Maria Aitken, who played Archie's wife Wendy, for example, recalls, 'John rang me to tell me about the part saying, "I think you could play it, but you are intrinsically too nice." I put the phone down in a flurry of despair and said to the man I live with "What shall I do?" He replied, "Leave it to me" and wrote to John – and said, "Dear John, Maria Aitken is my domestic and business partner and she's a total cunt." It was a gag, but it amused John, and they then saw me and auditioned me extensively. A lot of other people were up for it, and I was very lucky to get it.'

Even luckier, perhaps, was Cynthia Cleese, then seventeen and in the middle of A-levels at Millfield School. Using the name Cynthia Caylor, she got a small part as Portia, Archie Leach's daughter. 'I didn't want Cynthia started in acting with the name Cleese because there'd be such expectations. So she's taken her mother's mother's name,' Cleese explained, without even an apology for nepotism. 'Cynthia is very talented and helped me work out her character for the film. We would discuss things she said and did when she was young and throw ideas about until we evolved this nauseating girl she plays. Now I tease her that this awful character is based on the way she used to be. She hotly denies it!' The parent in him added: 'She's supposed to be about fifteen, playing two years younger than she is. A terrific brat. She's got a real gift for comedy. I think she's going to be an excellent actress, and that's fine, providing she's got another interest. Acting's not enough to engross people unless you're say, Jack Nicholson.' Wisely balancing the claims of his two daughters, Cleese also ensured that little Camilla got a part – albeit in the companion 45-minute video that eventually came out on the making of *Wanda*. She is seen sitting on her father's shoulders, as he explains to her why Daddy is about to be hung by his trouser legs 100 feet above London's docklands.

The cast received the first draft of the script in summer 1986, a year before they started making the film at Pinewood. On the first day of shooting, Cleese put a major Video Arts management technique successfully into operation, by confiding to the production team that he was still undecided how best to make the film, and inviting their input, which encouraged a relaxed and committed environment. 'I wanted to create an atmosphere and get the maximum impact from everyone in the room,' Cleese explains. 'I try as much as possible to get a feeling of play.' The non-authoritarian approach to direction made for an unusual film set; Kevin Kline describes Cleese as having 'hosted' the film.

He had been obliged in the early stages to be a generous host. Cleese spent around £100,000 of his own money funding *Wanda*, and still four of the five big Hollywood studios (including Dino De Laurentiis and Universal) passed it over before MGM/UA took it on and put up the $8 million budget. Cleese believes it helped that when he went to MGM for an hour's meeting on a Tuesday morning in February 1987, he took along the American studio-wise producer Michael Shamberg, whom he had met through Babs, and had a carefully worked out package of director, actors and script, although he didn't even have to produce it. He simply told them the story. 'We had only just driven away [on their way back to Malibu] when they called us on the car phone and said they wanted to do it.'

'After fifteen years making films about how to sell, I think I knew instinctively how to pitch,' he announced in the *Los Angeles Times*. 'And that is no different in Hollywood than anywhere else. You describe the benefits and not the features. In other words, you never talk about why you think the idea is great. You talk about it from their point of view, why they should want to take it. If I were selling you a mixer, I wouldn't say this has a revised version of the Gordonsplatz rotator valve – that is a feature – but that it can grind coffee in six seconds. That is the benefit. So I said to MGM that for $7.3 million – which is a cheap movie – they were getting a sexy package with a great old English director, Charles Crichton, and with me backing him up, plus a cast which consists of the two best-known Python names plus Kevin Kline and Jamie Lee Curtis.' (Cleese has subsequently admitted that he thought the American principals were more famous in the US than they actually were. Kline's reputation was based in New York theatre rather than film – *The Big Chill* and *Cry Freedom*; Curtis was known as a 'scream queen' because she'd appeared in several horror movies.)

Cleese was nearly fifty by the time he struck the deal with MGM, and made it a priority to get back to the sort of physical fitness he knew from his sporting past he could achieve. 'Vanity is a wonderful thing – if only you can tap it,' he said. The knee injury from the shooting of *Clockwise* in Hull meant he could not run, let alone hang from windows with ease, and years of enjoying large quantities of food while doing little exercise made him understandably wary of appearing nude in part of the film – he had not been entirely Adonis-like in his naked debut, the 1974 short film *Romance with a Double Bass*. As soon as he got back to London, he hired a trainer, a rabbi's son turned wrestling coach, Josh Salzmann from Connecticut, who was keen on 'muscular exhaustion' and was delighted with the result: 'I have had more attention from women in the last few months than in the whole of my life, and about time too,' he chortled to Hilary Bonner of the *Daily Mirror*. 'The most active sport I was involved in was snooker. But I was desperate not to look a fat slob for my nude scene, so I didn't care what kind of agony this guy put me through. He gave me all kinds of work-outs, some weight-training and plenty of jogging. He also put me on a strict diet, and it worked. I lost 15 lb and firmed up my whole torso. The best thing that happened was that after the film was previewed a lot of people came up and complimented me on my physique.' Cleese went from 14 st 12 lb to 13 st 11 lb.

A Fish Called Wanda cost £3.5 million to make and took £22 million in just seven weeks in the USA. It hit number two in the New York top ten movie list (behind *Die Hard*). Worldwide, it has made around £75 million, of which Cleese has seen at least £7 million, making him higher paid for one film than Sean Connery or Michael Caine. Cleese likes to maintain that the film flopped in Japan 'because the Japanese don't like fish' but he is wrong; it did as well as can be expected there, given the translation problems. Oddly, these had never prevented *Monty Python* becoming almost as big as golf in Japan. When *Python* was first shown, the sketches were interpreted by actors and afterwards followed by a grave discussion by a group of men in suits. Dubbed *Python* episodes were shown from 1976, however, and even in a culture where there is no word for 'funny', and 'interesting' and 'something to watch' are the same word, which is used in place of 'funny', *Wanda* is available in every suburban video shop as *Wanda, The Diamond and the Good Guys*.

Knowing with hindsight that *Wanda* was a vast financial success does not explain why someone who had decided that he hated work and neither wanted nor needed to become a 'star' went off and made a film which could just as easily have bombed as it boomed. Cleese made the film to show the world, but more specifically the rest of showbusiness, how good he was; he had once set out to create the finest ever sitcom and done it; now he would have another stab towards achieving what he calls 'the big three' – the stage play, the screenplay and the novel – and his immense sense of competitiveness defined that it would have to be superlative. Even that was not enough; although he deliberately went out to woo the American audience ('There doesn't seem to be any point in making a comedy unless it's accessible to Americans'), he also effectively handicapped himself by using an elderly director and a distinctly quirky story and by introducing elements of humour, especially cruelty (not least in the portrayal of Palin's stammering role), that would alienate a lot of the public. It was as if John Cleese's private joke at the world's expense was continuing, the feeling, though he would never be so arrogant as to express it, that he was just that crucial bit cleverer (or, more accurately, *capable* of being that little bit cleverer) than most of us. *Wanda* might, or might not, have been its punchline.

In the brief period since *Wanda*, a kind of conventional wisdom has grown up linking it more with financial success than being an especially good film. It happened that Cleese started to see the £7 million he earned from the film at the same time as he made another £7 million from the sale of Video Arts; all the John Cleese stories in the press for a while were about money, and it was forgotten that *Wanda* was also an enormous critical success. Cleese was named Film Actor of 1988 by the Variety Club and won the BAFTA Best Actor award. Palin won Best Supporting Actor and Curtis was nominated for Best Actress. In

1989, *Wanda* collected three Golden Globe nominations (given by Hollywood-based foreign press), for Best Film, Best Actress (Curtis) and Best Comedy Actor (Cleese). In the same year, Cleese was nominated for an Oscar for Best Comedy Actor, while Kevin Kline won an Oscar for Best Supporting Actor. In 1990, *Wanda* was named Best British Video of the Year and Best Comedy by the British Videogram Association; the film was America's most rented video in 1989.

A heaving awards cabinet was perhaps an unexpected pay-off for Cleese's policy of film direction on democratic principles; at the time of making the film, he also got free lessons in a lot of things he professed, as ever, to be unsure about. Not only was there Charles Crichton with his sometimes opaque and sometimes inaudible advice, but, as he told Penelope Gilliatt, 'Maybe the reason I find acting so boring is that I'm usually doing lines I wrote, so there's no sense of discovery. But on *Wanda* I got interested again, because when we came to the more romantic scenes with Jamie she said, "Don't let's rehearse them, let's just see what happens." I'd never done that. It's pretty scary if you're addicted to rehearsing, as I am – like pushing a boat off from shore without any oars. But Jamie said, "Trust it." And sometimes, between takes, she'd see me running lines in my head and she'd say "Don't," and wave a finger at me.'

Cleese was also perfectly happy to take advice on what he regards as his real craft, writing. He invited the actors in *Wanda* to participate in developing their lines to the extent that some are theirs rather than his. Palin even gave Curtis a T-shirt reading 'Wait, I have an idea'. Cleese obviously enjoyed the collaborative process, one difference between this and Python collaborations, which he grew to detest, being that he had final say in everything. On the other hand, he achieved the extended family feeling on the film that he has always striven for, only this time it was Hollywood and big money and big stars. There were the running jokes (Cleese, for example, thought it funny that Tony Curtis's real name was Bernie Schwartz and had his co-star referred to as Jamie Lee Schwartz on her call sheets) and a sense of happiness everyone seemed to share.

The scientist in Cleese put his own comic ability down to technique and planning rather than an innate funniness. Like

Fawlty Towers on an even grander scale, Cleese endlessly structured and restructured *A Fish Called Wanda* using flow charts and diagrams drawn with a felt tip pen on huge white pieces of paper. Julian Doyle, one of the most renowned of film technicians, who worked closely with Cleese on *Life of Brian* and other projects, confirms his dedication to structure but says: 'He's not good on the visual side – that's Terry Gilliam's area – and he has no sense of the sets, lighting and costume side, but structurally he's brilliant. In *Wanda*, he didn't worry about sets and lighting, and he used television lighting – it looked like a bad British production.' One might have thought that with Cleese's track record for structural ability, he would have considered that area of his education finished, but far from it. In 1990, Cleese earnestly explained to the author John Hind: 'The moment you get into anything other than a gag, you have to get structure right if it's going to work, and it becomes harder and harder the longer the piece becomes. Moving from a three-minute sketch to eight minutes is much harder, half an hour is very difficult, and 110 minutes is an absolute bugger. I certainly don't know how to do it yet, but I've just bought some books about the Three-Act Structure and I'm about to get to grips with them.' In 1990, Cleese enrolled for a Story Structure Course in London given at the Royal Society of Chemistry by Robert McKee, an intellectual, though paradoxically not very successful, Hollywood scriptwriter: 'If we had twenty people in this country who understood film story-structure we would have a British film industry,' Cleese said. The following year, he frustratingly found himself prevented from attending another lecture series by an American writer because he had not been on the first part of his course.

Charles Crichton found that mentoring Cleese could be a little tiring. 'We fought like mad sometimes, though he doesn't remember that,' Crichton says. 'John would have an idea fixed in his head because when he was actually writing the scene which we had talked about, he would write it remembering, shall we say, a certain place, and that's how he would remember it, in a certain place. I wouldn't like John to hear what I'm saying now, bless him. It can happen that an author sees something in a certain kind of a way. At the beginning he was a little bit in a straitjacket about how he saw it, which cinematically wasn't the best way to see it. So there were sometimes a few arguments because it wasn't precisely as he wanted it. It doesn't mean to say you're against each other – you're just working. There is this marvellous shot when they're [Cleese and Curtis] on the bed together in that flat and Otto comes up in between them. Now, in John's original vision, Otto was looking through a keyhole. But how much better that was. John was against it.'

Wanda was first seen in Britain at the Edinburgh Film Festival in August 1988 but did not open until October. It was out in America in July, but only after some of the cruelty, particularly involving animals, had been removed. Although in reality Cleese is as soft and sentimental about animals as any red-blooded Englishman (he wept when one of his cats was run over in Holland Park in 1991) Cleese was inclined intellectually to agree with Otto, who quoted Nietzsche to the effect that all higher civilization is based on cruelty. Cleese admits that his sense of humour may be a bit blacker (Crichton says more childish) than most people's: 'Do you know what W. C. Fields said?' he asked a *New York Times* interviewer. 'You can make the average man laugh by having a man dressed up as an old woman potter down the street and fall down a manhole. To make a professional comedian laugh, it really has to be an old woman.' (It was actually Groucho Marx who said: 'An amateur thinks it's funny if you dress a man up as an old lady, put him in a wheelchair, and give the wheelchair a push that sends it spinning down a slope towards a stone wall. For a pro, it's got to be a real old lady.')

Cleese sees a well-established tradition of cruel humour in film, starting with Chaplin and the Marx Brothers, right through to Ealing comedies – nine people die in *Kind Hearts and Coronets* – to W. C. Fields, to Bilko, Alf Garnett and the outspoken 'alternative' comics of the 1980s. 'Comedy that doesn't have that streak is essentially mediocre, safe and uninteresting. The question then is, is it really cruel? But I think, for example, when Tom is run over by Jerry on a steamroller you laugh, but you don't think, "God, that poor cat must have suffered dreadfully." You can see that it is an idea. Literal-minded people cannot see the difference between what happens on screen and what happens in reality, but more intelligent people understand that they can laugh at an idea which would not be funny in real life.'

Test screenings in Los Angeles, New York and England, however, proved that Nietzsche and Groucho Marx notwithstanding, audiences were upset by sections of *Wanda*, and MGM (and, in some cases, Cleese) asked for alterations. The end was softened when it was found that audiences did not think Curtis deserved to be on the plane with Cleese because she wasn't nice enough (about seventy-five additional seconds rectified all faults) and part of the squashed dog scene was reshot. A lingering view of the dog's entrails, lovingly laid-out in a pattern by Crichton, was omitted, a 'safety shot' taken at the producer's suggestion at the same time substituted. The scene where Ken's fish are eaten by Otto was also shortened because it distressed people so much, and some of Kline's more overpoweringly psychopathic sequences, such as using cat's tails for target practice, were cut. (On first reading his sociopathic part, Kline actually said to Cleese: 'You've written the John Cleese part for me.') Not everyone agreed that *Wanda* went over the top. According to Cleese, 'My favourite comment about *Wanda* came from two old ladies who came up to me in New York after a première. They approached me with a rather severe expression and one of them asked, "Why didn't you kill more dogs?"'

It is not even that they were especially bloodthirsty old ladies; even with its mean streak, seeing *Wanda* had, Cleese discovered, a strange ability to make people feel better, something he had never really explored in his comedy before. 'I learned something from Paul Hogan,' he reflected in an *LA Herald Examiner* interview. 'He has about as much charm as anyone can have on screen and *Crocodile Dundee* is a great hit, but it's not really very funny, is it? Still, people do come out feeling pretty good. He was on television recently and he said he'd seen a few of the Pythons. He said they were very clever but very cold. And you know, I think as you get older making people feel good is pretty important.'

The idea of a film wantonly perking the audience up was one of many concessions in *A Fish Called Wanda* to the overwhelmingly let's-be-happy American culture. If the film was some kind of personal catharsis for Cleese, it was not so much because it helped him exorcize all his English hang-ups but because it gave him a platform to explain his fascination with the differences between the English and the Americans, the introversion of the one compared to the extroversion of the other. His relentless publicity tour of America just before the release of *Wanda* almost took the form of a continuous monologue on the subject, although it was only on the British promotional tour that he let slip that the Wanda character was not originally going to be American – Cleese cast Curtis after seeing her in *Trading Places*. That shift in the story may well have been the reason for the film's success in the USA – the idea that a dull, pedantic English barrister could, with the help of American optimism, fall in love and reconstruct himself as a passionate, impulsive and lovable person. 'Because Europeans aren't as direct, they have something to teach Americans about irony, scepticism and ambivalence – the ability to hold conflicting attitudes at the same time, which I think is the essence of mental health,' Cleese said in Orange County, California. 'I mean that seriously. Healthy families are able to tolerate a high degree of ambivalence towards people.'

'I think we can learn a lot from that American openness and receptivity to new ideas – that great enthusiasm,' he continued in Hollywood, 'but Americans can also learn a certain scepticism from us, and a sense of ambivalence and irony. These ideas and my own love–hate relationship with both cultures were at the back of my mind when I wrote *Wanda*. Jamie's character frees me, and that's an experience I've had in real life when I've met American women. At the same time, I make it obvious that America has its absurdities and excesses, as symbolized by Otto. He's a totally ridiculous figure, bristling with lethal weaponry and without a shred of common sense. So it's a critical view, but then all comedy is critical, isn't it? And I really do care about America, you know. I even remember crying in 1968 when they elected Nixon.'

'The bitching between the Americans and the English on the set was nonstop,' he explained further in Philadelphia. 'Michael Shamberg was always moaning about the weather, never let up. Then he went back to Los Angeles and there was an earthquake. I sent him a telegram that said, "A little cool in London, chance of rain. But reassuring lack of motorways cracking up and buildings falling over." I was still laughing myself silly ten days later when the worst hurricane in history hit England and destroyed 10 per cent of all the trees.'

Despite his immense experience of America, Cleese confessed still to being baffled by aspects of the American way. He describes being introduced to a producer called Marvin in a Hollywood restaurant: 'He said, "What's your name?" I said, "John Cleese." He went back to talking for a long time with the man he was with. Then he came over to me and said, "Hey, I'm a big fan of yours."'

Drumming up publicity for *Wanda* in America, Cleese was funnier apparently off the cuff than he had ever been. The man to whom American chat shows were once vulgar, alien and to be avoided now seemed utterly relaxed on them. On David Letterman, he burbled on more in Michael Palin's style about the purpose of *Wanda* being 'to put fish on the map'. Acutely tuned as he is to cultural undercurrents, Cleese had noticed the growing mania in America – vastly greater than in Britain – for anthropomorphized (or just plain cute) animal gags, and exploited the cult ruthlessly. 'They're great pets,' he said of fish on Letterman. 'I mean, for a start they never wake you up by barking or anything like that. You always know exactly where they are, you never say, "The fish has escaped. Did somebody leave the back door open?" You don't have to give them shots, you don't have to brush them. If you forget to feed them they just eat each other. And they don't drown and the other thing is that they can breathe under water. If I could breathe under water I'd never stop talking about it. I mean, Albert Einstein couldn't breathe under water and the Buddha, who had extraordinary control over all his physiological processes, couldn't breathe under water, and even Our Lord, who could walk on it, couldn't inhale it.' He promptly did the same routine for *Playboy* magazine, with additional rude bits: '. . . even our Saviour, Jesus Christ, who could walk on the stuff, couldn't inhale it. Yet every single fucking fish can.'

Cleese also sold the Anglo-American divide astoundingly well, succeeding in being more funny for some viewers than *A Fish Called Wanda* itself. Asked by Letterman, it being around 4 July at the time, about public holidays in Britain, Cleese said, 'We have National Apology Day, when everybody apologizes to everyone that they haven't apologized to in the previous twelve months, or anyone that they haven't apologized to sufficiently in the previous twelve months. . . . That is August the 74th, because we're still on the old calendar. . . . And then we have another holiday – I don't know if you have this holiday in America – but we have a very special day, it's called Summer.' He went on, cunningly veering the subject back to his film, to mention that the British also had a National Day for Being Cruel to Animals.

Bill Bryson, an American writer living in England, caught up with Cleese in a Bristol television studio on the 46th day of his promotional tour for *Wanda*, which had now taken him to Britain. Cleese told Bryson it was his 150th interview. When Graham Purches, the television host, told him to feel free to plug *Wanda*, Cleese replied, 'Oh, don't worry. No matter what you ask me about – apartheid, jam-making, sexual preferences – I shall steer the subject relentlessly back to *Wanda*.' Bryson reported that Cleese mentioned *Wanda* five times and *Families and How to Survive Them* twice in the six-minute interview. Making all those Video Arts films on selling had been time well spent.

Cleese gave every interview an entirely appropriate spin. For the *Bristol Evening News*, he talked about choosing the name of the other local hero, Archie Leach aka Cary Grant. 'I suppose it's the nearest I will ever get to being Cary Grant, but it was also to do with my growing up in Weston and going to school in Clifton. I get some strange sense of contact or orientation driving around these streets I am so familiar with.' At a press conference in Venice to launch the film in Italy, he found himself at one with the earthy Italian sense of humour. Asked by an Italian correspondent whether the Pythons would ever regroup, he said No. Why not? demanded the journalist: 'Because they're all dead apart from me. Except, that is, for Terry Jones, and he's suffering from a terminal illness and has lost control of all his bodily functions. So if you go to see him, wear protective clothing.'

Palin, Kline and Jamie Lee Curtis joined the *Wanda* band-wagon. Cleese developed a running gag about Curtis insisting on taking her clothes off on the set at every opportunity as long as it was 'valid'. 'It takes a lot of guts for somebody to trust their talents enough and to believe in something over a long period of time. And for a very old man with bad teeth and little of his own hair, that's a real accomplishment,' Curtis said elsewhere. And in America, when asked about playing the nude scene with Cleese, she held up her thumb and forefinger about an inch apart and said, 'Short . . . attention span'.

Although the nude scene in *Wanda* was not a first for Cleese, he made maximum use of it. 'I must say taking my knickers off in front of the crew was like going through an emotional sound barrier,' he said in countless interviews. 'But I discovered that once you've done it, it gets easier. By the second day I was glancing down to see if I had my knickers on. And I spent so many years in *Monty Python* where you had to change like *that* from a knight in armour to an old woman in a supermarket, stripping off was something I got very used to.'

Having given birth to the concept of himself as a sex symbol, Cleese spent the next few months frantically trying to find reverse gear, to suggest, without doubt genuinely in his own mind, that the whole thing was a joke. Unfortunately, it had gone a little too far, and the albeit hazy image of a reborn John Cleese, mature, handsome and sexually successful, became burned on to the media's collective retina. Even though he has played on the image long after *Wanda* – he did a Schweppes television commercial as a sunbronzed beach bum – he vehemently insists that Cleese-as-sex-symbol was entirely fabricated by British journalists, whom he regards as the worst and least intelligent in the world. He finds it bizarre, for example, that he is frequently asked if choosing the name Archie Leach was some form of Cary Grant wish fulfilment. 'This is the closest to Cary Grant I'll ever get. It was not an attempt to suggest I was about to usurp Cary's mantle. I'm not only not good enough and not good-looking enough, I'm not sufficiently interested,' he averred in the *Guardian*. Elsewhere, he explained that he had given himself the name and written the part because it was the only way he could ever be sure of getting the girl at the end of a film.

Cleese is used to having his cake and eating it, balancing his conceitedness with an attractive self-deprecation and humility. This means he can indulge in, for example, the vanity of having hair transplants because he can also laugh at himself for doing so. Cleese, who shares his Parisian trichologist with Elton John, has had three hair transplant operations and, with his therapy-induced policy of *glasnost*, has shown a hearty refusal to be the slightest bit embarrassed about them, although it was not until he played a barrister at a rehearsal for a charity performance in January 1983, *An Evening at the Royal Court*, and his wig slipped to reveal a scabby scalp, that he was forced to come clean. Before the first night, he showed a newspaper diarist the seventy newly planted hairs: 'It works wonderfully; the silly little buggers think they're at the back of my head and keep on growing.'

He recently explained: 'I had a transplant done in '78 out of curiosity and vanity. I'm lucky because I can pretend I had it done for professional reasons. I was going a bit bald and a bit of hair suits my long skull. The advantage of being so tall is that the only people who see how bald I am are waiters. I first noticed it in 1973. I made the first training film for Video Arts and I saw this bloke walking along the street with this terrible bald patch and I suddenly realized it was me. And I had no idea because you never see that bit.

'The first one in '78 took an hour and a quarter and was slightly unpleasant. And the one I had done just before Christmas 1982 was a doddle. They move seventy little plugs. You look unsightly for about ten days. Barbara was quite happy about it because she got a very nice weekend in Paris. We had Friday, Saturday and Sunday. On Monday she went shopping and I had this done.' Cleese is enthusiastic about the results – 'About £500-worth, no pain, and the possibility that, as an actor, I might be able to claim the cost against my tax' – and sees no need to apologize for his vanity: 'The other day a woman asked me why I had a hair transplant. I asked her why she wore lipstick.'

In fact, the hair transplant has eased the passage of many an interview. 'It's all my own hair, just redistributed a bit, on a socialist principle,' he once joked. He told Hal Hinson of the *Washington Post*: 'Whenever anyone asks me to tell them something funny, I'm just going to say "toupee". It's all you need to say, isn't it? Do you say too-pay or toup?' Cleese still maintains that toupees are the 'funniest thing that exists in the world. We used to play a game on *Python* – when we were walking down the street and saw a toupee we'd all go "Bzzzt".'

Cleese has also happily admitted on the *Aspel* show that he has none of his own teeth: 'I was talking to my dentist only three weeks ago and I said, "I do have one tooth of my own, don't I?" And he had a glance and said, "No, that went two years ago."' Cleese actually exposed his naked gum on the lower left side of his mouth for a camera close-up and added, 'I'm going to have some implants that side because I'm told I'm a sex symbol now, and if I have the teeth implanted there I shall be able to chew both sides which is essential for a sex symbol.'

Cleese has also encouraged his reputation for being badly dressed. As far back as 1967, Marty Feldman confirmed that Cleese had 'very poor taste in clothes'. This has not deterred the British public from confusing their admiration of the man as a performer with their admiration of his sartorial elegance. In 1981, Cleese was named one of Britain's seven best-dressed men by the Fenton menswear chain, but some would say that this is a bit like getting a restaurant award from the Golden Egg chain. The other six were Terry Wogan, Bryan Ferry, Michael Crawford, the Earl of Lichfield, David Steel and Sir Michael Edwardes (then BL chairman). Cleese remarked: 'It was undeserved. In fact, when it was announced over the radio during the rush hour, three of my friends had accidents. I don't dress well, I dress disgustingly. I make a point of it, as I have never met a well-dressed man whom I liked. I went to lunch at Buckingham Palace once and discovered at 11.15 a.m. that I'd mislaid my shirt. My training-film company had it and sent it over by bike. I also have the finest collection of bad-taste ties in the free world. Most of them have a fishy leitmotiv. I choose suede socks, and Turnbull & Asser make me shirts with the buttons missing and holes in the sleeves.'

Dressed in a rugby shirt, faded jeans and Reeboks and a fractionally too small tweed jacket for an interview with American *Vogue*, Cleese told journalist Vicki Woods, doing a regular 'Talking Fashion' slot on him, that he got his clothes from rubbish dumps: 'In summer I wear jeans and tennis shoes and white tennis shirts. That kind of thing. In winter, I wear a winter version of this. Cords and soft shirts.' Self-deprecation is, of course, a useful method of anticipating criticism. What Cleese failed to mention was that most of his clothes – typically pastel sleeveless or V-necked sweaters over open-necked shirts and jeans or slacks and a sports jacket – come from one of the most expensive menswear shops in the world, Ralph Lauren. The joke is, presumably, that you can't tell. He is often seen around London wearing an excessively expensive Dolce e Gabbana coat, but with the hem hanging down as a concession to English shabbiness.

In the attempt to distance himself from the post-*Wanda* sex symbol angle, Cleese's natural modesty and reticence began to border on an unbecoming obtuseness. Does a man who writes himself a sexy part in 'the zaniest, sexiest adult movie entertain-ment of the summer' (*Chicago Sun Times*), casts the actress of his dreams opposite himself, undergoes a punishing exercise regime to look fit, plays in nude love scenes with the girl and contrives triumphantly to win her in the last sequence then have the right to say that those calling him a sex symbol are making the whole thing up? As he irritatedly explained in a local radio interview, apparently he has. 'There were a lot of stories about the sex symbol, all of which were totally a media invention,' he said. 'And it was quite interesting for me to watch it happen and to realize that what was going on in the media was entirely unrelated to anything out in the real world . . . but that's how the media operates. Most people wouldn't believe the extent to which each bit of the media feeds off every other bit. And once somebody's started a story going it just has a bandwagon effect.'

'When people ask him where he gets his ideas from,' Charles Crichton said of John Cleese during the filming of *A Fish Called Wanda*, 'John says, "a little man in Swindon. But I don't know where *he* gets them from."'

Very occasionally, it is possible to believe it.

12 *What It's Like Being English*

Oh don't the days seem lank and long
When all goes right and nothing goes wrong,
And isn't life extremely flat
With nothing whatever to grumble at!

W. S. Gilbert, *Princess Ida*, 1884

A few months before his divorce from Barbara Trentham came through, Cleese moved back into his Holland Park house, having bought Barbara another home round the corner. The huge Victorian villa was almost empty, and, alone in there (Cynthia was beginning her last year at Millfield), Cleese went off to Liberty's to buy furniture for it. Within a year, the house was buzzing with people again; a new girlfriend, Alyce Faye Eichelberger, had moved in, her two teenage sons were regularly around, and Cynthia, having completed her A-levels, decided not to move into the flat Cleese had bought her nearby, but to live with her father.

When Alyce Faye Eichelberger (née MacBride) was born in Frederick, Oklahoma, in the 1940s, the woman she was named after was a great musical star of the day. With her husband, bandleader Phil Harris, the original Alice Faye sang a lot of very corny songs and became an American emblem, so much so that the name is considered in American showbusiness somewhere between hilarious and a terribly sophisticated (and very Cleese) joke; combined with Eichelberger, to which Alyce Faye changed her name by marriage, it is apparently even funnier. An English equivalent would be something like Gracie Fields von Ribbentrop.

Alyce Faye Eichelberger's father died when she was at High School, her mother when she was at Oklahoma State University. An only child, she came to London University on a Rotary scholarship and developed a love of Britain. She got her master's degree at Baylor University in Waco, Texas, where she met Dave Eichelberger, her husband, a golf professional. She almost finished her Ph.D., and could become Dr Eichelberger by teaching in Waco for two semesters, but has never bothered to do so. She has two sons by Eichelberger: Martin, who graduated in Business Management from Boston University in 1991, and Clinton, the 'British' one, who finished at Westminster School in June 1991.

A Jungian psychoanalyst, specializing mainly in adolescents, Alyce Faye works at the Tavistock Institute and also has a burgeoning private practice in a former council flat in St John's Wood, where she counsels several famous clients, about whom she is totally discreet. She actually met Cleese through show-business, rather than psychiatric, contacts – after her divorce, she mixed in entertainment business circles in London.

Since he met Alyce Faye, Cleese has professed to being completely happy for the first time in his life. He calls her Dingbat, she calls him Jack, saying 'John is what we call a toilet in the States'. Oddly enough, Cleese has been desperately trying to be called Jack for years without much popular success, but the name is catching on with his more post-Alyce Faye friends. The couple occasionally argue, usually over the tricky question of Cynthia; he sometimes defuses the tension in rows by hopping around the house doing monkey impressions. He is often quite rude to her if she inadvertently says something illogical or less than perfectly thought out; she in turn is assertive with him. Friends and staff at Cleese's office see the partnership as his show but run in large part by her – for example, he often turns up late at his own dinner parties, even if he has only been doing something else in a different part of the house, but the guest list and menu will be designed entirely by her.

Alyce Faye is physically very similar to Connie Booth and

Barbara Trentham, as Linda Lee Potter noted in the *Daily Mail*. 'They're all slender, wholesome American blondes with clear-cut features who look a bit like crisp young doctors in an old Dr Kildare film.' In keeping with Cleese and Robin Skynner's observation in *Families and How to Survive Them* that people are attracted to mates who have similar characteristics to their own, both Cleese and Alyce Faye had elderly parents, are only children and regard themselves as bookish.

Cleese is enormously generous with Alyce Faye, constantly buying her presents of jewellery, clothes and, for her last birthday, a Mercedes sports car, which nestles with his green Bentley on the gravel drive. The generosity causes awkwardness with Cynthia, who with the best will in the world (and she tells friends she is very keen on her father's relationship with Alyce Faye) still cannot help noticing that her mother, Connie Booth, rarely received Mercedes as birthday presents.

Father and elder daughter are still extremely close – 'I am the only woman my father has ever had a close relationship with and the one woman who really knows and understands him,' Cynthia says proudly. She is an open, friendly girl, but nervous of relationships and wary of people interested in her because of her name. She likes to go around the house at weekends in her father's shirts and jackets, and wants to be an actress, but feels she lacks confidence. Cynthia and her father spend a lot of time discussing their respective love lives, and say they make each other laugh. When she used to stay with him after his separation from Barbara, rumours went around that he was going out with a girl young enough to be his daughter, which was technically correct at least; the American gossip columnist Gaile Robinson even reported in her Fashionable Liaisons column on Cleese's 'sex kitten date', unaware that Cynthia was his daughter.

Days before Alyce Faye moved into Cleese's household, and the day before the twentieth anniversary of *Monty Python* being broadcast for the first time, Graham Chapman died in a Kent hospital of spine cancer. A friend and contemporary dying of natural causes is a doleful landmark in a person's life, and Cleese was terribly distressed by Chapman's death. According to David Sherlock, Chapman's lover and companion for twenty-four years, 'John Cleese was so distraught we had to take him into the sister's office for privacy. His raw emotion was so great.' He was helped from the room in tears moments before Chapman died. Palin, who stayed with Chapman, told the *Sun* newspaper, which gave enormous and very sympathetic coverage to Chapman's illness and death, 'John and I chatted to him about two of Graham's favourite topics – other people's misfortunes and things going wrong.'

Two months later, at a memorial service in the Great Hall of Bart's, Cleese gave a eulogy of such precisely judged vulgarity that it was actually in immaculate taste. He began by parodying the parrot sketch from *Monty Python*: 'Graham Chapman, co-author of the parrot sketch, is no more, he has ceased to be, bereft of life. . . .' He continued into the sloppy bit, life tragically taken away at forty-eight and so on, then startled the mourners with: 'Well, I feel that I should say nonsense, good riddance to him, the free-loading bastard, I hope he fries.' Chapman would never have forgiven him, Cleese explained, for not scandalizing the service, and he went on to claim the honour of 'being the first person ever at a British memorial service to say "fuck"'.

Cleese had somehow turned the tragedy into a happy occasion, mirroring what was happening at alarming speed in his own life – the onset of a new and strange contentment. Parts of the house have become almost a shrine to his achievements. One room is full of trophies and framed awards; all around the house are pictures of Cleese with family, playing cricket and in performance. There are jokes; on his front gatepost is a sign: 'Attention – Chien Bizarre', and round the corner on his office door, 'Attention – Chat Lunatique'. There is a fish roller blind in one room, and on the bed in their room at the back of the house a wonderfully tacky, film-starry fur cover. Losing over a stone for *A Fish Called Wanda* created a precedent – in 1990 Cleese bought a £2,000 treadmill exercise machine, on which he spends half an hour a day; he has a television rigged up so that he can keep busy while taking his simulated walks on the machine.

When Alyce Faye arrived, she persuaded Cleese to buy four long-haired Siamese seal point kittens, increasing the house cat-count to six, one of whom is called Keith. Cleese also collects strange brands of whisky and some very valuable paintings.

Chris Beetles, a Ryder Street dealer who specializes in nineteenth- and twentieth-century watercolours, with an additional interest in illustrators and cartoonists, is a friend of Cleese as well as the man who has sold him much of his art. Beetles trained as a GP with Dr Rob Buckman, with whom he appeared in *The Secret Policeman's Ball* in June 1979 as a comedy duo. (Beetles and Buckman wrote the last *Doctor on the Go* series and the *Pink Medicine Show*.) Beetles has had his St James's gallery for ten years and also supplies Jeffrey Archer. 'John's a very shrewd buyer of watercolours and he has one marvellous Albert Goodwin painting of Venice. Goodwin's a wonderful nineteenth-century oil painter whom John's been collecting very wisely,' attests Archer. 'He's got a very good eye, but Chris advises both of us. Three years ago he bought a watercolour by Pamela Kay – a rather well-defined dining table with food on it, salmon and bread rolls – that I really wanted, but he got there a day before me. He said that if I joined the SDP he'd sell it to me at any price.' Cleese also appears to be going in for house collecting, at least in a small way. In 1990, he bought a second house next to his first. It was to be for Alyce Faye to use for her practice, but then they changed their minds. At the moment she uses this £1.4 million villa for her piano lessons.

John Cleese in maturity has absolutely no problem with wealth and status. 'He's a man's man and likes to be in the company of powerful people,' says one friend. 'People throw themselves into a frenzy simply because of what he is. And he laps it all up. He likes all of that. People keep wanting to please him, it's terrible. You find yourself wanting to do it, wanting to beam a smile and say, "Oh, how wonderful you are." He definitely doesn't take criticism at all.'

What will he do next? Leaving aside his regularly stated desire to retire and sit reading books in the garden, he has been consistently keen over the years on writing some kind of history book, possibly a funny one. This is all part of Cleese's Sisyphean task of getting himself educated. 'I've left it too late probably to do much original thinking in the areas that I am interested in like psychology, psychiatry and religion. I'd like to be able to understand a lot of things which I don't yet understand,' he says. 'I'm still trying to find something interesting to do. I spend my entire life trying to discover what I ought to be doing. I got into Cambridge and did law and was going to join a firm of lawyers. Then I got into this silly business – so I am really still looking.'

'I'm getting very curious about what I'm going to do after I'm dead,' he mused in *Playboy* magazine in 1988. 'I think once you're in your mid-forties and the grave begins to loom, there's something truly fatuous about continuing to clamber up career ladders trying to become more important. Surely, you should be moving into something a bit more interesting than that. People think I'm weird, of course. I think it's weird to believe that mental health consists in pretending you're immortal. Anyway, what's so bad about death? Most of the best people are dead, you know.'

He has been turning down film scripts, usually unread, since *Wanda*. He even refused the role of the dissipated British journalist in *The Bonfire of the Vanities*, which was played instead by Bruce Willis, disastrously as many reviewers thought at the time. Cleese spent three days in Malta as Haffdan the Black for Terry Jones's film *Erik the Viking* – 'I play the embodiment of evil. It's about time I tackled that,' he commented. He was offered £60,000 to appear in a second episode of *Cheers* as psychologist Dr Simon Finch-Royce; it did not work out.

As soon as *Wanda* came out, Cleese half-joked about making a sequel, *Death Fish II*, with the *Wanda* team, possibly as a thriller. 'Jamie's always wanted to do a spy movie, Mike's got an idea about a psychiatrist, I've always loved the Hitchcock genre, and Kevin will be in it provided he gets the girl,' he says. He is resolute that the 'sequel' will not be a sequel at all, but a completely different film. He has a persistent fear, however, that the next film will not live up to *Wanda*. 'I was terribly pleased with *Wanda*, and I know that the next thing won't be as good and won't work as well, because we were just lucky. Some projects are just lucky – things fall into place, and even the mistakes that you make are mistakes you can fix. But even knowing that the next one won't be as good, it will still be worth trying, with the same cast, but maybe a completely different style. I'll probably write it in autumn of next year and shoot in spring or summer of 1992, depending on how long it takes to write,' he said late in 1990.

The fear of indifference may turn out to be a great spur to Cleese to write more and even better comedy. Intellectually, he rejects the idea that personal contentment can work against a comedy writer's performance, but if he cares what people think – and there is plenty of evidence that he does – he will feel the need for decades ahead to prove himself the best. For a man in his fifties (who surely cannot be far off the ultimate indignity of being made Sir John Cleese), he still has an extraordinary hold over each new generation of young people; yet he is only too aware that among them there is a rumour abroad that John Cleese is not funny any more. Aside from buffoons who have never forgiven him for not being Basil Fawlty, Cleese will take such warnings seriously.

Psychiatry books may come and go, beards and tweedy social worker outfits may be donned and shed again. There is a history of longevity in Cleese's family. He will retire several more times, announce sabbaticals during which he may not be telephoned or spoken to by impertinent journalists. He will ridicule the press for trivializing his life, then give toe-curlingly candid interviews to the very newspapers he dislikes. He will explain a thousand more times, and still not be understood, that he thinks there is a very important difference between being serious, which he unapologetically is, and being solemn, which he finds too many Americans to be to their detriment. Cleese will continue to give a tenth of his after-tax income to charity, and will do something political, perhaps even stand for Parliament at some stage, if he can weather another flood of Minister for Silly Walks headlines.

But every now and again, among all these sideshows, he will create something so new and original and funny that when his obituaries are written, even if they are in forty years' time, we will reel off lists of comedians, some who have yet to be born, and conclude that, yes, John Cleese probably was the funniest man in the world.

Select Bibliography

Bailey, John, *Weston-super-Mare: Look Back with Laughter* (Redcliffe Press, 1986)

Banks, Morwenna, and Swift, Amanda, *The Joke's on Us: Women in Comedy from Music Hall to the Present Day* (Pandora, 1987)

Barker, Ronnie, *It's Hello From Him* (New English Library, 1988)

Beisly, Philip, *Weston-super-Mare: A History and Guide* (Alan Sutton, 1988)

Bennett, Alan, Cook, Peter, Miller, Jonathan, and Moore, Dudley, *The Complete Beyond The Fringe* (Methuen, 1987)

Bennett, J. G., *Gurdjieff: Making a New World* (Turnstone Books, 1973)

Bergan, Ronald, *Beyond The Fringe . . . And Beyond* (Virgin Books, 1989)

Bergson, Henri, *Laughter: An Essay on the Meaning of the Comic* (Macmillan, 1911)

Chapman, Graham, *A Liar's Autobiography* (Methuen, 1980)

Clifton College, *125 Years of Clifton College, 1862–1987* (Clifton College, 1987)

Dahl, Roald, *Boy* (Jonathan Cape, 1984)

Dahl, Roald, *Danny, The Champion of the World* (Jonathan Cape, 1975)

Davis, Anthony, *TV Laughtermakers* (Boxtree, 1989)

Durant, John, and Miller, Jonathan (eds), *Laughing Matters: A Serious Look at Humour* (Longman Group, 1988)

Frischauer, Willi, *David Frost* (Michael Joseph, 1972)

Hewison, Robert, *Monty Python: The Case Against* (Eyre Methuen, 1981)

Hewison, Robert, *Footlights!* (Methuen, 1983)

Hind, John, *The Comic Inquisition* (Virgin Books, 1991)

259

James, Clive, *May Week Was in June* (Jonathan Cape, 1990)

Johnson, Kim 'Howard', *The First 200 Years of Monty Python* (Plexus Publishing, 1990/St Martin's Press, New York, 1989)

Kingsley, Hilary, and Tibballs, Geoff, *Box of Delights: The Golden Years of Television* (Macmillan, 1989)

Lee, Laurie, *Cider with Rosie* (Hogarth Press, 1959)

McCall, Douglas L., *Monty Python* (McFarland & Co., 1991)

Moore, James, *Gurdjieff: The Anatomy of a Myth. A Biography* (Element, 1991)

Nathan, David, *The Laughtermakers* (Peter Owen, 1971)

Nicoll, Maurice, *Psychological Commentaries on the Teaching of G. I. Gurdjieff & P. D. Ouspensky*, vols 1–4 (Watkins, 1980)

Perry, George, *Life of Python* (Pavilion Books, 1983)

Staveacre, Tony, *Slapstick! The Illustrated Story of Knockabout Comedy* (Angus & Robertson, 1987)

Thompson, John O. (ed.), *Monty Python: Complete and Utter Theory of the Grotesque* (British Film Institute, 1982)

Took, Barry, *Laughter in the Air* (Robson Books, 1976)

Took, Barry, *A Point of View* (Duckworth, 1990)

White, Michael, *Empty Seats* (Hamish Hamilton, 1984)

Wilmut, Roger, *From Fringe to Flying Circus* (Eyre Methuen, 1980)

A Curriculum Vitae

Films

1968   *Interlude* (Columbia/Domino, UK)

1969   *The Magic Christian* (Commonwealth United Entertainment/Grand Films, UK)

1970   *The Rise and Rise of Michael Rimmer* (Warner Bros/Seven Arts. A David Paradine Film, UK)

1970   *The Statue* (Cinerama/Josef Shaftel Productions, US)

1971   *And Now For Something Completely Different* (Columbia/Kettledrum/Python. A Victor Lownes/GSF Organisation Presentation, UK)

1972   *It's a 2'6" Above the Ground World* [renamed *The Love Ban*] (British Lion/A Betty Box/Ralph Thomas/Welbeck Film Distributors Production, UK)

1974   *Monty Python and the Holy Grail* (EMI/Python (Monty) Pictures, in association with Michael White, UK)

1974   *Romance with a Double Bass* (CIC/Anton Films, UK)

1976   *Pleasure at Her Majesty's* (Essential/Amnesty International, UK)

1979   *Away From It All* (CIC/Taylor Hyde International/Python (Monty) Pictures, UK. Short film preceding *Life of Brian* and directed by Clare Taylor and with Cleese as narrator Nigel Farquhar-Bennett)

1979   *Monty Python's Life of Brian* (CIC/HandMade Films, UK)

1979   *The Secret Policeman's Ball* (Tigon/Films of Record. For Amnesty International, UK)

1981   *The Great Muppet Caper* (ITC, UK)

1981   *Time Bandits* (HandMade Films, UK)

1982   *The Secret Policeman's Other Ball* (United International Pictures, UK)
1982   *Monty Python Live at the Hollywood Bowl* (Columbia, US)
1982   *Privates on Parade* (HandMade Films, UK)
1983   *Monty Python's The Meaning of Life* (UIP, UK)
1983   *Yellowbeard* (Rank/Hemdale. For Orion, US)
1985   *Silverado* (Columbia-Delphi IV Productions, US)
1985   *Clockwise* (Columbia-EMI Warner/Moment Films. In association with Thorn-EMI, UK)
1988   *A Fish Called Wanda* (UIP/Prominent Features. For MGM, UK)
1988   *The Biggest Picture* (Columbia, US)
1989   *Erik the Viking* (UIP/Prominent Features, UK)

Books

1971   *Monty Python's Big Red Book* (Methuen UK/1975 Warner US)
1973   *The Brand New Monty Python Bok* (Methuen UK/1976 Henry Regnery US – hardback identical to the paperpack above, bar tits 'n' bum cover)
1974   *The Brand New Monty Python Papperbok* (Methuen UK/ 1976 Warner US)
1977   *The Strange Case of the End of Civilisation as We Know It*, John Cleese, Jack Hobbs, Joe McGrath (Star Book/ Wyndham Publishers – script and stills of LWT film)
1977   *Monty Python and the Holy Grail* (Methuen)
1977   *Fawlty Towers*, Cleese and Booth (Futura/Contact Publications – 'The Builders', 'The Hotel Inspectors', 'Gourmet Night')
1979   *Monty Python's Life of Brian/Monty Python Scrapbook* (Methuen UK/Fred Jordan Books/Grosset & Dunlap US)
1979   *Monty Python's Life of Brian* (Ace Books – as above but smaller and without scrapbook)
1979   *Fawlty Towers* (Weidenfeld & Nicolson – 'The Wedding', 'A Touch of Class', 'The Germans')
1981   *The Complete Works of Shakespeare and Monty Python: Volume One – Monty Python* (Methuen – compilation of

Monty Python's Big Red Book (1971) and The Brand New Monty Python Bok (1973))

1981   The Secret Policeman's Other Ball (Methuen – with an introduction by John Cleese, three sketches in which he appears and photographs)

1983   Monty Python's The Meaning of Life (Methuen UK/Grove Press US)

1983   Families and How to Survive Them, Cleese and Robin Skynner (Methuen)

1984   Freaky Fables, by J. B. Handelsman, with a Foreword by John Cleese (Methuen)

1984   The Golden Skits of Wing-Commander Muriel Volestrangler FRHS & BAR, Muriel Volestrangler (Methuen – collation of skits written and co-written by Cleese from Cambridge to The Meaning of Life)

1988   The Monty Python Gift Boks (Methuen – repackaged first two books and poster)

1989   Monty Python's Flying Circus: Just the Words (Methuen Mandarin UK/Pantheon US – twentieth anniversary compilation of television scripts, in two volumes)

1992   Life and How to Survive It, John Cleese and Robin Skynner (Methuen)

Albums

1965   Cambridge Circus (Odeon PCS 3046 Original Broadway Cast)

1966   The Frost Report on Britain (Parlophone PMC 7005 – Cleese in 8 out of 13 sketches)

1967   The Frost Report on Everything (Janus JLS-3005 – Cleese [misspelled as 'Clease'] in 5 out of 11 sketches)

1967   I'm Sorry, I'll Read That Again (EMI M-1164 & BBC Records REH 342 – Cleese as the Doctor, Mary's John, Little John, Sir Angus of the Prune, the MC, Baby Rupert, Captain Cleese and Wong Tu)

1970   Monty Python's Flying Circus (BBC Records)

1971   Another Monty Python Record (Charisma)

1972   Monty Python's Previous Record (Charisma)

1973   The Monty Python Matching Tie and Handkerchief (Charisma/Arista)

1974   *Monty Python Live at The Theatre Royal, Drury Lane*
(Charisma, UK only)

1975   *The Album of the Soundtrack of the Trailer of the Film of
Monty Python and the Holy Grail* (Charisma)

1976   *Monty Python Live at City Center* (Arista, US only)

1976   *The Worst of Monty Python* (Kama Sutra – a repackaging
of *Another Monty Python Record* and *Monty Python's Previous Record*)

1976   *A Poke in the Eye With a Sharp Stick* (Transatlantic
TRA, UK only – first Amnesty International benefit
concert)

1977   *The Mermaid Frolics* (Polydor Special 2384101 – Cleese,
Booth, Jones, Jonathan Miller and Peter Ustinov)

1977   *The Monty Python Instant Record Collection* (Charisma)

1979   *Monty Python's Life of Brian* (Warner Bros)

1979   *The Secret Policeman's Ball* (Island LPS 9601)

1979   *Fawlty Towers* (BBC Records REB 377 – 'Hotel Inspectors' and 'Mrs Richards')

1980   *Monty Python's Contractual Obligation Album* (Charisma/
Arista)

1981   *Fawlty Towers: Second Sitting* (BBC Records REB 405 –
'The Builders' and 'The Rat')

1981   *The Secret Policeman's Other Ball* (Island)

1982   *Fawlty Towers: At Your Service* (BBC Records REB 449
– 'The Germans' and 'Death')

1983   *Monty Python's The Meaning of Life* (MCA Records)

1988   *Monty Python's The Final Ripoff* (Virgin)

1988   *The Screwtape Letters* (Audio Literature Inc. – cassette
only. A three-hour, two-cassette version of Cleese
reading the book by C. S. Lewis)

Radio (as performer/contributor)

1963 30 December   *Cambridge Circus*

1964   3 April   *I'm Sorry, I'll Read That Again*, 3
                             pilot programmes (BBC Home
                             Service)

       14 May   co-wrote *Emery At Large*
        5 July   co-wrote *Not to Worry*

1965	September	radio show with Jack Palance (US)
1966	14 March	*I'm Sorry, I'll Read That Again*, 2nd series (BBC Home Service)
	12 September	*David Frost at the Phonograph* (BBC Light Programme)
	3 October	*I'm Sorry, I'll Read That Again*, 3rd series (BBC Home Service)
	8 October	*David Frost at the Phonograph* (BBC Light Programme)
	29 October	*David Frost at the Phonograph* (BBC Light Programme)
1967	26 January	*Call my Bluff* (BBC Light Programme)
	23 March	*I'm Sorry, I'll Read That Again*, 4th series (BBC Home Service)
	17 December	*Down Your Way* (Radio 4)
1968	14 April	*I'm Sorry, I'll Read That Again*, 5th series (Radio 4)
	6 July	*Galaxy* (Radio 2)
	26 December	*I'm Sorry, I'll Read That Again*, Special (Radio 4)
1969	12 January	*I'm Sorry, I'll Read That Again*, 6th series (Radio 4)
	8 April–3 June	*What's So Funny About . . .?* (Radio 4)
	25 December	*I'm Sorry, I'll Read That Again*, Special (Radio 4)
1970	15 February	*I'm Sorry, I'll Read That Again*, 7th series (Radio 4)
	4 July	*The Clever Stupid Game* (Radio 4)
1971		guest of panel game *Right or Wrong* (throughout the year) (Radio 4)

1973	4 November	*I'm Sorry, I'll Read That Again*, 8th series (Radio 4)
1974	6 June	co-wrote *Sheila Hancock's Sketchbook* (Radio 4)
1975	25 August	*The Summer Show* (Radio 4)
	21 September	*Celebration: 'The Art of Musical Parody'* (Radio 4)
1978	17 December	*Black Cinderella Two Goes East*, by Rory McGrath/Clive Anderson (BBC)
1989	25 December	*I'm Sorry, I'll Read That Again*, reunion programme (Radio 2)
1990	12 December	*Families and How to Survive Them* (Radio 4)

Radio (as interviewee)

1966	1 April	*Late Night Extra* (Light Programme)
1968	11 November	'Movie-Go Round', on *Interlude* (BBC)
1970	1 September	*Today* (with Ed Boyle) (Radio 4)
	22 December	*Woman's Hour* (Radio 4)
	23 December	picked funny books for *Now Read On* (Radio 4)
1971	5 March	*Woman's Hour* (Radio 4)
	21 April	*News Desk*, re Rectorship of St Andrews (Radio 4)
	17 July	*Desert Island Discs* (Radio 4)
	20 November	*Film Time* (Radio 4)
1972	29 April	*Sports Report* (BBC)

1973	5 July	*Weekend Woman's Hour* (Radio 4)
1975	11 April	*Open House* (with Pete Murray) (Radio 2)
1976	20 February	*Newsbeat* (Radio 1)
	29 October	*First Impression*, on favourite childhood books (Radio 4)
1978	20 May	*Away From It All* (with Joan Bakewell) (Radio 4)
1979	16 February	*Around Midnight*, on *Fawlty Towers* (Radio 2)
	27 March	*PM*, on training films (BBC)
	26 June	*Today*, on *The Secret Policeman's Ball* (Radio 4)
	28 June	*Kaleidoscope*, on *The Secret Policeman's Ball* (Radio 4)
	5 November	*Kaleidoscope*, on *Life of Brian* (Radio 4)
	7 November	*Today*, on *Life of Brian* (with Brian Redhead) (Radio 4)
	31 December	*Today* – celebrities' hopes for the 1980s (Radio 4)
1980	16 August	*Sport on 4*, on interest in squash (Radio 4)
1983	31 January	*John Dunne Show*, on *Privates on Parade* (Radio 2)
	2 February	*Gloria Hunniford* (Radio 2)
	24 February	*Star Sound Extra*, on *Privates on Parade* (Radio 2)
	28 September	*Woman's Hour*, on *Families and How to Survive Them* (Radio 4)
	30 September	*Gloria Hunniford*, on *Families and How to Survive Them* (Radio 2)

1984 13 September   *Round Midnight*, on *Families and How to Survive Them* (Radio 2)

     17 September   *Today*, on a TV Advert Award for Sony compact disc (Radio 4)

1985 24 May   *Book Plug*, on *Muriel Volestrangler* (Radio 4)

1986 20 March   *Gloria Hunniford*, on *Clockwise* (Radio 2)

     21 June   *A View from the Boundary* (with Brian Johnston) (Radio 3)

1990 17 May/24 May   *How Far Can You Go?*, on blasphemy and *Life of Brian* (Radio 4)

     13 August   *Funny That Way* (with Barry Cryer) (Radio 4)

     17 September   *Today*, at the Liberal Democrats' Party Conference (Radio 4)

     6 December   *Bookshelf* (Radio 4)

     25 December   Orchard FM, Taunton, interviewed by Phil Easton

Television (as performer/contributor)

1963 28 September–21 December   contributed to *That Was The Week That Was* (BBC)

     28 December   contributed to *That Was The Year That Was* (BBC)

1966 10 March–28 April   *The Frost Report* (BBC)

     19 October–4 January   *The Frost Programme* (Rediffusion)

1967 15 February–22 March   *At Last the 1948 Show* (Rediffusion)

     6 April–18 May   *The Frost Report* (Rediffusion)

     26 September–7 November   *At Last the 1948 Show* (Rediffusion)

1968	8 August	*The Goon Show* – 'Tales of Men's Shirts' (Thames)
1969	5–26 October, 23 November– 11 January 1970	*Monty Python's Flying Circus* (BBC)
1970	15–29 September, 20 October–22 December	*Monty Python's Flying Circus* (BBC)
1972	19 October– 21 December, 4–11 January 1973	*Monty Python's Flying Circus* (BBC)
1973	18 January	*Elementary, My Dear Watson* (BBC1, Comedy Playhouse)
	3 February	*Doctor in Charge*: 'No Ill Feelings', Fawlty prototype (BBC)
1974	22 February	*Sez Les* (ITV)
	22 April	*A Place in History* (ITV)
	28 June	*Sez Les* (ITV)
1975	20 September	*Fawlty Towers* (BBC2)
	6 October– 24 November	*The Selling Line*, 1st episode: 'Who Sold You This, Then?' (BBC2)
1976	14 November	*Read All About It*, a books discussion (BBC1)
1977	18 September	*The Strange Case of the End of Civilisation As We Know It* (LWT)
	21 October	*The Muppet Show* (ATV)
1979	1 January	*Grandstand*, film (BBC1)
	19 February	*Fawlty Towers* (BBC2)
	18 March	*Company Account*: 'The Balance Sheet Barrier' (with Ronnie Corbett) – 5-part series (BBC1)

May	*Norway: Land of Giants!* (BBC2)
17 October	cameo appearance on *Ripping Yarns* ('Golden Gordon') (BBC1)
20 October	cameo appearance on *Dr Who* (BBC1)
1980 2 March	*The Office Line*: 'The Secretary and her Boss', the first in a series of 8 training films (BBC1)
23 October	Petruchio in *The Taming of the Shrew* (BBC2)
1982 March	*Whoops Apocalypse* (LWT)
1985 3 December	SDP party political broadcast
1986	wrote and appeared in a commercial for the BBC
1987 1 April	SDP party political broadcast
1989 end May	SDP party political broadcast (old footage)
6 December	appeared on BBC's *Network*, against the Broadcasting Bill (BBC1)

Television (as interviewee)

1970 12 January	Guest on *Late Night Line Up* (BBC2)
1976 20 February	Profiled by *Tonight* (BBC1)
16 August	*Festival 40*, special *Monty Python* edition (BBC1)
1977 14 December	*Pebble Mill* (with Donny Macleod) (BBC1)

1979	20 June	*The Pythons*, commemorative documentary (BBC1)
	22 June	*Tonight In Town*, on *The Secret Policeman's Ball* (BBC1)
	9 November	*Friday Night, Saturday Morning*, discussing *Life of Brian* (BBC2)
	23 November	*The Pythons* (BBC2)
1980	22 October	*Parkinson* (BBC1)
1982	12 December	*Film '82*, on *Privates on Parade* (BBC1)
1983	29 January	*Wogan* (BBC1)
	31 January	*Nationwide*, on *Privates on Parade* (BBC1)
1984	October	Appeared on Miriam Stoppard's *Where There's Life* (ITV)
1986	31 January	*South Bank Show Special* (LWT)
1988	October	*Aspel*, on *A Fish Called Wanda* (ITV)
1990	October	*Omnibus*: 'Life of Python' (BBC1)
	December	*Wogan* (BBC1)
1991	30 January	*This Morning* (ITV)

Index